.63

D0712823

*Political Power in*

*the Soviet Union*

AN ADVANCED STUDY IN POLITICAL SCIENCE

# Political Power in the Soviet Union

A STUDY OF DECISION-MAKING

IN STALINGRAD

*Philip D. Stewart*
THE OHIO STATE UNIVERSITY

THE BOBBS-MERRILL COMPANY, INC.
*A Subsidiary of Howard W. Sams & Co., Inc.*
*Indianapolis and New York*

James A. Robinson
*The Ohio State University*

**CONSULTING EDITOR**

*To my parents*

# Preface

🔲🔲

This book analyzes the structure of influence in decision-making at the regional level of the Soviet Communist Party through an intensive study of one Party committee—the Stalingrad obkom. The study argues that there exist in the Soviet Union "institutional" interest groups that exert varying degrees of influence on political decision-making. Five major channels are analyzed through which these groups might acquire and utilize influence: (1) participation in the Party conference, (2) membership on the Party committee, (3) participation in obkom plenums, (4) membership on the bureau or participation in its sessions, and (5) work in the secretariat.

What clearly emerges here is that a small group of professional Party secretaries can and do control all the channels of access to the decision-making bodies of the obkom. Rather than acting as forums for active discussion and decision-making, the Party conferences and obkom plenums are platforms for persuading the rank and file of the correctness of new policies and calling to task the leaders of organizations who fail to fulfill sufficiently the demands made upon them by Party officials. The membership of the Party committee and its bureau is structured to assure the dominant position of the Party secretaries, who account for at least 40 per cent of obkom membership. The next largest group consists of those most closely subordinated to Party control—the local Soviet officials. For nearly all other major groups in the oblast representation is limited to the head of their corresponding oblast organization. The purpose of this membership structure is to give the leaders of the most important organizations in the oblast the opportunity to become acquainted with bureau decisions quickly. In this way, they become transmission belts between the Party committee bureau and the organizations responsible for executing its decisions. Analysis of the patterns of participation in obkom plenums shows that those groups most heavily represented in the membership are, in general, those who participate most frequently, although considerable specialization by issue area is evident. On the assumption that both membership and participation are related to potential influence on decision-making in the obkom, these two factors are used to bring out variations in the potential ability of groups included in the obkom to influence its decisions. Those groups with the highest potential influence include the Party secretaries, the heads of the Soviets, the trade-unions, the Komsomol, and the leaders of some major industries. Others, such as literary, scientific, general educational and engineering groups are noticeably absent from those with a measurable degree of influence.

The evident tendency of the Party secretaries to consult with interest groups in the policy-making process indicates that now many of these institutional interest groups may be able to translate their potential influence into actual influence.

As the success of any study of power and influence will depend upon the sources to which the researcher has access, a few words about the sources used for this study are appropriate. Any student of the Soviet Union is beset by problems of access to relevant source materials, and this is especially true of those who seek to analyze the process of Soviet politics. Although the U.S.S.R. publishes vast amounts of material about the system, most of this is political propaganda designed to persuade the Soviet masses and the outside world to accept the official Soviet view of what the system is like and how it works. However, there are certain publications that are especially designed to speak to the Soviet elite. While using the same terminology as political propaganda, some articles in *Pravda,* and in such journals as *Partiinaia Zhizn'* (*Party Life*) and *Kommunist* (*Com-*

*munist*), discuss in some detail many of the real problems faced by the local Party committees. At times, through fierce criticism of instances of arbitrary rule, articles give clues to the local Party officials that they are now expected to be more responsive to the suggestions of other bureau members, etc. When similar articles appear over a long period of time, the Western analyst can safely assume that this is not an isolated problem, but one that is persistent and may be deeply rooted in the nature of the system. Other articles citing the good example shown by a particular Party committee in carrying out the harvest provide an ideal for local leaders to live up to. The analyst of Soviet behavior may use both types of articles as indicators of the extremes of Soviet behavior, somewhere in the middle of which may be found the normally functioning committee.

The lack of information on these normal Party committees is precisely the chief difficulty of these materials. A scholar is apt either to lean too heavily on the critical materials for his picture of Soviet reality, or to go too far in accepting the ideal examples as the real thing.

In addition to the data that may be obtained from an analysis of the central press and Party journals, several other sources lend valuable insight into the decision-making process at the oblast level. One of the most important of these is the recent novel, *Secretar' Obkoma* (*The Obkom Secretary*), by the Soviet novelist Vsevolod Kochetov. This book portrays the experiences of two fictional obkom first secretaries. One, Denisov, represents most of the characteristics desired by the Soviet leadership in its middle level officials. The other, Artamonov, is an example of the old, outmoded bureaucrat who uses methods no longer considered proper to achieve successes in production. Although it is probable that neither of these characters represents the "typical" Soviet politician, nevertheless this novel is very useful for the insights it provides into the daily routine of an up-and-coming Party secretary. In his descriptions of the way Denisov handles problems that arise in the course of his daily work we are given what is probably a quite accurate picture of whom a Party secretary would consult in real life. For example, when making inspection trips to the countryside, Denisov is accompanied by the second secretary in charge of agriculture and the chairman of the oblast Soviet executive committee. When combined with the material compiled from journals and the press, such insights as these help the researcher to gain a better feeling for the realities of Soviet politics.

Other sources of particular value include collections of lectures delivered at higher Party schools, written largely by Party officials for the instruction of other professional Party workers; collections of Party resolutions such as the series, *Spravochnik Partiinogo Rabotnika* (*Handbook of a Party Worker*), and *KPSS v Rezoliutsiiakh* . . . (*The CPSU in Resolutions* . . .). Of special interest is a book, based upon Party archives, that describes some of the activities of the Stalingrad Party organization, entitled *Iz Istorii Stalingradskoi Partiinoi Organizatsii* (*From the History of the Stalingrad Party Organization*). Unfortunately this book provides no information more recent than 1957, but what it does contain proved quite useful for this study.

As valuable as these sources may be, this book would not have been possible without the material gathered from the Stalingrad oblast Party newspaper. To the everlasting misfortune of American scholarship on the Soviet Union this paper, as well as all other regional and local newspapers in the Russian Republic, cannot be exported from the Soviet Union. (The papers from the union-republic capitals and from Moscow and Leningrad may be ordered from this country.) However, from the Soviet point of view, perhaps this is understandable for these local newspapers contain a wealth of information on local politics completely unobtainable from any other available source. If the time and opportunity were available for sufficiently thorough analysis, it is not inconceivable that a picture of oblast politics could be compiled nearly equaling in detail that presented in Fainsod's *Smolensk Under Soviet Rule*, based entirely upon captured Party archives. Apparently the Soviets realize this too, for while not forbidding the use of these papers in the U.S.S.R., they are quite reluctant to give an American complete freedom to read and analyze them. At least this was my experience in Moscow, and that of a fellow researcher in Leningrad. However, I consider myself especially fortunate to have had the opportunity, as a member of the Soviet-American faculty-student exchange program for the 1962–1963 academic year, to gather considerable material for this study from one provincial newspaper, *Stalingradskaia Pravda*, for the period 1954–1962. A special debt of gratitude for making this possible is owed the Inter-University Committee on Travel Grants.

For his invaluable assistance, and constructive criticism of the manuscript I am grateful to Darrell P. Hammer. Appreciation goes to Robert C. Tucker for stimulating my interest in obkom politics and for guidance and inspiration in the early phases of this work. In addition, I wish to express my thanks to the Foreign Area Fellowship Program for providing financial assistance to make possible completion of the research and writing the manuscript. A note of gratitude and appreciation is also owed my wife, Nancy, for her patience, encouragement, and moral support throughout this project. Of course, the responsibility for any errors or misstatements rests entirely with the author.

PHILIP D. STEWART
*Columbus, Ohio*
*November 1966*

# Contents

🔳🔳

# Tables and Figures

**1:1**

*Political Power in*

*the Soviet Union*

# ONE

# Measuring Influence in
# Soviet Politics

[1:1]

## CONCEPTUAL CONSIDERATIONS

Making decisions is one of the universal phenomena of political life.
One of the major efforts toward understanding the way decisions get
made in political systems is the interest group approach. The major
tenets of this approach suggest that political decision-making in all
systems results from the claims made upon the government by the
existing social and economic groups, channeled through interest
groups and political parties. The function of the political leadership, according to this notion, is to assess these claims, to provide for
compromise, and to articulate them in the form of authoritative
rules or decisions.[1] When an effort is made to examine the Soviet
political process in the light of such propositions, several problems
immediately arise. First, it may be argued with some justification,
that it is impossible to describe the Soviet system in these terms because interest groups, in the Western sense, either do not exist or

---

[1] The basic work in this approach is David B. Truman, *The Governmental Process* (New
York: Knopf, 1951).

are so controlled that they lack the political resources necessary to translate their claims into public policy, i.e., to achieve effective access. An interest group is, according to the commonly accepted Western notion, usually a voluntary organization, such as the N.A.M. or the Farm Bureau, with independent resources, whose leaders are more or less responsive to the shared interests of the members. In the Soviet Union a Party unit is formed in all organizations that functions to ensure that no policy is adopted contrary to the general line of the Party. Further, since all leading positions within Soviet society come within the *nomenklatura* of the Party committees, there are not nor can there be any groups with autonomous political power. As Brzezinski and Huntington point out in their recent work, "In the Soviet Union economic or social power is not an autonomous political resource."[2]

Yet, to ignore completely the role of groups in the Soviet political process because they may lack much of what Dahl calls "potential" for influence on political decision-making would be, it seems to me, a mistake. After all, it is indisputable that groups do exist in the Soviet Union, and they—or at least some officials from these groups—do participate in the political process. Indeed, according to the definition of an interest group as a "shared attitude" that makes certain claims upon other groups in society,[3] such Soviet groups as the industrial managers, the trade unions, and the local Soviet officials should probably be considered as interest groups. While the question of the degree to which the leaders of these groups are responsive to the common shared interests of their members remains unanswerable, nevertheless to the extent that the leaders share common career experiences with the rank and file of their occupation group it would seem reasonable to assume that the former, at least indirectly, represent some of the professional interests of the latter.

Nor would it be wise to assume, *a priori*, that the existing groups in the Soviet Union lack all potential for political influence. After all, while the Party can replace any industrial manager it wishes, the overall success of its plans remains dependent in large part upon the voluntary and energetic cooperation of the industrial

[2] Zbigniew Brzezinski and Samuel P. Huntington, *Political Power: USA/USSR* (New York: Viking Press, 1964).

[3] Truman, p. 37.

officials, as well as officials in every other branch of activity. Many of these men possess special knowledge and skills on which the Party is also dependent. To assume that the Party can ignore altogether the interests of these groups would, it seems, be naive.

In talking about interest groups in the Soviet context it is well to bear in mind several ways in which they differ rather significantly from the type of interest groups commonly studied in the United States. Although our definitions are not quite so limited, most interest group studies tend to concentrate on voluntary associational groups, such as the farmers' unions, or manufacturers associations. The reason for this focus seems to be related to the situation that these groups, possessing their own bases of wealth and prestige, have the possibility of entering into a negotiating relationship with the political organs they seek to influence. However, as was pointed out in a recent study of the Italian interest group system, our concept of interest groups need not be limited to the independent associational type. Certain other groups in society, not possessing the independent resources of associational groups, may still exercise influence on political policy-making. These groups have been called "institutional" interest groups,[4] and are directly dependent upon the political decision-makers for their existence and for their position in the political structure. Such an interest group in Italian politics would be the public school teachers, who are directly dependent upon the government as employees of the Ministry of Public Instruction.[5] In speaking of interest groups in the Soviet Union, it seems much more appropriate to classify them as "institutional" rather than as "associational" interest groups. Thus, most groups in Soviet society, from the Komsomol (Communist Youth League) to the industrial managers, and possibly the military, are much more similar to the institutional interest groups described in LaPalombara's study than to the associational groups commonly studied in the United States.

The way "interest group" is defined is of central importance in any attempt to apply elements of group theory to analysis of Soviet politics. If it is assumed that an interest group must possess independent sources of wealth and prestige in order to achieve ef-

[4] Joseph LaPalombara, *Interest Groups in Italian Politics* (Princeton: Princeton University Press, 1964), pp. 293–294.
[5] *Ibid.*

fective access to political decision-making, then such a study as this is doomed from the outset. One need simply show that groups within Soviet society are all highly dependent upon the Party and subject to its control and direction in order to invalidate any attempt to demonstrate the existence of group politics in the Soviet Union. On the other hand, if we conceive of these groups as the institutional type, an analysis such as this one becomes feasible. Thus, as LaPalombara made clear, although the Italian teachers are very dependent upon the Ministry and subject to its control, they nevertheless operate as an interest group in Italian politics.[6]

When approaching the study of institutional interest groups, it is necessary to remember that there is a major difference in the methods of operation of these groups compared with the associational interest groups. Associational groups are able to enter into a bargaining, negotiating relationship with the political decision-makers, while the institutional groups may depend primarily upon the willingness of the political authorities to *consult* with them in the formation of policy. While it is true that the various institutional groups may make better or worse use of their position, or that their ability to demand a hearing, or otherwise exercise a positive influence on policy-making may vary from time to time and from group to group, the important point is that the possibility of these groups exercising influence cannot easily be denied. Rather than denying the possibility of influence, then, it becomes the task of the researcher to determine the extent to which consultation actually does or might take place, to analyze the potential of various institutional groups for exercising influence on policy formation.

Even when it is recognized that interest groups of a sort do exist in the Soviet Union, it may be objected further that any attempt to study the role of these groups in the Soviet political process is futile because of the lack of necessary data. Robert Dahl, who has devoted considerable attention to problems of measuring influence,[7] or even potential influence, gives some indication

6 *Ibid.*

7 For a pertinent critique of Dahl's definition and measures of influence and power see William H. Riker, "Some Ambiguities in the Notion of Power," *The American Political Science Review,* 58 (June, 1964), 341–349; and Peter Bachrach and Morton Baratz, "Two Faces of Power," *The American Political Science Review,* 56 (December, 1962), 957–962.

of the amount and kind of data that are necessary for such analyses:

> If you want to refer to the potential influence of a particular group of individuals, all I ask is that you specify certain conditions—in particular the *level* at which members of this and other groups *use* their resources, and also your assumptions as to how skillful or efficient they are in employing them.[8]

At another point, summarizing the complexity of this problem, even in the American situation where access to data is incomparably greater than it is for students of Soviet politics, Dahl states, through one of the participants in an imaginary dialogue, "I must say, all this presents me with a task of such formidable proportions that from now on I shall hesitate to speak of potential influence at all!"[9]

In general, Dahl is making a plea for as much precision as possible in the use of the concept "potential influence." While it is true that the lack of adequate information on the Soviet political process makes it impossible to achieve the level of precision desired by Dahl, it does seem that the spirit of exactness can be maintained by making our estimations of variations in potential influence as definite as permitted by the evidence available, and by using measures that seem best suited to bring out differentials in potential influence in Soviet conditions.

As a step in this direction the following paradigm proposed by Dahl for formulating statements about power and influence has been adopted for this study: "_____ is more influential than _____ with respect to _____ as measured by _____ and _____."[10] Three important factors in measuring potential influence are suggested by this paradigm. First, it indicates that measures of potential influence are more meaningful when they are comparative. This can be illustrated by some propositions from this study. One such proposition might be as follows: "The officials of the local Soviets have great potential influence." What is meant by the phrase "great potential influence" is not at all clear in this formulation. On the other hand, if the statement is made compara-

[8] Robert A. Dahl, *Who Governs?* (New Haven: Yale University Press, 1961), p. 272.
[9] *Ibid.*, p. 273.
[10] Robert A. Dahl, *Modern Political Analysis* (Englewood Cliffs: Prentice-Hall, 1963), p. 47.

tive its meaning becomes more evident. Stated comparatively the proposition might take this form: "The officials of the local Soviets have greater potential influence than officials of local industry." Now the hypothesis is made more specific and its significance is more obvious. Yet, this formulation is still too general. As it stands it is not possible to judge whether this relationship holds in all instances or only in relation to certain types of questions. The second element in the paradigm is designed to cope with this problem. The phrase, "with respect to," implies that statements of potential influence are more useful when they are related to the specific type of question or scope of activity with respect to which such potential influence is said to exist. An example of such a statement might be: "Local Soviet officials have greater potential influence than local industry officials with respect to questions of industrial policy." It now becomes possible to perceive at once the range of issues over which the measured potential influence exists. However, even momentary consideration will indicate that the relationships observed—who turns out to have how much potential influence —will depend in large part on the measures used. The relationships indicated by one set of measures may not be the same as those indicated by a different set. The third factor suggested by the paradigm relates to this point. The phrase, "as measured by," is intended to draw attention to the limitations of the findings by indicating the specific measures on which they are based. The principal measures adopted for this study are (1) the official offices and elective positions held by individuals or groups, and (2) participation in the public aspects of the oblast Party committee's work, primarily in obkom plenums. When these measures are applied to the illustration used above the following proposition emerges: Local Soviet officials have greater potential influence than local industry officials with respect to questions of industry as measured by the greater frequency with which local Soviet officials participate in the discussions of industrial questions at obkom plenums and the relatively higher elective office occupied in the Party committee by the participants from the local Soviets.

Each of the measures used in this study deserves comment. The first measure employed here is the official offices and positions held by individuals within the region. Included in this measure are the positions held in a professional capacity, such as director of a factory, secretary of a Party committee, or chairman of a collective farm. Also included are "elective" positions within the Party hierarchy that are not full-time, professional positions, such as simply membership on the Party committee, or membership on its bureau. In addition, positions that are largely honorary are considered. Examples of such positions include membership on the directing presidium of a Party conference, delegate to the Party Congress, or the Supreme Soviet.

This measure was selected on the assumption that an individual's potential influence is closely correlated with his position in an official or semiofficial hierarchy. In addition, the abundance of relevant information available in the Party journals and the local press on both the positions occupied by particular individuals and the relative importance attributed to various positions combine to recommend this measure for the present study. Comparisons using this measure are based upon analyses of such information. For example, it is quite obvious from the literature that the position of chairman of the oblast or city Soviet executive committee is regarded as much more important in terms of obkom politics than the position of director of an enterprise concerned with local industry. This is confirmed, in Stalingrad at least, by the evidence that the oblast Soviet chairman is always a member of both the oblast and city Party committee bureaus, while few local industry managers are even members of the oblast Party committee.

While analysis of potential influence on the basis of offices, or positions held by individuals or groups may be very useful in pointing up relationships among different groups involved in the political process, it must be recognized that this is not a very firm indicator; formal position is not necessarily correlated with influence. At the same time, Armstrong did find this to be a useful indicator of the relative importance of members of the elite in the Soviet context. His study, based primarily on examination of the career patterns of elite members, led him to conclude that the relative importance of particular individuals among the elite "depends *primarily* on the positions they hold in the bureaucratic structure" (italics mine).[11] For the purposes of this study, then, official and

11 John A. Armstrong, *The Soviet Bureaucratic Elite* (New York: Praeger, 1959), p. 11.

elective positions are used as one tentative indicator of the relative potential for influence of various individuals and groups in political decision-making.

The second measure adopted for use here is participation in the public aspects of the obkom's work. While it would be most desirable to study actual participation in decision-making—to examine who makes what proposals, whose suggestions are most frequently adopted, and who participated in several or many different areas of decision-making activity—such information is almost completely unobtainable for the Soviet Union since actual decision-making occurs almost entirely in closed sessions whose records are not made public. What is available, however, is the record of participation by various individuals in the public aspects of the obkom's work. That segment of the obkom's activity for which the most complete information is available and which appears to provide the best reflection of obkom decision-making is the obkom plenary session. These sessions are held four or five times a year and discuss a wide range of topics. In addition, over a long period a great number of individuals participate in these plenums. On the basis of this data it is possible to investigate which individuals participate most frequently in this aspect of obkom politics and which participate in the discussion of one or several types of questions. In this manner individuals can be compared on the basis of (1) the frequency of participation and (2) the scope of participation.

To illustrate, we may refer once again to the local Soviet officials and the local industry officials. On the basis of their records of participation in obkom plenums, we may find that not only do the local Soviet officials participate more frequently in obkom plenums than local industry officials, but in addition they participate in the discussion of a wider range of issues. Such a finding would indicate that, in terms of this measure, the local Soviet officials have greater potential influence over a greater range of issues than the local industry officials.

Obviously, this is not an entirely reliable measure; participation is not necessarily the same thing as potential or actual influence. It is entirely possible that those who participate most frequently in a given problem area have the least influence on decisions relating to it. As the price for opposing the dominant faction and losing, they may be made to make the public presentation of the policy. Nevertheless, it does still appear that visible participation is a useful factor to consider as one measure of potential influence. Summarizing one of Truman's hypotheses regarding potential influence, LaPalombara states:

> A group's ability to intervene efficaciously in authoritative decision-making varies directly with the nature of the group's access to decisional information and to the centers of decisional authority.[12]

On the basis of this hypothesis it does seem that there is a relationship between participation and potential influence. It seems reasonable to assume that a person who participates in the public aspects of obkom affairs probably has greater access to decisional information than most of those who do not participate, other things being equal. While this relationship will not always hold when correlated with the position held by the participant it may be taken as at least a tentative indicator of potential influence. In full recognition of the weaknesses of this method, then, these two indices will be used as a tool for drawing some tentative conclusions regarding the relative potential influence of various individuals and groups in the Soviet political process.

Several factors combine to recommend the oblast or regional level as a focus for this study. First, since it is the highest of the "local" Party organs, it must make policy decisions affecting the success of the entire Party. Although the central leaders can invoke powerful sanctions and offer great rewards, in the long run their authority depends directly upon the effectiveness with which the officials at the oblast level fulfill their responsibilities. Second, there is available a relative abundance of materials on the oblast level of the Communist Party. These provide much information and offer many insights about the Soviet system not easily available elsewhere.[13]

To give this analysis greater concreteness and a sense of "realism," one particular obkom,[14] the Stalingrad oblast Party commit-

[12] LaPalombara, p. 22.
[13] The sources used in this study are described in the Preface.
[14] In this study the Soviet terminology, oblast Party committee and the abbreviation for this—obkom, are used in preference to the English translations.

tee, has been selected as a principal focus. The reasons for choosing Stalingrad are (1) in terms of size, location, industrial and agricultural development Stalingrad seems to be fairly typical of the oblasts within the Russian republic, and (2) it proved possible to examine a large number of issues of the local Party press for this oblast—Stalingrad. In order to avoid some of the pitfalls of a single case study, and particularly to place in broader perspective the details of the Stalingrad Party organization, extensive use is made of information on practices in other obkoms and in the Party as a whole.

In approaching the analysis of potential influence in the Communist Party, in order to bring out most effectively as many as possible of the relevant factors affecting the potential influence of various groups and individuals within the obkom, five questions are asked of the data in this study:

1. What is the composition of the decision-making organs?
2. What is their competence?
3. What are the patterns of participation in the deliberative process?
4. How are policy proposals formulated?
5. On the basis of the answers to these questions, what are the patterns of potential influence in the decision-making process of the Stalingrad oblast Party organization?

The first question seeks to determine who are the members of the decision-making organs, how they are selected, what groups are included among the membership, and in what proportions. If one or several groups are heavily overrepresented, while others receive little or no representation on the decision-making bodies, it may indicate that some groups have a favored position in terms of their opportunities for influencing Party policy.

The second question is directed at revealing the decision-making competence of the obkom as a whole, and of its subunits, the large committee and the small bureau. The competence of each of these decision-making units will determine, to a large extent, the degree of potential influence the members of each unit will have on particular areas of policy-making.

The third question focuses attention on what persons from which groups directly take part in the deliberative process through

making major speeches or contributions to the discussions at Party
committee plenums or bureau sessions. Are only committee members allowed to speak, or are nonmembers invited to participate?
What is the effect of this on the level of discussion? Does any one
group dominate the deliberations? Answers to these questions will
throw more light on the degree to which various groups participate
in political decision-making.

The fourth question examines the problem of the formation
of policy proposals prior to their discussion and either adoption
or rejection by the decision-making units. Analysis of the processes
for collection and assessment of information on policy problems
and the formation of project decisions will provide insight into
what groups are likely to exercise some influence on decision-
making through access to this segment of the decision-making
process.

The answers to these questions should help to elucidate the
basic problem of this study; namely, to what extent do interest
groups possess the potential for influencing Party policy? To what
extent do scientists, for example, have a measurable potential for
influence on Party decisions? What are the differentials in potential
influence between various occupational, or interest groups? Finally,
what are some of the factors that may account for the measurable
differences in potential influence between groups?

On a more general level, this study points to the possibility of
approaching the study of Soviet politics with tools now applied
almost exclusively to Western societies. Specifically, when interest
groups are thought of more as "shared interests" or institutional,
occupational groups, rather than formal, independent organizations; and when the concept of potential influence is introduced,
these tools can be used to assist us in constructing a more systematic,
and hopefully more revealing picture of the Soviet political system.
Of course, the more important goal of such an approach is not simply to analyze variations in potential influence of various individuals and groups, but to assess their actual influence on the political
process. In this study I attempt to point out some of the factors
that seem to condition the actual influence that groups might have.
Yet, given the present state of our knowledge, given the existing
difficulties of access to reliable information on the decision-making

process within the Communist Party, we cannot, at present, hope to do much more than experiment with different approaches attempting to develop analytical tools that enable us to attain the most significant findings possible from the available data.

Before proceeding directly to an analysis of political life in Stalingrad, it may be well to describe the city's physical and economic setting since this to a large extent will determine the problems the obkom must face as well as the kinds of resources it may bring to bear in attempting to fulfill the tasks placed upon it.

### THE SETTING OF STALINGRAD POLITICS

Stalingrad[15] spreads out for nearly 50 miles along a high bank of the lower Volga River. It was originally built as a small frontier fortress and, during the sixteenth and seventeenth centuries, it was frequently attacked by roaming tribes. In 1670, the Cossack Stenka Razin and his robbers took the city. From 1773 to 1775, the Pugachev Rebellion brought hostilities to the area. During the nineteenth century Tsarytsyn experienced rapid growth and became an important transshipment point for goods from the Volga to the Don River. The arrival of the railroad served as a further stimulus to its development. The city served as a key defense point in the civil war against Krasnov's White Army attacks from 1917 to 1920. The capture of the White controlled city by the Red Army was personally directed by Joseph Stalin, in whose honor the city was renamed Stalingrad in 1925.[16]

During the early five-year plans its industry developed rapidly, so that by 1929 its population had increased 300 per cent over its 1917 level.[17] World War II brought world-wide fame to the city as a result of the Battle of Stalingrad.

Stalingrad oblast has an area of 44,100 square miles and borders Voronezh and Saratov oblasts on the north, West Kazakhstan oblast on the east, Astrakhan oblast and Kalmyk Autonomous Republic on the south, and Rostov oblast on the west.[18] In 1963

---

[15] Before 1925 the city was called Tsarytsyn, and in 1961 its name was changed to Volgograd.

[16] "Stalingrad," *Collier's Encyclopedia*, 1961 ed., XVII, 627.

[17] *Ibid.*, p. 628.

[18] *SSSR: Administrativno-Territorial'noe Delenie Soiuznykh Respublik* (Moscow: "Izvestia," 1963), p. 66.

the population was 1,972,000 in the oblast—1,190,000 city dwellers, and 782,000 rural inhabitants. The population of Stalingrad, the oblast center, numbered 570,000.[19]

Stalingrad oblast is important both as an industrial and as an agricultural producer. Up until 1954, production of the main crop, spring wheat, was concentrated largely on the pre-Volga plateau to the west of the Volga River. This region consists of fertile chestnut-brown soils, and is located so as to receive whatever moisture the prevailing westerly winds may bring. Yet the average annual precipitation for the oblast as a whole is only 14 inches, and it frequently falls below this amount.[20] Other crops that grow in the pre-Volga region include winter rye, oats, spring barley, sunflower seeds, mustard seed, and grapes.

The area to the east of the Volga River, because the high eastern bank of the river acts as a barrier to the moisture bringing winds, is still drier and less fertile. Here the major agricultural undertaking until 1954 was sheep raising. Between 1953 and 1956, under the Virgin Lands program, the sown area in the oblast increased 72.9 per cent.[21] Much of this increase undoubtedly occurred on the eastern steppe regions. Although Stalingrad oblast was awarded the Order of Lenin in 1958, for overfulfilling its plan for grain deliveries,[22] the problems of grain production occupied a major part of the time and energy of the oblast level decision-makers throughout the period of this study— 1954 to 1962.

Live-stock production, for meat, milk, cheese, and other products, also constitutes an important part of Stalingrad's agricultural output. In a report to an oblast Party committee plenum, the obkom first secretary stated that the kolkhozes (collective farms) and sovkhozes (state farms) of the oblast, as of April 12, 1957, possessed 407,000 head of large-horned cattle, including 126,000 cows, 247,-000 hogs, and 1,697,000 head of sheep.[23]

As of 1957, the rural agricultural population was organized into 418 kolkhozes and 71 sovkhozes. These farms were serviced by

19 *Ibid.*
20 *Collier's Encyclopedia*, XVII, 628.
21 *Stalingradskaia Pravda*, April 12, 1957.
22 *Ibid.*, September 20, 1958.
23 *Ibid.*, April 12, 1957.

118 Machine Tractor Stations with tractors and other mechanized equipment totaling 358,000 horsepower.[24]

Not all agricultural production is carried on in the collectivized or state economy, however. As is well-known, each peasant family on the kolkhoz has the right to a small garden plot on which they may grow foods for their own use or for sale in the peasant markets. In Stalingrad oblast many peasants and even enterprising employees appear to spend considerable time and energy in developing their own plots and enlarging their own animal herds. At a Central Committee meeting in January, 1962, for heads of organizational otdels (departments)[25] of obkoms and raikoms (rural district Party committees), one raikom official from Stalingrad oblast complained that there was a tendency to expand the output of private plots, to the detriment of communal production:

> Individual kolkhozniki, workers, and employees of the sovkhozes and enterprises of our raion have two to three pigs, up to 20 sheep, about 3 cows, more than 50 ducks and geese, and as many chickens. . . . This does harm to the communal economy, and affects labor discipline.[26]

In addition to having a highly developed, diversified agriculture, Stalingrad is an industrial center of major importance for the country as a whole. In April, 1957, there were 656 enterprises and construction organizations.[27] In addition to the well-known Stalingrad Tractor Factory, other major enterprises include the steel factories—Red October and Petrov. Just outside Stalingrad a large oil refinery complex was completed in 1959, as was a major textile mill in the city of Kamyshin.[28] Some idea of the diversity of Stalingrad's industry can be gained from the evidence that before the 1957 industrial reorganization, economic leadership of her industry was exercised by 43 ministries and departments.[29] After the reorganization the Council of the National Economy (Sov-

---

[24] *Ibid.*

[25] Otdel is a Russian term referring to an administrative department. The Russian term is used in this study in preference to the English translation.

[26] "Let's Improve the Management of Agriculture," *Partiinaia Zhizn'*, No. 5 (1962), p. 26.

[27] *Stalingradskaia Pravda*, April 12, 1957.

[28] *Ibid.*, January 28, 1959.

[29] *Ibid.*, April 12, 1957.

narkhoz) assumed direction of the major 250 enterprises in the oblast. At this time Stalingrad's industry employed 140,000 workers and employees, including 12,000 engineers and technicians.[30]

Construction also occupies an important position in the economy of Stalingrad oblast. The total investment in construction projects and the construction materials industry of the oblast in 1956, amounted to 2,408 million rubles ($240,800,000).[31] Control over the work of construction was exercised by 46 construction organizations prior to the industrial reorganization. However, after 1957, these were amalgamated into six general construction trusts, three special trusts and two subordinate trusts.[32] The largest single construction project in the oblast at this time was the Stalingrad Hydroelectric Station with a planned capacity of 2,300,000 kilowatts. This project alone employed nearly half of the 80,000 construction workers in the oblast.[33]

Another major area of construction work consisted of housing construction—this would be expected after the nearly complete destruction of the city in World War II. At the city Party conference in 1959, the first secretary of the Stalingrad gorkom (city Party committee) stated:

> At the present time the housing fund of the city consists of 3,400,000 square meters; that is, nearly two times greater than the housing fund of the pre-war period.[34]

However, as the next sentence shows, the need for housing in Stalingrad had far from fully been met. "There are now 5.7 square meters of housing space for each inhabitant, on the average."[35] By 1960 this figure had reached 5.9 square meters per person.[36] The relatively low priority of housing construction can be judged from the evidence that fully 40 per cent of the housing construction in the

30 *Ibid.*

31 *Ibid.* The dollar amount is figured at the official rate of exchange as of 1956—ten rubles to the dollar.

32 *Ibid.*, June 13, 1957.

33 On April 12, 1957, the obkom first secretary, Zhegalin, stated in *Stalingradskaia Pravda*, that 80,000 persons were engaged in construction in the oblast, while on June 13, 1957, the Sovnarkhoz chairman, Sinitsyn, stated that except for the trust, Stalingradhydrostroi, 41,000 persons were engaged in construction in the oblast.

34 *Stalingradskaia Pravda*, November 14, 1959.

35 *Ibid.*

36 *Ibid.*, January 28, 1960.

postwar period consisted of privately built and owned structures, primarily of the log cabin type.[37]

Another indicator of the attention given to public services in the overall construction plans for Stalingrad is this statement by the obkom first secretary from 1957:

> In Stalingrad there are at present more than 550,000 inhabitants, and we have more than 100 schools, 43 hospitals, 3 theaters, 22 movie houses and movie squares (*kinoploshchadki*), 56 palaces of culture and clubs, 92 libraries, and 590 stores and cafeterias.[38]

The very difficult situation implied by these figures was made graphically clear several months later when it was explained that for each seat in the cafeterias, restaurants, and cafés in the city, there were 36 inhabitants, and in one of the major industrial districts, Krasnooktiabr'skii, one seat for every 54 inhabitants.[39]

If housing construction and public services were given a low priority, then consumer goods production was given even less attention. Of the 656 enterprises in Stalingrad oblast in 1957, only 40 of them were producing consumer goods. While all of these were "meeting their production plans," their products were described as "of poor quality, expensive, and limited in assortment."[40] Even though shortages in the consumer sector, and a lack of investment funds in the agricultural sector continually plagued the oblast decision-makers throughout the period of this study, their efforts to remove such shortages were hampered by limitations imposed on them from above. For example, the 1957 plan for capital investments in Stalingrad oblast, compiled by the planning agencies and ministries in Moscow, directed 70 per cent of such funds into heavy industry, leaving only 30 per cent to satisfy the needs of agriculture and of the city dwellers for communal services, housing, and consumer goods.[41]

Stalingrad's five higher educational institutions, including one of the country's best-known medical schools, help to keep its industry and agriculture supplied with educated specialists. In 1956

[37] *Ibid.*, April 19, 1956.
[38] *Ibid.*, April 12, 1957.
[39] *Ibid.*, October 24, 1957.
[40] *Ibid.*, February 12, 1957.
[41] *Ibid.*

these institutions graduated 1,300 students specializing in various branches of the economy. In addition to the advanced schools there are 31 secondary specialized educational institutions in the oblast that in 1956 graduated 3,700 specialists.[42]

These, then, are some of the objective factors conditioning and limiting the decision-making activities of the Stalingrad obkom. While striving to achieve a maximum level of agricultural and industrial output—particularly the products of heavy industry—the obkom would always have to consider the minimum needs of the local population for such products as housing and communal services.

[42] *Ibid.*, April 12, 1957.

# TWO

# Political Organization at
# the Oblast Level

[1:1]

## HIGHER AND LOWER PARTY ORGANS

The structure of the Communist Party is usually analyzed in terms of four levels: (1) the central organs; (2) the republic, krai, and oblast; (3) the district and city; (4) and the lowest and most widespread layer—the primary Party organs.[1] The higher Party organs include the Party Congress, the Central Committee of the Party and its Presidium. Local Party organs include the two middle layers: the oblast, republic and krai, on the one hand, and the raion and city on the other.[2] These are the territorial Party organs, forming the connecting link between the Central Committee and the primary Party organs and responsible to the former for the execution of its policies and decisions.

The number of local Party organizations has often varied. In

[1] L. Slepov, *Vysshie i Mestnye Organy Partii* (Moscow: Higher Party School, 1958), p. 11.

[2] B. F. Shilov, "Local Party Organs—Organs of Political and Organizational Leadership," *Voprosy Partiinogo Stroitel'stva* (Leningrad: Leningrad Publishing House, 1962), p. 238. (Hereafter cited as *VPS.*)

1958, the Communist Party included 14 union-republic Party organizations, 6 krai,[3] 154 oblast (including 70 in the Russian Republic), 10 okrug,[4] 577 city, 411 city district, 3,908 rural district Party organizations, and 351,249 primary Party organizations.[5] By October 1, 1961, the number of oblast Party organizations had decreased to 137, while the number of city Party organizations had increased to 602. At the same time, the number of district committees in cities had decreased to 343, rural district committees to 3,202, and the number of primary Party organizations dropped by nearly 55,000.[6]

### SIGNIFICANCE OF THE LOCAL PARTY COMMITTEES

The significance of the local Party committees arises partly from the strategic position they occupy in the intermediate ranges of policy-making and policy execution. Their importance is fully recognized by Party theorists. Slepov has stated that "it is difficult to imagine leadership of the country without these intermediate links of Party leadership."[7] The Vice-Chairman of the Department of Party and Soviet Construction of the Leningrad Higher Party School goes even further:

> It can be stated boldly that there are no questions in the life of the Party and of the Soviet state the successful solution of which to a significant, and very often decisive degree does not depend on the level and quality of organizational activity of the local Party organs, on their ability to lead and direct the initiative and creative activity of the wide masses of working people.[8]

[3] A kraikom occupies exactly the same position and exercises the same rights as an obkom.

[4] An okruzhkom occupies exactly the same position and has the same rights and responsibilities as a raikom.

[5] Slepov, p. 9.

[6] "The CPSU in Figures," *Partiinaia Zhizn'*, No. 1 (1962), p. 53. The decrease in the number of primary Party organizations included nearly 36,000 collective farm (kolkhoz) organizations—chiefly in connection with the enlargement of kolkhozes, nearly 9,000 organizations in Repair Tractor Stations, nearly 14,000 in state and economic administrative organizations and institutions in connection with the reduction of excess branches of the bureaucracy, and nearly 8,700 in rural territorial institutions, as well as other reductions. At the same time, the number of primary Party organizations in construction projects increased by nearly 3,400, in state farms (sovkhozes) by more than 6,700, and in educational, scientific, cultural, and health organizations and institutions by approximately 6,000. Similar increases occurred in trade, procurement, and communal service organizations.

[7] Slepov, p. 37.

[8] *VPS.* p. 252.

Thus, the local Party organs are seen as connecting links between the Central Committee and the primary Party organizations, whose "first obligation" is the "precise and unconditional fulfillment of the Party's directives."[9] The central leaders themselves feel that the local Party organs should serve primarily as a "disciplined phalanx" to execute their will.[10]

### ORGANIZATIONAL PRINCIPLES

The organizational structure of the Party is based on the principle known as "democratic centralism." The relationship of the local Party organizations to the Central Committee[11] is based on "the unconditional obligatory nature of decisions of higher organs for lower bodies."[12] The Party is conceived as a single system of organizations, with higher and lower governing bodies, in which practical decisions are binding on all Party members. Centralism is said to be necessary to secure unity of will and action.[13] This, in turn, "gives the Party mobility, enabling it to reform its ranks rapidly as the situation changes, to concentrate the efforts of the whole Party on accomplishing the historic tasks of communist construction."[14]

Although there are 14 Communist Party organizations in the union republics, each with its own name and Central Committee, their relationship with the Central Committee of the CPSU is much the same as that of an oblast Party committee. The Communist Party of the Soviet Union is not a "federation of national Parties," but a "united monolithic Party." This means that the republic Party organizations exist and work within the same rights and duties as the oblast Party organizations and have no special

---

9 Slepov, p. 39.

10 Merle Fainsod, *How Russia is Ruled*, 2nd ed. (Cambridge: Harvard University Press, 1963), p. 215.

11 The term "Central Committee" is used here to denote the central Party organs, including the Central Committee, the Presidium or Politburo, and the Secretariat. This is in line with general Soviet usage.

12 G. Shitarev, "Democratic Centralism and the Guiding Work of the Party Organs," *Kommunist*, No. 18 (1953), p. 55. The other elements usually included in democratic centralism are the electivity of all leading Party organs, from the bottom to the top; the periodic accountability of Party organs before their Party organizations; strict Party discipline; and the subordination of the minority to the majority.

13 *Ibid.*

14 *Pravda*, October 29, 1961, p. 5.

rights.[15] The largest of the republics, the RSFSR, has no national Party organization, but rather the oblast and krai Party organizations within the Russian Republic are directly subordinate to the Central Committee of the CPSU through its bureau for the RSFSR.[16]

GENERAL COMPETENCE

While stressing the strict subordination of local Party organizations to the Central Committee, Party theoreticians are also quick to point out that whereas under Stalin and the personality cult there occurred "excessive" centralism, the proper Leninist understanding of centralism also includes the "display of creative initiative" by the local Party organizations.[17] The Party Rules define the area in which the local Party organs may exercise their initiative by stating that they are "autonomous in the solution of local questions, if these solutions do not contradict Party policy."[18] Autonomy in the Soviet context is interpreted quite narrowly. It is not to be construed as allowing the local Party organizations to act "in isolation from the center," to "shut themselves up within the limits of their own local region."[19] Most important, the principle of local autonomy does not permit the local organizations to "act wilfully in matters of politics."[20] The local Party organizations must bear in mind constantly the directives, policies, and programs of the central organs when seeking the solutions to tasks and problems facing them.

While the general competence of the local Party organs appears from the above discussion to be restricted to mere execution of decisions taken at a higher level, in practice it can be, indeed must be, quite far reaching. The reasons for this are made clear by the Party theoreticians themselves. "No directive from above," Slepov states, "regardless of how excellent it may be, can take into account all local potentialities and resources." For this reason, he

15 *VPS*. p. 243.
16 *Ibid*. RSFSR is the abbreviation for the Russian Soviet Federated Socialist Republic.
17 Slepov, p. 22.
18 *Programma i Ustav KPSS* (Moscow: Gospolitizdat, 1962), art. 21.
19 Slepov, p. 43.
20 *Ibid*.

continues, "Party decisions define only the general outlines of what must be achieved."[21] Local Party organs must fill in the detail, make the decisions applicable to their region, find the local resources necessary to fulfill the plan, and take the responsibility for the overall fulfillment of higher decisions. Yet, no local Party leaders can limit themselves to mere fulfillment of specific Central Committee directives and hope for longevity in their positions. The Party committees and Party secretaries must be concerned with everything, as was emphasized in a lecture read at the Central Committee Higher Party School:

> One of the distinguishing features of the activity of a Party committee as an organ of political leadership is that it answers for everything: for the state of the economy, for cultural work, for any other branch. The Party organs encompass all questions which are of vital concern to the toilers. There is no Soviet, economic, or cultural institution whose activity would not be given direction by a Party organ. There is not one question concerning the life of the toilers in relation to which a Party organ could say, "This is not my affair." As the organ of political leadership, everything is of interest to the Party committee; it must be concerned with everything that is connected with the execution of the Party's policies, with the interests and needs of the toilers.[22]

Although this statement gives the impression that the competence of the local Party organizations is universal within their territorial area, such a conclusion would be quite misleading. In actual practice, the area in which the local Party organizations may take authoritative (binding) decisions, as opposed to recommendations, or suggestions, has varied considerably. Generally, during the period under study, the trend has been toward increasing the range of matters concerning which local committees may take binding decisions.[23] Before making a detailed analysis of decision-making in the Stalingrad obkom, we must examine its structure.

21 *Ibid.*, p. 41.
22 *Ibid.*, p. 45.
23 See Chapters 5 and 6.

THREE

# The Oblast Party
# Conference

3.1

The Stalingrad oblast Party organization in January, 1960, included 89,609 full members, and 7,085 candidates, or in all 96,694 Communists.[1] The Party Rules stipulate that the highest organ within the oblast organization is the oblast Party conference, and in the periods between conferences, the oblast Party committee. Conferences are held on the decision of the obkom, but, in any case, must be held at least once every two years. The Party conferences hear the reports of the Party committee, discuss at their discretion other questions of Party, economic, and cultural work, and elect the new Party committee.[2] During the period under study, five conferences were held in Stalingrad. The ninth oblast Party conference was held in February, 1954; the tenth in January, 1956; the eleventh in December, 1957; the twelfth in January, 1959; and the thirteenth in January, 1960.[3]

[1] *Stalingradskaia Pravda,* January 27, 1960.
[2] *Programma i Ustav KPSS,* art. 44.
[3] *Stalingradskaia Pravda,* February 10, 1954; January 18, 1956; December 26, 1957; January 8, 1959; and January 28, 1960.

The norms for representation at the Party conferences are established by the corresponding Party committee, in this case, by the Stalingrad obkom. At the eleventh Party conference there were 783 delegates with a decisive vote and 74 with a consultative vote, making approximately one delegate for every hundred Party members.[4]

The primary responsibility for selecting delegates, arranging the conference agenda, and formulating the list of candidates for election to the conference presidium, secretariat, and mandate commission appears to lie with the obkom Party organs otdel.[5] Delegates to the oblast Party conference are formally elected at the district and city Party conferences that are held several weeks before the oblast conference; and, as stated by an obkom secretary, "as a rule at the conferences the candidates recommended by the obkoms are amicably supported."[6]

At the conference itself, each delegate's credentials are examined by the mandate commission. At four of the five oblast conferences, the head of the Party organs otdel was named chairman of the mandate commission. At the 1957 Stalingrad Party conference this responsibility was fulfilled by the former head of the Party organs otdel who was about to be elected obkom secretary in charge of work with cadres and relations with other Party organizations.[7] This latter fact is significant as evidence that the obkom secretaries probably play an active role in supervising and approving all conference arrangements.

The delegates to the Stalingrad conferences included the major Party officials in the oblast, officials of the local Soviets, the trade-union and Komsomol organizations, executives from the most important industrial enterprises, scientific, cultural, and artistic workers. At the 1957 conference, rank and file workers and kolk-

---

[4] *Ibid.*, December 26, 1957. At the 1960 conference it was stated that the oblast Party organization had grown by about 9,000 members in the past two years, or about 5 per cent per year. Calculating back, this would mean that the oblast Party organization had about 76,000 members in 1957. Unfortunately, no exact data is available as to the number of delegates at the other Stalingrad oblast Party conferences.

[5] This would be consistent with the overall responsibility of this otdel for the selection of leading cadres, and its function as organizer and supervisor of meetings and conferences of lower Party committees. An article in *Partiinaia Zhizn'*, No. 22 (1960), p. 15, describes the "chief business" of the otdel of Party organs as "the selection of cadres and the verification of fulfillment." See also, *Partiinaia Zhizn'*, No. 23 (1957), p. 28, for a discussion of the role of the Party organs otdel in organizing and supervising meetings and elections in lower Party organs.

[6] "From the City and Raion Party Conferences," *Partiinaia Zhizn'*, No. 23 (1957), p. 28.

[7] *Stalingradskaia Pravda*, February 10, 1954; January 18, 1956; December 26, 1957; January 8, 1959; and January 28, 1960.

hozniks accounted for nearly 40 per cent of all delegates.[8] At the eleventh conference the delegates included two deputies to the Supreme Soviet of the USSR, four to the Supreme Soviet of the RSFSR, eight "Heroes of Socialist Labor," four "Heroes of the Soviet Union," and 714 persons who had been decorated with Soviet orders and medals.[9]

ORGANIZATION

In Stalingrad, the oblast Party conferences are held in the Gor'ky Drama Theater. The arrangements in the foyer of the theater indicate one major purpose of the conferences. Here exhibits are set up, including examples of products produced by Stalingrad's enterprises, as well as charts and diagrams showing "the successes of the rural working people, and how they are struggling to fulfill the decisions of the Party."[10] As a result of having attended the Party conference, the rank and file Party workers are expected to return to their work with greater zeal and determination, and with a clearer idea of the place their work occupies in the overall tasks and plans of the oblast Party organization in particular, and of the Party as a whole.[11]

While the rank and file delegates are assembling in the main auditorium, the "leading comrades," slated for election to the presidium, usually "go through the side entrance, direct to the stage, avoiding the hall."[12] Some Party members protest that a place in the presidium often becomes *nomenklaturny,* that is, it seems to come with a certain post and is permanently occupied by one person. Moreover, the same seating arrangement is nearly always used. Thus, the presidium chairman, who is usually the obkom first secretary, sits in the center; on his left is the chairman of the oblast Soviet; next to him, the director of the most important enterprise in the oblast, and so on.[13]

8 *Ibid.,* December 26, 1957. It is probable that kolkhoz chairmen, and other agricultural officials, as well as shop foremen and employees are included under the designation "rank and file."

9 *Ibid.*

10 *Ibid.*

11 See especially, "From the Raion and City Conferences," *Partiinaia Zhizn',* No. 21 (1956), p. 5; and "Centralism and the Guiding Work of the Party Organs," *Kommunist,* No. 18 (1953), p. 64.

12 "On Presidiums at Party Meetings," *Partiinaia Zhizn',* No. 20 (1955), p. 63.

13 *Ibid.*

At ten A.M. the obkom first secretary rises and declares the oblast Party conference open. The presidium, already seated on the stage, is then elected unanimously. At the 1957 and 1959 conferences, the presidium consisted of 49 and 42 persons respectively. Table 1 shows the composition of each presidium by occupational

*Table 1: Membership in the Presidium of Stalingrad Oblast Party Conferences by Occupational Position—1957 and 1959*

| OCCUPATIONAL POSITION | NUMBER OF PRESIDIUM MEMBERS | |
|---|---|---|
| | 1957 | 1959 |
| Obkom bureau members and candidates | 11 | 11 |
| Obkom secretaries | 5 | 5 |
| Obkom apparat officials | 0 | 1 |
| Oblast Soviet executive committee chairman and members | 4 | 3 |
| City Party committee first secretaries | 3 | 3 |
| City Soviet executive committee chairman | 1 | 0 |
| District Party committee secretaries | 10 | 6 |
| District Soviet executive committee chairmen | 2 | 1 |
| Heads of oblast trade-union and Komsomol organs | 2 | 2 |
| Managers of industrial enterprises | 3 | 3 |
| Oblast Sovnarkhoz chairman | 1 | 1 |
| Military officials | 2 | 3 |
| Editor of Stalingradskaia Pravda | 1 | 1 |
| Director, oblast agricultural institute | 1 | 1 |
| Secretary, primary Party organization | 1 | 1 |
| State farm and MTS directors, and chairmen of kolkhozes | 1 | 3 |
| Old Bolshevik | 1 | 1 |
| Rank and file workers and peasants | 1 | 7 |
| Central Party and Government officials | 0 | 2 |
| Members of the oblast Party committee | 39 | 29 |
| Not identified | 6 | 0 |
| Total number of presidium members[a] | 49 | 42 |

SOURCES: *Stalingradskaia Pravda*, December 26, 1957, and January 8, 1959. Data on positions held by presidium members was compiled on the basis of information from *Stalingradskaia Pravda*, 1954–1961.

[a] Columns do not equal totals given because individual persons may occupy two or more positions.

position of each member.[14] Analysis of the Table lends support to
the protest that Presidium places always go to the same "leading
comrades."

All five obkom secretaries and all other members of the obkom
bureau—the most important Party body at the oblast level—[15] were
included in the presidium at both conferences. The first secretaries
of the three city Party committees were also "permanent" presidium members.[16] The director of the Stalingrad Tractor Factory, the
oblast's most famous and one of its most important factories, was
elected in both instances, although in 1957, he was joined by the directors of two construction trusts and the director of the hydroelectric construction project. In 1957, the secretary of the primary
Party organization of the Stalingrad Tractor Factory sat on the
presidium, but in 1959, he was replaced by the secretary from the
Red October steel plant Party organization. Although the number
of district Party committee secretaries varies from six to ten, it
seems to be the practice to honor with a position on the presidium
those who have performed exceptionally well. This is also true regarding agricultural officials and rank and file workers. Thus, of ten
raikom secretaries elected to the presidium in 1957, one had been a
delegate to the twentieth Party Congress, another was a "Hero of
Socialist Labor," six were first secretaries of continuously successful agricultural districts, and two were representatives from major
industrial districts in Stalingrad, including the Tractor Factory
district.[17]

FUNCTION

If the Party conference presidium exercised a purely honorary
function, its composition would be of little consequence. However,
this is not the case. A major part of the work of the conference is to
pass judgment on the activities of the leading Party organs for the

14 Only the data for the 1957 and 1959 oblast Party conferences are used here because
this information is not available for the other conferences.
15 See Chapter 6 for an analysis of the place of the bureau in the structure of the obkom.
16 The city Party committees included are those of Stalingrad, Kamyshin—the site of an
important textile mill—and Volzhki, a new city built to house construction workers
at the Stalingrad Hydroelectric Station.
17 This information was compiled on the basis of data from *Stalingradskaia Pravda*,
1954–1961, but especially from material published during 1957 and 1959.

previous two years, and to subject the performance of the responsible Party officials—primarily the oblast Party secretaries—to intensive and thorough criticism.[18] In this way the rank and file, represented by the conference delegates, are supposed to "direct" their
elected bodies. The effectiveness of debate and discussion at the
conference will, of course, be determined largely by what topics are
discussed and who is permitted to speak. As the directing body of
the conference, it is the presidium that has the responsibility for
directing all its activity. In this light it is very significant that the
largest group in the presidium consists of the Party secretaries—
precisely those whose work is supposed to be under scrutiny.[19]
Thus, not only do the Party secretaries in general and the obkom
secretaries in particular have the determining voice in selecting the
delegates to the conference, but they also occupy the crucial positions at the conference itself.

Following the election of the working presidium, beginning
with the 1956 conference and continuing at each conference thereafter, the Presidium of the Central Committee of the CPSU was
unanimously elected by "long and stormy applause" as an honorary
conference presidium.[20] It is worth noting that no such action was
taken at the 1954 oblast Party conference. The symbolic election of
the Central Committee Presidium may be seen as a reflection of
Khrushchev's efforts to build support for himself through use of his
patronage powers. As first secretary of the Central Committee, he
would have the decisive voice in determining whether an obkom
first secretary would remain in his post, be promoted, or face removal and disgrace.[21] A "long and stormy" display of loyalty and
devotion to the Central Committee Presidium may be one way for
oblast secretaries to improve their chances for a long and successful
career.

The conference agenda usually consists of three to four items.
The first item is the report on the work of the oblast Party commit-

18 *Stalingradskaia Pravda*, February 10, 1954.

19 The 1957 and 1959 conference presidiums included 19 and 15 Party secretaries respectively.

20 *Stalingradskaia Pravda*, January 18, 1956; December 26, 1957; January 8, 1959; and
January 28, 1960.

21 For an analysis of the changes that occurred among the secretaries of the Stalingrad
obkom from 1954 through 1961 see Chapter 6, pp. 89–99.

tee, given, as a rule, by the first secretary.[22] In abbreviated form this report normally fills one to two pages in *Stalingradskaia Pravda*. Major emphasis is placed on economic achievements in heavy industry, while difficulties and failures in the production of consumer goods, housing, and municipal services are given only cursory treatment. Problems and prospects in agricultural production are discussed prominently and extensively. Concluding sections deal briefly with problems of Soviet, Komsomol, trade-union and other mass organizations, and with questions of the Party organization's political and organizational work.[23]

The second item on the agenda is the discussion of the major report. The opportunity to participate in the discussions theoretically is available to all delegates. It has been reported that 75 to 100 persons frequently express a desire to speak at an oblast Party conference.[24] However, in Stalingrad the participants are normally chosen before the conference begins and are limited to about 25 or 26 speakers.[25] Soviet theorists justify this practice on the basis of the general duty of the Party committee to see that everything is well-organized, that nothing is left to chance.[26] One practical reason cited for limited participation is that "the conference cannot go on for more than two or three days."[27] Moreover, Lenin gave support to selecting participants before the opening of the conference when he urged the Party committees to ". . . turn the conferences and meetings not into organs of endless discussion, but into organs of the verification of economic successes, into organs in which we can study economic work in a real way."[28]

---

22 Although the obkom first secretary made the report at all other conferences, in 1956 this duty was performed by the second secretary. Since the new first secretary had been appointed just a month before the conference, this may be considered a special case.

23 For example, see *Stalingradskaia Pravda*, December 26, 1957, pp. 2–3.

24 "Let's Improve the Practice of Party Leadership of the Economy," *Partiinaia Zhizn'*, No. 8 (1960), p. 27.

25 This was true in Stalingrad for 1956, 1957, and 1959, but in 1960 there were only 12 speakers in the discussions. See *Stalingradskaia Pravda*, January 20, 1956; December 27, 1957; January 8, 1959; and January 28, 1960.

26 "Consistently Practice and Develop Inner-Party Democracy," *Kommunist*, No. 12 (1954), p. 5.

27 "Let's Improve the Practice of Party Leadership of the Economy," *Partiinaia Zhizn'*, No. 8 (1960), p. 27.

28 *Ibid.*

PARTICIPATION

Examination of the list of speakers in the discussions points up the essentially pedagogical orientation of the Party conference. Rather than effective participation by the rank and file, we see the discussion dominated by the Party secretaries and members of the obkom bureau. In 1956, out of 26 speakers 12 were Party secretaries from the obkom, gorkom, and raikoms, and six were industrial managers or oblast level ministry officials, but only one rank and file worker was permitted to speak—and then he talked only about reasons for the failure of a construction trust to fulfill the housing construction plans. Eight of the speakers were members of the obkom bureau.[29]

Even though the speakers criticize other officials for their errors and point out some of their own mistakes, one gathers the impression that these revelations are made not so much for the officials' benefit as to instruct the 700 or so delegates, who are mostly middle and lower level Party workers, as to what is expected of them. The very titles of the speeches ring with admonitions: "Delve Deeper into the Work of the Enterprises!" "Know the State of Affairs in Each Raion!" "Build Quickly but Well!" and "Pay Daily Attention to the Oil Workers' Needs!"[30] It would be incorrect to imply, however, that the conference is not or may not be used as a forum for severely criticizing and disgracing certain officials who have lost favor or failed miserably in their work. At the same time it must be stated that although certain individuals were quite strongly criticized, at the Stalingrad conferences there were no instances where such workers were publicly disgraced and ousted from the Party.

At two conferences, 1956 and 1959, the agenda included discussions of projects of new economic plans—the projected Sixth Five-Year plan in 1956, and the projected Seven-Year plan in 1959.[31] The inclusion of such items in the agenda points to another

[29] *Stalingradskaia Pravda*, January 19, 1956. The other speakers included one official of the obkom apparat, the chairman of the oblast Soviet, three directors of MTS's, the heads of the oblast organizations of the Komsomol and trade-union organization, and the chief of the oblast administration of the All-Union Society for the Dissemination of Political and Scientific Knowledge.

[30] *Ibid.*

[31] *Ibid.*, January 18, 1956, and January 8, 1959.

purpose of the Party conferences: namely, to help the local Party and state officials to gain some perspective of the place their work occupies in the overall plans and programs of the Party. This aspect of the conference has been summed up as follows:

> The responsibility of the leaders is to assure such a preparation for the conference and its execution that it becomes a really important occurrence in the life of the organization, that it gives a good experience and a good plan for the struggle to successfully fulfill the decisions of the 20th Party Congress.[32]

While the Party conference, then, may serve at times as a forum for criticizing, disciplining, and disgracing particular Party officials, and thus "steering" the work of the Party committee, it seems to serve primarily as a school or training session for lower level Party and state officials. Participation in this school should help these local workers to acquire some of the attitudes and values necessary for making decisions in their own area of competence that are correct from a Party point of view.

After a concluding statement by the obkom first secretary, the discussion comes to an end, and the conference "recognizes the work of the oblast Party committee for the accounting period as satisfactory," and adopts a resolution, "directed to improving further the work of the oblast Party organization."[33] Beginning with the first oblast Party conference after the June, 1957 Presidium power struggle and continuing thereafter, the conference resolutions also "expressed confidence [*uverennost'*] that the oblast Party organization, as never before, is united and devoted to the Leninist Central Committee. . . ."[34] Even more than the election of the Central Committee Presidium as an honorary conference presidium, this statement, appearing only after Khrushchev had finally routed his rivals, seems to be an affirmation of personal loyalty to him on the part of the oblast Party committee leadership.

ELECTING THE PARTY COMMITTEE

The final item on the conference agenda is the election of the oblast

32 "From the District and City Conferences," *Partiinaia Zhizn'*, No. 21 (1956), p. 5.
33 *Stalingradskaia Pravda*, January 19, 1956.
34 *Ibid.*, January 8, 1959. The 1957 statement is identical except that it omits the phrase, "and devoted," while the 1960 statement is identical to that quoted in the text.

Party committee and revision commission.[35] Although the Party conference is called the "highest organ of the oblast Party organization,"[36] nevertheless, it has only a formal part in selecting the committee entrusted with directing the affairs of the Party organization between conferences. The same procedure for selecting conference delegates and the members of the conference presidium appears to be used in the selection of members for the oblast Party committee. Here again the list of nominations is prepared by the obkom bureau, probably with the assistance of the otdel of Party organs.[37] The extent to which the obkom bureau is free to select the candidates it desires cannot be determined exactly, but certain limiting factors may be cited.

In discussing the new procedures for electing leading bodies envisaged in the new Party Rules, Frol Kozlov pointed out that "as hitherto" all details relating to the election of Party organs will be determined by instructions from the Central Committee of the CPSU.[38] Among the items these instructions probably include are the approximate size of the Party committee and its composition according to groups of the population. Thus, *Partiinaia Zhizn'* stated in 1955 that ". . . in recent years, the Party expanded the size of committees."[39] The reference to "the Party" normally means its leading bodies, the Central Committee and the Presidium. Somewhat later *Kommunist* stated that "considerable numbers of workers, collective farmers, and representatives of the intelligentsia, all directly engaged in production, have now been elected to district, city, and oblast Party committees."[40] An across-the-board change in the composition of local Party committees can reasonably be attributed to Central Committee instructions.

In addition to its influence on the size and composition of the

---

[35] The revision commission, which is charged with reviewing budgetary and other Party housekeeping matters, is of no real consequence to oblast level decision-making and so is omitted from our discussion.

[36] *Programma i Ustav KPSS*, art. 43.

[37] Unfortunately the oblast press does not provide much useful detail on the procedures for selecting the members of the oblast Party committee. The best that it does offer is its failure to disconfirm the conclusions regarding these procedures found in the standard works. See, for example, John N. Hazard, *The Soviet System of Government*, 2nd ed. (Chicago: University of Chicago Press, 1960), p. 17.

[38] *Pravda*, October 29, 1961, p. 1.

[39] "What are the Rights and Responsibilities of a Party Committee Member?" *Partiinaia Zhizn'*, No. 12 (1955), p. 68.

[40] "Fully Restore the Leninist Norms of Party Life," *Kommunist* No. 4 (1956), p. 5.

oblast Party committee, the Central Committee has a decisive voice in selecting certain of its members. Before the 22nd Party Congress, the Party Rules specified that the election of obkom secretaries was "subject to the confirmation of the Central Committee of the Party."[41] In the new Rules, as adopted at the 22nd Congress, there is no direct reference to the confirmation of obkom secretaries by the Central Committee, still the latter is given the power to "select and distribute leading cadres."[42] On the basis of this power, the Central Committee may appoint and remove an indefinite number of obkom members. In practice, however, the Central Committee seems to limit itself to the appointment of secretaries and either appointment or simply confirmation of the bureau, depending upon the circumstances under which changes are being made.[43]

The oblast Party committee is given a list of candidates for election. This list is drawn up by the obkom bureau with reference to the Central Committee's wishes and in accordance with its instructions. What is left for the conference delegates to do? The statements in *Stalingradskaia Pravda* on the election of the Party committees give the impression that the delegates simply turn in their ballots with little or no discussion before they vote.[44] However, the Party Rules state that "each candidate shall be voted upon separately, every Party member being ensured the unlimited right to challenge the candidates and to criticize them."[45] Actual practice probably varies somewhere between these two extremes.

Under the Rules in effect prior to the 22nd Party Congress, candidates were considered elected in the order of the number of votes cast for them individually. If 100 obkom members were to be elected from 110 candidates, then the ten candidates with the least number of votes would be counted as not elected. According to the Party Rules adopted at the 22nd Party Congress, the total num-

---

[41] *KPSS v Rezoliutsiiakh i Resheniiakh S"ezdov, Konferentsii i Plenumov Tsk*, 4 vols., 7th ed. (Moscow: Gospolitizdat, 1954–1960), III, art. 42, 588. (Cited hereafter as *KPSS v Rezoliutsiiakh*...).

[42] *Programma i Ustav KPSS*, art. 35.

[43] Fainsod, p. 325. The practice in Stalingrad is, apparently, to make changes in obkom secretaries and other leading personnel at plenums, rather than at conferences. See Chapter 6, 88–99, for more discussion of this.

[44] *Stalingradskaia Pravda*, January 28, 1960. The statement is nearly always the same: "As a result of secret voting, the oblast Party committee and the oblast revision commission are elected."

[45] *KPSS v Rezoliutsiiakh*..., art. 26, p. 584.

ber of candidates to be elected would have to be flexible since "those candidates are considered elected who received the affirmative votes of more than half of the participants. . . ."[46] While this change appears to be a move in the direction of greater democracy in the election of Party committees, the real choices are made by the obkom bureau and the Central Committee prior to the voting at the Party conference. Although at the level of the district and primary Party organizations, candidates suggested from above occasionally do not receive enough votes for election, at the obkom level where discipline is perhaps more effective such occurrences are probably very rare.[47]

After the voting is completed, the delegates rise and sing the Party hymn, the "International." The obkom first secretary then declares the oblast Party conference closed.

A major purpose of the oblast Party conference is to help the lower level cadres gain a better sense of the place of their work in the overall activities of the oblast Party organization. For the oblast leadership itself, the oblast Party conference is of more than passing importance. From the tone of the speeches and the reactions of the delegates, the leadership may gain fresh insight into what areas of the work must be pushed, what problems are being overlooked, and what opportunities are not being fully utilized. From analysis of proposals put forth at the conference the leadership may broaden its own experience, and improve the quality of its day-to-day decisions.[48]

The Party Rules notwithstanding, the oblast Party conference cannot be considered the highest Party organ in the oblast. Although it theoretically "guides" the actions of the oblast Party committee and its leaders, the entire conference is organized and directed by the professional Party secretaries and bureau members. Decision-making power and responsibility reside not in the oblast Party conference but in a narrower collegium.

[46] *Programma i Ustav KPSS.*, art. 24.

[47] For an instance where a raikom refused to accept a candidate suggested by the obkom, see "From the City and Raion Party Conferences," *Partiinaia Zhizn'*, No. 23 (1957), p. 28.

[48] The purpose of the Party conferences from the leadership's point of view is discussed in "Centralism and the Guiding Work of the Party Organs," *Kommunist*, No. 18 (1953), pp. 51–66.

# FOUR

# The Oblast Party
# Committee—Membership

🄳🄳

## SIZE

The last ten years have seen a considerable increase in the number
of Communists elected to the local Party committees. In June,
1955, the district and city committees consisted of more than
200,000 members, and the oblast committees of nearly 14,000.[1] In
1957, more than 250,000 members and candidates were elected to
raion and city Party committees, and about 20,000 to obkoms.[2] By
1961, on the eve of the 22nd Party Congress, the former had increased to 286,000 and the latter to 20,821.[3] This growth, however,
was more than offset by increases in the size of the Party as a
whole. Between February, 1956 and July, 1961, while the Party
grew from 7,215,505 to 9,626,740 members, the membership of all
district and city Party committees decreased from 3.4 to 2.9 per

---

1 "What are the Rights and Responsibilities of a Member of a Party Committee," *Partiinaia Zhizn'*, No. 12 (1955), p. 68.
2 "From Party History," *Partiinaia Zhizn'*, No. 20 (1957), p. 92.
3 "Democratic Centralism—The Guiding Principle of Party Organization," *VPS*, p. 152.

cent of the entire Party.[4] At the same time obkom membership dropped from slightly more to just less than two-tenths of one per cent of the Party as a whole. In Stalingrad the oblast Party committee grew from 77 members in 1954 to 96 in 1956 and 131 in December, 1957, remaining at the same level in 1961.[5]

## COMPOSITION

Before proceeding to an analysis of the membership structure of the obkom it is necessary to clarify the meaning of the term "representative" as it is used in this study. In the Soviet context this term is not meant to denote an individual who speaks for the majority of, or who is responsible to the particular occupational, institutional, or social group of which he may be considered a member; that is, this term cannot be understood as connoting or denoting the normal meaning associated with it in democratic countries. Rather representative and representation as used here are more akin to the practice observed in some European states whereby major associational interest groups are accorded formal corporative representation on certain organs within the bureaucracy. In this sense representative denotes an individual who, while not necessarily speaking for the majority or even a large segment of the group he represents, normally may be presumed to speak from a point of view common to at least the leading strata of his group.[6] At least to some degree, for example, an industrial manager can be said to speak from the point of view of managers in general; at any rate, he may be presumed to view problems and possible solutions from a perspective having more in common with the outlook of his own occupational group than, say, with that of trade-union or professional Party secretaries. At the same time it must be made perfectly clear that this suggested commonality of outlook by no means implies that all the members of any particular group, managers, or Party officials for example, hold identical views on current

---

4 "From Party History," *Partiinaia Zhizn'*, No. 20 (1957), p. 93, and "The CPSU in Figures—1956–1961," *Partiinaia Zhizn'*, No. 1 (1962), p. 48.

5 *Stalingradskaia Pravda*, February 10, 1954; January 18, 1956; December 26, 1957; and January 28, 1960.

6 Robert Conquest offers a similar concept of representation in the Soviet political system in his book, *Power and Policy in the U.S.S.R.* (London: St. Martin's Press, 1962), p. 48.

issues. Indeed, it is well-established that conflicting viewpoints exist within each occupational or social grouping in the Soviet Union—just as elsewhere.[7]

Although the Soviet form of representation is similar in most respects to the European concept of corporate-state representation, several critical differences between these forms must be stressed. The first major difference relates to the question: What groups will be accorded representation? Whereas in most European countries any group may seek openly to establish channels of influence to the government, and generally, may select the individuals who act as their spokesmen, in the Soviet Union the central Party organs largely decide which groups are to be accorded representation on the Party committees, as well as the persons to serve as representatives. This practice may lead to more or less arbitrary manipulation of various social groupings. Indeed, this appears to be the case with most cultural groups such as writers and actors as well as with peasants and workers. The first of these groups, as will be shown (p. 41), are largely excluded from this form of representation. Although a few peasants and workers are included on the Party committees, there is little evidence to suggest that they act as spokesmen for their respective social groups. Most evidence suggests, on the contrary, that individual peasants and workers are chosen as committee members on the basis of their ability to act as spokesmen for the Party among their respective classes rather than as advocates of peasant and worker interests.

A second critical difference is the role of the individual representative. In the system of corporate-state representation the individual representative is directly and unabashedly a spokesman for particularistic interests and values. His role is to protect and promote the interests of his group in governmental policy-making. In the Soviet Union the individual member of the Party committee is considered, first of all, a member of the Party, dedicated to the attainment of its goals. Only secondarily is he considered a spokesman for a particular social or economic group. Even then his role is not seen as directly promoting special group interests, but rather as assisting in integrating his group and its activities into larger Party goals. This means that the Soviet representative may act to

---

[7] *Ibid.* See also Wolfgang Leonhard, *The Kremlin Since Stalin* (New York: Praeger, 1962), p. 17.

protect and promote his group's special interests only indirectly and within the context of his Party responsibilities. In effect, the Soviet group representative functions within the context of a deliberate effort to submerge disparate group interests, the interests of the diverse subcultures composing Soviet society, within an overriding "Party"culture. If this policy were ever entirely successful the concept of representation of anything but Party interests would have little meaning in the Soviet context. However, it is precisely the continued existence of distinctive subcultures of special and divergent interests that makes meaningful the concept of representation.

The local Party committees consist of representatives from many sectors of Party and state activity, including officials from the industrial, Soviet, and agricultural hierarchies, and the mass organizations. In addition, especially since 1956, worker and peasant representation on the Party committees has also increased. People of diverse backgrounds and varied experience are elected, *Partiinaia Zhizn'* has emphasized, so as to make it possible for a Party organ "to examine any question in an all-round and objective manner, and to take qualified decisions and organizational measures."[8] Although the Party committees do include various segments of the population, there is a wide divergence between group representation in the Party as a whole and on the district and city committees, as shown in Tables 2 and 3.[9]

The most obvious conclusion emerging from analysis of these two Tables is the underrepresentation of workers and peasants and the overrepresentation of white collar workers on the local Party committees. In 1961, the first two groups comprised 52 per cent of the entire Party but represented only 37.9 per cent of district and city Party committee membership, while white collar workers accounted for only 48.0 per cent of the former but 62.1 per cent of the latter. The most striking fact is that although the leaders of all organizations, institutions, and production units, including the Party officials, made up only 5.0 per cent of the entire Party in 1961, they comprised 36.4 per cent of all city and district Party committee members. Moreover, more than two-thirds of this leadership group consisted of Party and Soviet officials.

8 "What are the Rights and Responsibilities of a Member of a Party Committee," *Partiinaia Zhizn'*, No. 12 (1955), p. 67.

9 For comparative figures on the size of these groups in the whole population, see Appendix, p. 218.

## Table 2: Distribution of All Party Members by Social Position and Occupation

| SOCIAL POSITION OR OCCUPATION | JANUARY 1, 1956 | JULY 1, 1961 |
|---|---|---|
| *Workers* | 32.0% | 34.5% |
| *Peasants* | 17.1 | 17.5 |
| *White collar workers and all other* | 50.9 | 48.0 |
| INCLUDING: <br> Leaders of organizations,[a] institutions, enterprises, construction projects, sovkhozes, RTS, and their structural divisions | 7.0[b] | 5.0 |
| Engineering-technical personnel, agricultural specialists, economists and architects | 10.2 | 15.0 |
| Scientific, educational health, literary, and artistic workers | 9.8 | 10.6 |
| Trade and communal dining workers | 2.4 | 2.5 |
| Control, accounting, and clerical workers | 6.6 | 5.8 |
| Others—communications, communal economy, etc. | 14.9 | 9.1 |

SOURCE: "CPSU in Figures (1956–1961)," *Partiinaia Zhizn'*, No. 1 (1962), pp. 47–48.
[a] Includes leaders of Party and Soviet organizations.
[b] Figures refer to percentage of group in entire Party.

## Table 3: Distribution of Gorkom and Raikom Members by Social Position and Occupation

| SOCIAL POSITION OR OCCUPATION | JANUARY 1961[a] |
|---|---|
| *Workers and Peasants* | 37.9[b]% |
| *White collar and all other* | 62.1 |
| INCLUDING: <br> Leaders of organizations, institutions, enterprises, construction projects, sovkhozes, kolkhozes, and their structural divisions | 36.4 |
| INCLUDING: Party and Soviet officials | 26.3 |
| Engineering-technical personnel, agricultural specialists, scientific, educational, health, literary, and artistic workers | 17.4 |
| *All other* | 8.3 |

SOURCE: "CPSU in Figures (1956–1961), *"Partiinaia Zhizn'*, No. 1 (1962), p. 53.
[a] The comparable figures for 1956 are not available.
[b] All figures refer to percentage of group among all raikom and gorkom members.

In accordance with the stress on concrete Party leadership, backed up by detailed knowledge of technical processes in both industry and agriculture, the proportion of engineer-technical personnel, agricultural, and other specialists among Party members increased from 10.2 to 15.0 per cent between 1956 and 1961. However, this group including the scientific, educational, cultural, and similar groups that account for more than 25 per cent of the Party, comprise only 17.4 per cent of city and district committee membership. All other white collar Communists were similarly underrepresented on the local Party committees. Study of the membership of the Stalingrad oblast Party committee shows an even heavier weighting in favor of the professional Party secretaries and Soviet officials, to the disadvantage of all other groups.

*Table 4: Distribution of Obkom Membership by Social Position and Occupation*

| SOCIAL POSITION OR OCCUPATION | 1/54 | 1/56 | 12/57 | 1/60 |
|---|---|---|---|---|
| *Workers and Peasants* | | | | |
| identified | 0.0% | 3.1% | 3.8% | 6.7% |
| estimated[a] | 10.2 | 10.8 | 13.3 | 16.3 |
| *White collar and all other* | 89.8 | 89.2 | 86.7 | 83.7 |
| INCLUDING: | | | | |
| Leaders of organizations, institutions, enterprises, etc. | 70.0 | 67.8 | 64.8 | 58.6 |
| INCLUDING: | | | | |
| Managerial of all types | 5.1 | 11.6 | 12.9 | 6.7 |
| Party and Soviet officials | 64.9 | 56.2 | 51.9 | 51.9 |
| *Engineering-technical personnel, agricultural specialists, etc.* | | | | |
| identified | 1.2 | 2.1 | 0.7 | 2.2 |
| estimated[a] | 13.5 | 9.8 | 9.7 | 12.9 |
| *All other* | 6.5 | 11.6 | 12.2 | 12.2 |
| Total Membership (actual) | 77 | 96 | 131 | 131 |

SOURCES: This information is compiled from lists of obkom members and articles identifying individual members, published in *Stalingradskaia Pravda*, 1954–1961.

[a] The estimated figures are derived in the following manner: Out of the membership lists for the obkom from 1954 through 1960, 17, 16, 25, and 27 persons respectively were not positively identified. Since most Party, Soviet, and managerial officials' names appear in the press, and whereas this is true of very few workers, peasants or engineering-technical personnel, it was assumed that the unidentified members belong to these groups. Finally, because approximately equal numbers from each group were identified, it was decided to divide the unidentified members equally between the two groups. The results seem consistent with the Tables on page 41.

Table 4 shows a trend toward increasing the relative representation of workers and peasants in the obkom. However, even by 1960, worker and peasant representation amounted to a mere 16.3 per cent of total obkom membership. Most of the workers and peasants positively identified were "Heroes of Socialist Labor," and appear to have been elected to the obkom for that reason. At the same time, the position of the oblast Party committee as the coordinating body for all the positions of leadership in the oblast is emphasized by the evidence that, in 1961, more than 83 per cent of its members were white collar workers, whereas in the raikoms and gorkoms and the Party as a whole the corresponding figures were 62.1 and 48.0 per cent. Within this leadership group the position of the Party and Soviet officials is paramount, amounting to more than twice the percentage for the raikoms and gorkoms and more than ten times that for the whole Party.

It is worthwhile noting that the relative percentage of Party and Soviet officials showed a marked decrease between 1954 and 1956. The initial benefactors from this were the managerial personnel, who increased from 5.1 per cent in 1954 to 11.6 per cent of the oblast Party committee membership in 1956. Once the Party's ascendency over the industrial hierarchy had been assured by the industrial reorganization of 1957, and by Khrushchev's assumption of formal direction of both the Party and state hierarchies in 1958, the representation of managerial interests on the Stalingrad obkom was reduced to near the 1954 level.

The representation of engineering-technical personnel on the oblast Party committee is of interest in that the same phenomenon noted in regard to this group's representation on the gorkoms and raikoms is repeated in the obkom. At a time when technical expertise is called for in the exercise of Party leadership, the proportion of engineering-technical workers decreased significantly, not even meeting the 1954 level by 1960.[10]

The residual category in Table 5 includes such officials as the heads of the oblast trade-union and Komsomol organizations, military commanders, and police chiefs. Most of these officials occupy a place on the obkom by virtue of their position as head of a

[10] It should be pointed out here that the engineering-technical category in Table 4 includes agricultural specialists, scientific, educational, health, literary, and artistic workers. Thus the percentage of strictly engineering-technical workers on the obkom must be considerably lower than the most inclusive figure given in the Table.

*Table 5: Distribution of Party and Soviet Officials on the Obkom*

|  | 1/54 | 1/56 | 12/57 | 1/60 |
|---|---|---|---|---|
| *Party officials* | 48.0ª% | 43.3% | 40.6% | 40.9% |
| *Soviet officials* | 12.9 | 12.9 | 11.3 | 10.0 |

sources: This information is compiled from lists of obkom members and articles identifying individual members, published in *Stalingradskaia Pravda*, 1954–1961.

ª All figures refer to group distribution as a percentage of total obkom membership on the date indicated.

particular mass organization or military-legal administrative structure and, for this reason form a small, yet relatively stable, segment of the Party committee membership.

Up to this point we have discussed the Party and Soviet officials as a single grouping. While there is some validity to this conception, owing to personnel crossover from one occupation to the other, it is necessary and desirable to make quite clear the unequivocal ascendency of the Party officials over the Soviet and all other groups represented on the obkom. Table 5 indicates the relative positions, in terms of sheer numbers, of the Party and Soviet officials on the Stalingrad obkom.[11]

While the proportion of Party officials decreased from 48.0 per cent in 1954 to 43.3 per cent in 1956, its relative stability since that time points to continued domination of the oblast Party committee by the Party officials in general and the Party secretaries in particular.

Table 6 presents a detailed analysis of the entire membership of the Stalingrad oblast Party committee by occupation and elective position. For purposes of comparison with the Tables on relative positions of the various occupational groups within the obkom, this Table may be divided into several sections. Items 3, 4, 5, 7, and 8 identify the Party officials; 9 through 12, the Soviet officials; 14 through 16, the managerial personnel; and 17, the engineering-technical and cultural workers. The workers and peasants are identified in item 25. The trade-union, komsomol, military, police officials, and similar entries—items 18 through 24—belong to the

11 Unfortunately, no information is available on the proportion of professional Party workers in the city and raion committees, but it is enough to point out that the proportion of Party officials alone on the obkom is nearly twice the figure for both groups on the gorkoms and raikoms.

residual category "all other," used in the previous Tables. Item 6 points out the overlap between obkom and city Party committee membership, while item 27 shows the number of oblast committee members who are also elected deputies to the oblast Soviet.

A particularly significant feature of the structure of the oblast Party committee is that, whereas the group of Party officials is drawn from all levels of the Party hierarchy—from the obkom bureau itself down to the primary Party organizations—nearly all the other members (excluding the small group of workers and peasants) are heads of major organizations or administrative structures located predominantly in the oblast center. Thus, the spokesmen for those engaged primarily in industrial administration include the directors of the Stalingrad Tractor Factory, the Red October steel plant, and, in 1956, the chief of the oblast administration for the construction materials industry.[12] After the industrial reorganization, the chairman of the Sovnarkhoz and several vice-chairmen are included in the obkom, but, so far as is known, none of the Sovnarkhoz department heads is given this privilege. Similarly, the trade-unions, the Komsomol, the Military, and the procuracy have an official voice on the obkom only in the heads of their oblast organizations. Cultural and educational organizations are not even this fortunate. The only "permanent" representative of a cultural or an educational institution on the obkom is the director of the Stalingrad agricultural institute. In 1956, he was joined by the director of the Institute for Engineers Specializing in the Local Economy, and in 1960, by the chairman of the Department of the Fundamentals of Marxism-Leninism of the Stalingrad Medical Institute.[13] As a minimum, it would seem the obkom would include such cultural officials as the head of the oblast division of the Writers' Union or the director of the Gor'ky Drama Theater!

In analyzing the membership of the obkom in general terms we included engineering-technical personnel in the same category with cultural officials, scientific workers, and agricultural specialists. However, there is no information to indicate that persons from any of the former groups were elected to the Stalingrad oblast Party committee.

[12] *Stalingradskaia Pravda*, January 20, 1956.
[13] *Stalingradskaia Pravda*, February 13, 1954; January 20, 1956; February 5, 1957; January 8, 1959; and January 28, 1960.

## Table 6: Obkom Membership by Occupation and Elective Position

| OCCUPATION OR ELECTIVE POSITION | 1/54 | 1/56 | 12/57 | 1/60 |
|---|---|---|---|---|
| 1 Obkom bureau members | 9 | 11 | 11 | 11 |
| 2 Candidate obkom bureau members | 3 | 2 | 3 | 3 |
| 3 Obkom secretaries | 4 | 5 | 5 | 5 |
| 4 Obkom apparat officials | 8 | 8 | 10 | 12 |
| 5 Gorkom secretaries and bureau members | 3 | 4 | 7 | 8 |
| 6 Gorkom members | 19 | 15 | 17 | 17 |
| 7 Raikom first secretaries | 21 | 25 | 29 | 31 |
| 8 Primary Party organization secretaries | 1 | 1 | 2 | 0 |
| 9 Oblispolkom chairman, vice-chairmen, and members | 6 | 5 | 9 | 7 |
| 10 Oblispolkom officials | 6 | 3 | 5 | 3 |
| 11 Gorispolkom chairman, vice-chairmen | 1 | 1 | 2 | 2 |
| 12 Raiispolkom chairmen | 1 | 1 | 2 | 1 |
| 13 Sovnarkhoz and ministry officials | 1 | 2 | 4 | 3 |
| 14 Industrial managers | 3 | 6 | 5 | 4 |
| 15 Local industry managers | 0 | 1 | 2 | 0 |
| 16 Sovkhoz, MTS directors, and kolkhoz chairmen | 1 | 2 | 6 | 2 |
| 17 Cultural officials, directors of educational institutions | 1 | 2 | 2 | 3 |
| 18 Trade-union and Komsomol officials | 2 | 2 | 2 | 2 |
| 19 Oblast Trade-Union Council Presidium members | — | — | — | 5 |
| 20 Oblast Komsomol Committee members | — | — | — | 1 |
| 21 Oblast MVD or KGB chiefs | 1 | 2 | 2 | 1 |
| 22 Oblast military commander and other military officials | 1 | 1 | 4 | 3 |
| 23 Oblast prosecutor | 1 | 1 | 1 | 1 |
| 24 Editor of Stalingradskaia Pravda | 1 | 1 | 1 | 1 |
| 25 Workers and peasants | 0 | 2 | 5 | 9 |
| 26 "Old Bolshevik" | 0 | 1 | 1 | 0 |
| 27 Oblast Soviet deputies | — | 32 | 34 | 18 |
| 28 Not identified | 17 | 16 | 25 | 27 |
| Total obkom membership | 77 | 97 | 131 | 131 |

SOURCES: This information is compiled from lists of obkom members and articles identifying individual members, published in *Stalingradskaia Pravda*, 1954–1961.

Item 4 refers to the full-time, paid staff of the Party committee. In most cases, only the heads of the Party committee otdels are elected to the committee itself.

Items 9–12 refer to the executive committees of the oblast, city, and district

Thus, while the Party officials on the obkom include the five obkom secretaries, the heads of nearly all obkom otdels, all three secretaries of the Stalingrad city Party committee, plus the first secretaries from 21 to 31 of the oblast's 47 district Party committees, as well as the first secretaries from three other gorkoms, nearly all other groups are limited to either the head of their oblast organization, to the directors of a few of the largest enterprises, or they are left out of obkom membership altogether, as in the case of engineering-technical personnel. Here, in graphic form, is an illustration of Party supremacy at the oblast level.

Although the professional Party officials are by far the largest group within the oblast Party committee, and are thus in a position to exercise a high degree of influence on whatever decisions may be taken by the obkom, the inclusion on the Party committee of the top leaders from many major non-Party organizations and institutions is important for several reasons. One stated purpose of a large and diverse membership on the Party committees is that this enables the committees "to strengthen their ties with the masses and lower organizations," while enhancing the growth of local leading cadres. The experience of active participation in the work of a Party committee should help these people to "acquire the habits of leading work, to multiply their experience, and expand their political field

---

Soviets respectively. The oblispolkom officials includes the heads of executive committee departments who are not members of the executive committee itself.

In item 13, Sovnarkhoz is the Russian abbreviation for the Council of the National Economy for Stalingrad oblast, established in June, 1957.

Item 14 includes only managers of major industries, subordinated to the ministries, or, later, to the Sovnarkhoz.

Included under item 18 are the Chairman of the Oblast Trade-Union Council, and the first secretary of the Oblast Komsomol Committee.

Complete information on items 19 and 20 is available for only 1960; however, the heads of these organizations were always members of the obkom.

In item 21, *MVD* refers to the oblast department of the Militia (police), and *KGB* refers to the oblast department of the Committee of State Security of the USSR Council of Ministers (security police). The head of the *KGB* was always elected to the obkom, while the head of the *MVD* was positively identified as a member only in 1956 and 1957.

The data for item 27 can be considered complete only for 1957, since only in that year was a complete list of deputies to the oblast Soviet published. The data for the other two years is based on the assumption that those obkom members who were elected deputies to the oblast Soviet in 1957 would also have been elected in 1955 and 1959.

The data in each item include only those persons positively identified. As explained in the note to Table 4, p. 42, it is believed that most of the unidentified persons belong under items 17 and 25.

of vision."[14] This essentially tutorial function is probably most important at the city and district level since the oblast leadership may be presumed to have acquired already the habits of leading work. Probably a more valid reason for the composition of the obkom is that this provides the Party officials with a large reservoir of knowledge and experience in the major areas of Party concern within the oblast.

I. Spiridonov, at the time the first secretary of the Leningrad obkom, supported this point in an article for *Partiinaia Zhizn'*:

> The highest principle of Party leadership is collectivity. Only by relying on the experience and knowledge of many people, the collective, is it possible to avoid mistakes and one-sidedness in the decision of this or that question.[15]

So that the Party officials may avoid narrowly conceived and mistaken decisions, affecting, say, industry or agriculture, they should seek the advice of the leaders of the organizations concerned. This is the essence of "collective leadership." In terms of obkom decision-making in any particular instance, this may well be the most important purpose of a diversified Party committee membership.

Over the long run, such a membership structure may serve another purpose as well. As we have seen, one of the general functions of the obkom is to be the responsible supervisor of all sectors of the oblast's activity—economic, social, and political. The Party committee is not supposed to run everything itself, but rather it must coordinate the work of all other organizations and institutions. One of the most effective ways of assuring such coordination is to put the responsible officials from the major non-Party organizations and institutions in a position where they have the opportunity to become acquainted quickly with Party decisions and directives, where they are especially responsible before the Party, and where they can come into frequent and easy contact with the Party officials. This is accomplished, in part, by bringing such leaders into the oblast Party committee. The persistence of a relatively stable distribution of occupational and elective positions

---

14 "What are the Rights and Responsibilities of a Member of a Party Committee," *Partiinaia Zhizn'*, No. 12 (1955), p. 68.

15 "Under the Sign of Reestablishing the Leninist Norms of Party Life," *Partiinaia Zhizn'*, No. 2 (1959), p. 17.

within the oblast Party committee,[16] in spite of a fairly high rate of turnover among individual members, lends support to this conclusion.

TURNOVER

A certain degree of turnover in the personnel elected to Party organs is a natural phenomenon and has occurred since the inception of the Party. But not until the 22nd Party Congress was regular renewal of the membership of Party organs incorporated into the Party Rules. The new Program explained that systematic turnover is necessary "in order to effect consistently the Leninist principle of collective leadership, to ensure a greater influx of fresh Party forces into the leading Party organs, to properly combine old and young cadres, and to rule out the possibility of an excessive concentration of power in the hands of individual officials, and prevent cases of their getting beyond the control of the collective. . . ."[17]

The most significant aspect of this explanation is the emphasis placed on keeping the Party officials under the control of the rest of the Party committee membership. For example, in his speech explaining the changes in the Party Rules, Frol Kozlov told of the first secretary of the Tyumen obkom who had decided that "for him, 'no holds were barred'." Because he abused his position, he was removed and punished.[18] While it is true that the new emphasis on systematic turnover is aimed, in part, at keeping the Party officials under control, it would be incorrect to conclude that it is the rest of the Party committee that is to do the controlling. The membership lists for election to the Party committees are still prepared under the direction of the Party officials, with the guidance of the Central Committee. The other committee members would have very little influence on the re-election or removal of a Party official. Rather, the new Rules provide a "legal" basis for the removal of any Party or other official from the Party committee on the "recommendation" of the Central Committee. This is a warning to committee members as a whole, and to Party officials in

16 See Chapter 4, Table 6, p. 46.
17 *Programma i Ustav KPSS*, p. 231.
18 *Pravda*, October 29, 1961, p. 5.

particular, that continuity in office will depend to a large degree upon their responsiveness to the lead of the Central Committee. Kozlov's statement clearly points this out:

> The wisdom of this system of elections to Party bodies is plain. New people, Party workers who are developing and are full of initiative, should be moving steadily into positions of leadership. At the same time firm steps must be taken to rid the executive bodies of the Party of persons who have been in office too long, who have come to believe themselves irreplaceable, have stopped growing and though they cannot cope with the tasks assigned them, cling tenaciously to executive positions.[19]

The possibility of advancement and the threat of removal and disgrace are powerful motivational forces acting to assure that the oblast level decision-makers remain responsive to the Central Committee.

The new Party Rules are quite explicit as to the amount by which the local Party committees are to be renewed at each election. The oblast Party committees are to be renewed by not less than one-third, while a turnover of one-half is required for city and district Party committees. At the same time, individual members are not to be re-elected for more than three terms in succession. Exceptions to this rule are made for particular Party leaders who show exceptional political and organizational abilities. Such persons can be re-elected if they receive not less than three-fourths of the votes cast by secret ballot.[20] This is justified by the need for a more or less stable leadership group.[21]

Although systematic renewal of leading Party organs was not raised to an official principle until the 22nd Party Congress, its essential features are evident in the life of the Stalingrad obkom throughout the period under study. Table 7 shows the number of new members elected to the Party committee at each of three oblast Party conferences. The figures given in this Table are quite close to those cited by Kozlov as the average for union-republic Central Committees, territorial, and oblast Party committees. In his speech at the 22nd Congress, he stated that 45 per cent of the membership of these committees was newly elected. Further, he

---

19 *Ibid.*
20 *Programma i Ustav KPSS*, art. 25.
21 *Pravda*, October 29, 1961, p. 5.

Table 7: Turnover in Obkom Membership 1956–1960 I

|  | 1956 | 1957 | 1960 |
|---|---|---|---|
| Number of new members elected | 46 | 60 | 62 |
| Per cent of total obkom membership | 47.9 | 45.8 | 47.3 |

SOURCES: *Stalingradskaia Pravda*, February 13, 1954; January 20, 1956; February 5, 1957; and January 28, 1960.

declared, regular turnover of the membership of executive Party bodies had become the rule in recent years.[22] If allowances are made for the growth that occurred in the size of the obkom between 1954 and 1957, however, a quite different picture emerges. Table 8 shows the number of members actually replaced at each election in absolute terms and as a percentage of total committee membership.

A comparison of Tables 7 and 8 shows that the appearance of a high rate of turnover in obkom membership in 1956 and 1957 is more the result of increases in the total number of obkom members than of the nonelection of former members who failed to prove themselves. This is not true for the obkom elected in 1960, however. Although the obkom remained at 131 members at both the 1957 and 1960 Party conferences, in the latter year 62 persons were elected for the first time, and 62 former members failed to be re-elected.

Table 8: Turnover in Obkom Membership 1956-1960 II

|  | 1954 | 1956 | 1957 | 1960 |
|---|---|---|---|---|
| Total obkom membership | 77 | 96 | 131 | 131 |
| Increase in size | — | 19 | 35 | 0 |
| Members not re-elected | — | 27 | 25 | 62 |
| Per cent not re-elected[a] | — | 34.1 | 26.1 | 47.3 |

SOURCES: *Stalingradskaia Pravda*, February 13, 1954; January 20, 1956; February 5, 1957; and January 28, 1960. Figures on turnover are not available for 1954.

[a] The percentages given refer to the number of members not re-elected as a per cent of total obkom membership elected at the previous conference. Thus, 34.1 per cent of obkom members elected in 1954 were not re-elected in 1956.

[22] *Ibid.*

*Table 9: Turnover in the Obkom Leadership Group 1956–1960*

|  | 1954 | 1956 | 1957 | 1960 |
|---|---|---|---|---|
| *Total leadership group* | 16 | 22 | 25 | 24 |
| *Number not re-elected* | — | 6 | 4 | 6 |
| *Per cent not re-elected*[a] | — | 37.6 | 18.2 | 24.0 |

SOURCES: *Stalingradskaia Pravda*, February 13, 1954; January 20, 1956; February 5, 1957; January 28, 1960; and other articles identifying individual officials.

[a] The percentages given refer to the number of leaders replaced as a percentage of the total leadership group elected to the obkom at the previous conference. Thus, 37.6 per cent of the obkom leadership group, elected in 1954, was replaced in 1956.

While actual turnover in the membership of the Stalingrad obkom did not approach 45 per cent before 1960, it nevertheless exceeded the norm of one-third in 1956 and approached it in 1957.

Systematic renewal of the leading Party organs, Kozlov indicated, must be accompanied by continuity of leadership.[23] While turnover of the Stalingrad leadership group[24] was, indeed, somewhat less than the rate for the committee as a whole in both 1957 and 1960, in 1956 the former actually exceeded the latter, as shown in Table 9. Although turnover among the members of the leadership group as a whole varied considerably, from a high of 37.6 per cent to a low of 18.2 per cent, the rate for bureau members alone remained fairly stable. In 1956, the bureau was renewed by 25 per cent, in 1957, by 23.1 per cent and in 1960, by 21.5 per cent. In spite of the rather high turnover among both the rank and file committee members and the leadership group, a certain degree of continuity is still evident. Among members of the obkom elected in 1960, 22 persons (16.7 per cent), including two obkom secretaries, had been elected for four successive terms; 10 persons (7.6 per cent), including two more obkom secretaries, had been elected three times; and 37 persons (28.2 per cent), including one obkom secretary, had been elected for two successive terms.[25]

[23] *Ibid.*

[24] The term "leadership group" is used here to designate all obkom bureau members, candidate members, and obkom members who are also members of the city Party committee. For a further discussion of this group, see Chapter 9.

[25] *Stalingradskaia Pravda*, February 13, 1954; January 20, 1956; February 5, 1957; and January 28, 1960.

# FIVE

# Obkom Plenary
# Sessions

## FUNCTION

The work of the Party committee as a whole is conducted at periodic plenary sessions. Although the Party journals describe that the purpose of these sessions is to "Discuss and decide the more important questions of the Party organization's work,"[1] their primary function is not policy-making. Rather, plenary sessions serve, fundamentally, as a forum for assessing progress made in implementing current programs and for detailing new policies, or courses of action. The discussion at committee plenums revolves not around whether to adopt policy "A" or proposal "B," but around how best to implement a previously formulated decision, adopted either by the Central Committee or the obkom bureau. The decision-making function of oblast committee plenums amounts to defining the specific tasks of various oblast organizations and motivating the affected leaders and workers to expend greater effort for their fulfill-

---

[1] "What are the Rights and Responsibilities of a Member of a Party Committee," *Partiinaia Zhizn'*, No. 12 (1955), p. 68.

ment. Such a conception is clearly evident in this statement by a former first secretary of the Stalingrad obkom:

> The present plenum of the Party obkom must define clearly just what must be done by each Party, Soviet organization, and land organ, by each kolkhoz, MTS, and sovkhoz. The decision adopted by the plenum must mobilize the workers of the oblast to increase live-stock production at a more forced pace.[2]

This interpretation of the decision-making function of plenary sessions is confirmed by analysis of those held by the Stalingrad oblast Party committee from 1954 to 1961.

### FREQUENCY

The Party Rules adopted at the 19th Party Congress in 1952 changed the period for holding plenary sessions of oblast Party committees from once every three months to once every two months.[3] At the Congress, Khrushchev explained that the change was necessary in order to "bring the leadership of the local Party bodies closer to the life of the Party organizations," and "to increase the role and activeness of Party committee members in resolving the tasks facing the Party organizations."[4] More frequent plenums, Khrushchev continued, would also encourage "criticism from below," and make possible more intensive and frequent checkups on the fulfillment of Party directives and decisions of local Party organizations.[5] Even before the end of the Congress, Khrushchev's proposal met with some criticism. While agreeing with the reasons for the change "in principle," the first secretary of the Velikii Luki obkom pleaded that the existing intervals for plenums should not be changed "because much time is required to prepare for every plenary session."[6] At the 20th Party Congress, the Party Rules were amended to require that plenary sessions of oblast Party committees be held at least once every four months.[7] This same stipulation was retained at the 22nd Congress.[8] While frequent

---

2 *Stalingradskaia Pravda*, May 22, 1954.
3 *KPSS v Rezoliutsiiakh. . .* , Vol. III, art. 44, p. 588.
4 *Pravda*, October 13, 1952, p. 2.
5 *Ibid.*
6 *Ibid.*, October 15, 1952, p. 5.
7 *Ibid.*, February 21, 1956, p. 1.
8 *Programma i Ustav KPSS*, art. 46.

meetings of Party committees may be desirable "in principle," apparently they are not quite important enough to justify requiring them more than three times a year.

The frequency with which plenary sessions of the Stalingrad oblast Party committee were convened has little relation to the exact requirements of the Party Rules, except that more than the required number of sessions always were held. In 1956 and 1959, four sessions were held; in 1954 and 1958, five; and in 1957 and 1960, six plenums were convened.[9] For the six years examined, the Stalingrad obkom averaged five plenums every year, with an average interval between plenums of just under two and one-half months.

The responsibility for supervising the preparations as well as directing the course of the plenary sessions themselves rests with the bureau of the oblast Party committee.[10] The bureau, consisting of 11 full and two or three candidate members, which maintains the highest political authority in the oblast, is discussed in detail in Chapter 6.[11]

COMPETENCE

The preparation of the agenda, the selection of both the major reporter and the speakers for the discussion, and the preparation of reports are the most important aspects of the organizational work carried out before a Party committee plenum takes place. While there can be little doubt that every detail of oblast Party committee plenums is well organized before the session begins, at various times the Party press and journals have been critical of too much rigidity in this matter. *Kommunist,* in a 1954 article, came out against the extreme regimentation of the agenda that occurred in many Party committees. This, it stressed, led to meetings taking place in a "listless" and "mechanical" fashion, to meetings where only "results and resolutions" were discussed.[12] At the same time, it strongly criticized trying to do away with an agenda altogether:

> The practice of conducting Party meetings without an agenda has long been condemned. At such meetings businesslike discussion of

---

[9] The data for 1955 are not available.

[10] "Who Directs the Plenary Sessions of Party Committees," *Partiinaia Zhizn',* No. 11 (1954), p. 67.

[11] See Chapter 6.

[12] "The Development of Internal Party Democracy is a Most Important Requirement for Increasing the Activeness of Communists," *Kommunist,* No. 12 (1954), p. 5.

fundamental and burning questions is replaced by pointless and general talk, and such meetings do not further the mobilization and unity of Communists. But it is this erroneous path that some insufficiently experienced Party officials have taken, apparently in an effort to liven up Party meetings.[13]

Similar criticisms have been advanced in regard to the selection of speakers before the plenum begins. In a letter to *Pravda,* a rank and file Communist complained that such a practice leads to a situation where the same persons always make the speeches, and so many Party members who would like to speak cannot succeed in getting the floor.[14] The point of such complaints, the letter makes clear, is not that the bureau should not organize such details, but that a wider circle of committee members should be drawn into the preparation of reports and project resolutions and contribute to their discussion at plenary sessions.[15] By 1959, it was reported that in many Party committees the members "are actively brought into the preparation of decisions, to practical participation in leadership of the Party organizations."[16]

The nature of this participation, under ideal conditions, was brought out in a letter to *Partiinaia Zhizn'*: When an important report is to be made, for example, by a Party committee secretary, a large group assists in its preparation. First the secretary gathers the members of the Party committee apparat and tells his own ideas about the report. Then, ideas and opinions are exchanged, after which the apparat goes about collecting the materials for the report. Material may come from committee members, Soviet or industrial officials, or members of the group of Party activists. After receiving all the materials the secretary writes up the report. Prior to the plenum, the text is circulated to all Party committee otdels to be read. Any comments are then considered by the reporter before the preparation of the final text.[17]

A somewhat similar practice is described in Kochetov's novel,

13 *Ibid.*

14 *Pravda,* May 4, 1956, p. 2.

15 *Ibid.* See also, *Voprosy Partiinoi Raboty,* (Moscow: Gospolitizdat, 1958), p. 82. (Hereafter cited as *VPR.*)

16 "How We Prepare for a Plenum in the Party Obkom," *Partiinaia Zhizn',* No. 21 (1959), p. 44.

17 "On the Preparation of Reports and Speeches," *Partiinaia Zhizn',* No. 21 (1957), p. 59.

*Secretar' Obkoma:* In preparing a report to be read in the Central Committee Bureau for the RSFSR on the results of the winter and spring agricultural work, the obkom first secretary gives his project report to the second secretary (who is in charge of agriculture), to the chairman of the oblast Soviet executive committee, and to the head of the Party committee agricultural otdel for their study and comments. After considerable discussion of the proper emphasis to be given questions of perspective long range planning, a final draft is agreed upon.[18] What is particularly significant in these two examples—both instances of the correct way (in the Soviet view) to draw up major reports and project decisions—is that the actual decision-makers are the Party secretaries, other Party officials, and the head of the oblispolkom. When others are involved, their participation is limited basically to providing information.[19]

The Party journals are replete with articles declaring that there must be full and free discussion at the plenary sessions of Party committees.[20] The Party Rules proclaim that "the free and businesslike discussion of questions of Party policy . . . is the inalienable right of every Party member. . . ." Such free discussion is necessary, the Rules continue, because only in this way "is it possible to develop self-criticism and to strengthen Party discipline, which must be conscious and not mechanical."[21] At the same time, the very next sentence of the Rules, as confirmed at the 20th Party Congress, imposes very severe limitations on the scope of discussion:

> But wide discussion . . . must be so organized as to prevent it leading to attempts by an insignificant minority to impose its will upon the majority of the Party; or to attempts to form factional groupings which break the unity of the Party; attempts to cause splits which may shake the strength and stability of the socialist system.[22]

The curb against formation of any grouping to support a particular

---

[18] Vsevolod Kochetov, *Secretar' Obkoma* (Moscow: Molodaia Gvardiia, 1961), pp. 56-59.

[19] This is not meant to belittle the role of information in decision-making, but to distinguish between those who actually make authoritative choices and those who provide the information on which such choices are based.

[20] For two examples, see "The Development of Internal Party Democracy is a Most Important Requirement for Increasing the Activeness of Communists," *Kommunist*, No. 12 (1954), pp. 3–11; and "What are the Rights and Responsibilities of a Member of a Party Committee," *Partiinaia Zhizn'*, No. 12 (1955), pp. 66–68.

[21] *KPSS v Rezoliutsiiakh . . .* , Vol. III, art. 28, pp. 584–585.

[22] *Ibid.*

proposal—different from that presented by the Party committee leadership—has served to hold Party discussions to very strict limits since its first enunciation at the 10th Party Congress in 1921.[23] The Rules adopted at the 22nd Party Congress continue this restriction in essentially the same form.[24] In his speech on the Party Rules, Frol Kozlov gave the official "reasons" for the limits on free discussions in Party meetings. "Naturally," he explained, "one must not allow a situation to come about in which the Party can be drawn into a sterile discussion at the whim of some small group of muddle-headed or immature people in which individual anti-Party elements can undertake actions leading to the subversion of Party unity. . . ."[25]

It is largely as a result of these restrictions on discussion and the corresponding organization by the bureau of every aspect of the Party committee plenums that these cannot be viewed as having a policy-making function, but rather must be seen as forums where those responsible for carrying out Party policy can be called to give an accounting before the Party officials and committee members, where the course of fulfillment of current programs can be assessed, and new policies announced. Analysis of the plenums held by the Stalingrad obkom further confirms this conclusion.

The reports of obkom plenums in *Stalingradskaia Pravda,* for 1954 and 1956 through 1960, show that 37 topics were discussed at 30 plenums held during this period. Of the questions discussed 11 concerned agriculture; 5, industry; 7, ideology; 4, work with Party cadres; 7, Party-organizational matters; and 3 discussed topics that were not announced. Table 10 shows the number of times these topics were discussed for each year under study.

The direct and continuing concern of the obkom with problems of agricultural production is evident from the frequency with which plenums were held to discuss this topic. In the spring of each year, except for 1959, an obkom plenum discussed either the preparation for or the results of the sowing campaigns, and in the latter half of the year one plenum was always devoted to assessing the fulfillment of the plan for delivery of agricultural products.

[23] The original resolution, "On Party Unity," is published in *KPSS v Resoliutsiiakh . . . ,* I, 527–529.
[24] *Programma i Ustav KPSS,* art. 27.
[25] *Pravda,* October 29, 1961, p. 1.

*Table 10: Topics of Stalingrad Obkom Plenums 1954–1960*

|  | 1954 | 1956 | 1957 | 1958 | 1959 | 1960 |
|---|---|---|---|---|---|---|
| Agriculture | 2 | 2 | 2 | 2 | 1 | 2 |
| Industry | 0 | 1 | 2 | 1 | 1 | 0 |
| Ideology | 1 | 0 | 2 | 0 | 1 | 3 |
| Cadres | 0 | 1 | 0 | 1 | 1 | 1 |
| Organization | 2 | 1 | 2 | 0 | 0 | 2 |
| Unknown | 0 | 0 | 0 | 2 | 1 | 0 |

SOURCE: *Stalingradskaia Pravda*, 1954, 1956–1960. The data for 1955 are not available to this writer.

While some of these plenums appear to have been held on the obkom's initiative, in at least seven instances the influence of the Central Committee is quite evident. Thus, the topics at two agricultural plenums were related directly to the decisions of Central Committee plenums in the description of the questions under discussion. The third obkom plenum, in May, 1954, discussed the question, "On the course of fulfillment of the decisions of the September (1953) plenum of the CC CPSU on measures for the further development of live-stock production in the kolkhozes and sovkhozes of the oblast."[26] In July of the same year, the fourth plenum discussed the report, "On measures for the fulfillment of the June plenum of the CC CPSU."[27] The Central Committee directed its own representatives to "participate and speak" in agricultural plenums in May, 1956, and June, 1958, sending A. M. Puzanov, a member of the Central Committee Bureau for the RSFSR and also the first vice-chairman of the Council of Ministers of the RSFSR, in the former instance, and V. P. Mylarshchikov, also a Bureau member and head of the Central Committee agricultural otdel for the RSFSR, in the latter case.[28] Three other agricultural questions were directly related to decrees or resolutions made by the central organs.[29]

[26] *Stalingradskaia Pravda*, May 20, 1954.
[27] *Ibid.*, July 12, 1954.
[28] *Ibid.*, May 30, 1956, and June 28, 1958.
[29] The December, 1956 plenum discussed the question, "On the course of fulfillment of the decisions of the 20th Congress on the question of the further upsurge of livestock production. . . ." The obkom plenum of May 7–9, 1957, followed by three days the Central Committee decree, "On improving the leadership of agriculture in Vologodskoi oblast." The January, 1960 plenum was devoted to discussion of the results of the December (1959) Central Committee plenum, and the tasks of the oblast Party organization.

The first obkom plenum to discuss problems of industry in the period under study was held in September, 1956, nearly six months after the 20th Party Congress. This plenum was devoted to a general discussion of industry, transportation, and construction in the oblast, as can be seen from the title of the major report—"On the state and measures for improving the work of industrial, transport, and construction organizations."[30] The four industrial topics discussed at obkom plenums since that time are all directly related to industrial policies formulated in the Central Committee. Khrushchev's theses for the reorganization of industrial administration were approved at the April, 1957 plenum; in October of that year, a plenum was devoted to measures for fulfilling the decree of the Central Committee and Council of Ministers, "On the development of housing construction in the USSR." The May, 1958 plenum examined "The results of the May plenum of the Central Committee on the development of the chemical industry and the production of synthetic materials." Finally, the November, 1959 obkom plenum discussed the course of fulfillment of the resolution of the June (1959) Central Committee plenum, "On speeding up the construction of enterprises."[31] With the possible exception of the 1956 plenum, questions of industry and construction were discussed in the Stalingrad obkom only on the initiative of the Central Committee, or on the basis of its resolutions and decisions.

A similar pattern is evident in regard to questions of ideological work. In December, 1954, the fifth obkom plenum examined the question, "On measures for improving ideological work in the oblast Party organization."[32] While not explicitly connected to it, this plenum occurred within three weeks of and discussed the same question as the Central Committee plenum of November 10, 1954.[33] In March, 1957, an obkom plenum discussed, as the first of three questions, "On strengthening political work among the population."[34] This followed by five days the decree of the Central Committee Bureau for the RSFSR, "On the unsatisfactory state of

---

[30] *Stalingradskaia Pravda*, September 13, 1956.

[31] *Ibid.*, April 10, 1957; October 19, 1957; May 15, 1958; and November 13, 1959.

[32] *Ibid.*, December 1, 1954.

[33] *KPSS v Rezoliutsiiakh* . . . , IV, 46–50. The topic at the Central Committee plenum was "On mistakes in the conduct of scientific-atheistic propaganda among the population."

[34] *Stalingradskaia Pravda*, March 10, 1957.

political work among the intelligentsia in the Tomsk Oblast Party Organization."[35] Since the main question of the day concerned the preparations for spring sowing, and since it is not usual for two major questions to be discussed at the same plenum, it seems reasonable to conclude that the question on ideological work was included at the last minute on the basis of the decree.

Just five days after the conclusion of the June, 1957 plenum that ousted the "anti-Party group," the Stalingrad obkom met in plenary session to discuss the Central Committee's action. In its resolution, the obkom approved the Central Committee's action and "called upon all Communists to unite their ranks under the invincible banner of Marxism-Leninism and direct all their energies to the successful solution of the tasks of Communist construction."[36] This plenary session illustrates a function somewhat different from those enumerated above that the obkom may be required to fulfill. Rather than assessing current programs, or approving new policies, this plenum was called upon to participate, albeit *post facto*, in Khrushchev's struggle for ascendency in the Party Presidium. While this participation in higher Party politics served to increase the importance of the obkom plenum as a political body, in terms of decision-making it remains limited to the ratification of decisions made by others. It is interesting to note, however, that in this politically important instance, the Stalingrad obkom's approval of the Central Committee resolution does not appear to have been unanimous. Whereas a meeting of the Stalingrad Party activists[37] approved the Central Committee's action "unanimously" *(edinoglasno)*, the obkom plenum expressed its support "in one spirit" *(edinodushno)*.[38] It is perhaps significant in this connection that neither the major report nor any of the discussion was reproduced in *Stalingradskaia Pravda* after this plenum, in contrast to the usual practice of publishing extracts of plenum speeches.

The May, 1959 plenum discussed "The tasks of the oblast Party

---

[35] *Spravochnik Partiinogo Rabotnika,* (Moscow: Gospolitizdat, 1957), pp. 378–380. (Hereafter cited as *SPR.*)

[36] *KPSS v Rezoliutsiiakh* . . . , IV, 271–277, and *Stalingradskaia Pravda,* July 4, 1957.

[37] The designation of Party activist, or *aktiv,* is applied to all those Party members who actively participate in the work of a Party organization, whether or not they are elected members of its committee. The *aktiv* encompasses a considerably larger group than the committee itself.

[38] *Stalingradskaia Pravda,* July 4–5, 1957.

organization in improving ideological work in the light of the de-cisions of the 21st Congress."[39] This session was supervised by K. P. Rybakov, the assitant head of the otdel of propaganda and agitation of the CC CPSU.

Three topics relating to questions of ideological work were discussed at obkom plenums in 1960. Only one of these, "On mea-sures for fulfilling the resolution of the CC CPSU, 'On the tasks of Party propaganda in contemporary conditions,' " can be directly related to a Central Committee decision.[40] At the May plenum, where the main question involved assessing the results of the spring sowing, a second problem, "On measures for improving the training of children," was also discussed. So far as can be ascertained this is the first time that ideological work was brought up at a plenum on the initiative of the obkom. In October of the same year, an entire plenum was devoted to analysis of mass propaganda work in two raions, again with no evident connection to any immediate Central Committee decision.[41]

Several conclusions regarding the discussion of problems of ideological work in the Stalingrad obkom emerge from this analysis. Under normal conditions, questions of ideological work are brought up for discussion at an obkom plenum only on the initiative of the Central Committee, or in connection with the promulgation of a Central Committee resolution or decree affecting such questions. On the other hand, if such problems assume unusual proportions, or if the Central Committee displays unusual interest in problems of ideological work in the oblast, as it did in March, 1960, by sending its representative to the obkom plenum, then the obkom may return to these problems on its own initiative at future plenums. These con-clusions appear to be equally relevant to questions of work with Party cadres.[42]

At the 20th Party Congress, the Stalingrad obkom was seriously criticized for not admitting enough new members to the Party, and

39 *Ibid.*, May 29, 1959.

40 *Ibid.*, March 26, 1960. The Central Committee decree was adopted on January 9, 1960. See *KPSS v Rezoliutsiiakh* . . . , IV, 590–610.

41 *Ibid.*, October 17, 1960.

42 In strict Soviet usage, the Party cadres are those Party members who are assigned to a particular position in the economy either by the Party committee directly, or with its approval. The term *nomenklatura* also refers to the Party cadres, but it is most often used with reference to the particular positions involved, rather than to their occupants. For purposes of this discussion, problems of admissions to the Party and supervision of lower Party committees are also included under the cadres category.

the Congress demanded that the obkom begin to pay more attention to this matter.[43] As a means of making this change in policy well understood by the raion secretaries and other local Party officials, this topic was added to the agenda of the regular agricultural plenum at the end of May, 1956.

In addition to discussing preparations for the spring sowing, the February, 1958 plenum examined the question, "On work with cadres in the oblast Party organization." At this session it was brought out that the problem of selecting, training, and promoting Party cadres had not been discussed at a plenum of the Stalingrad obkom for four years.[44] It appears to have been brought up at this time only with the intervention of the central officials, represented at this plenum by a certain Polekhin, the assistant head of the Central Committee otdel of Party organs.[45]

In March, 1959, an obkom plenum took up the question of improving the work of the primary Party organizations, apparently on its own initiative. Although precise information on this plenum is not available, this session possibly may have been connected with preparations for the formation of commissions within the primary Party organizations to control the work of enterprise administrations. The official announcement of these commissions was made in a Central Committee resolution of June 26, 1959.[46] As an alternative, discussion of this topic at an obkom plenum may be interpreted simply as an exercise of the direct responsibility of the obkom, as stated in the Party Rules, to supervise and guide the work of the lower Party committees.[47]

The obkom plenum of March 26, 1960, returned to the question of the selection, training, and promotion of Party cadres. The stated purpose of this plenum was to discuss progress made in fulfilling the decision taken at the 21st Party Congress relating to this question.[48]

Immediately after the conclusion of each oblast Party conference, an organizational plenum is held to elect the Party committee bureau, and to confirm the heads of the Party committee otdels, and

[43] *Stalingradskaia Pravda*, June 2, 1956.
[44] *Ibid.*, February 21, 1958.
[45] *Ibid.*
[46] *SPR* (1959 ed.), p. 575.
[47] *Programma i Ustav*, art. 47.
[48] *Stalingradskaia Pravda*, March 26, 1960.

the editor of the oblast newspaper. In Stalingrad, such plenums were held in February, 1954; January, 1956; December, 1957; and January, 1960. Three other organizational plenums during this period were concerned with removals and appointments of obkom secretaries.[49] The first two involved changes in the staff of subordinate secretaries, while the November, 1960 plenum removed the first secretary in connection with his promotion to an ambassadorial post.[50] Direct evidence of the Central Committee's influence on these organizational plenums is available only for the last mentioned instance, when V. M. Churaev, the head of the otdel of Party organs for the union-republics of the CC CPSU, "took part" in the plenum.[51] The Party Rules, however, indicate that the Central Committee retains full control over the selection of obkom secretaries. Article 42 of the Rules confirmed at the 20th Congress states that "the appointment of the latter [is] subject to the confirmation of the Central Committee of the Party."[52] While this phrase is deleted from the Rules adopted at the 22nd Congress, nevertheless, the right of the Central Committee to "select and distribute leading cadres" is retained.[53] Fainsod points out that in addition to appointing obkom secretaries, the Central Committee also controls the selection of the entire obkom bureau.[54]

This analysis of the agendas of the Stalingrad oblast Party committee plenary sessions has shown that while they extend over five broad areas of concern, from agriculture to organizational questions, the selection of particular topics, in most cases, appears to follow the lead of the Central organs. With the possible exception of the annual May plenums devoted to analysis of the spring agricultural work, it may be said that the effective competence[55] of the obkom in plenary session is defined by the current decisions of the Central Committee.

---

49 *Ibid.*, March 27, 1954; March 9, 1957; and November 27, 1960. In December, 1955, an organizational plenum removed Grishin as first secretary and elected Zhegalin to replace him. See Chapter 6, pp. 88-89 for more detail on the turnover of obkom secretaries.

50 *Ibid.*

51 *Ibid.*, November 27, 1960.

52 *KPSS v Rezoliutsiiakh* . . . , Vol. III, art. 42, p. 588.

53 *Programma i Ustav KPSS*, art. 35.

54 Fainsod, p. 225.

55 By "effective competence" is meant those questions actually discussed, as contrasted with the general range of problems for which the obkom is responsible, as defined in the Party Rules.

PARTICIPATION

The normal procedure in Party plenums is for one person to make a major report on the topic of the day. This is followed by a series of shorter speeches, called the "debates" *(preniia),* or discussions. In 20 of 27 instances, for which such information is available,[56] the major speakers were Party committee secretaries. The remaining seven included six major reports by the chairman of the oblast Soviet executive committee, and one, in 1959, by the chairman of the Sovnarkhoz.[57]

A certain degree of specialization is evident among the major speakers. Thus, of 11 reports on agricultural topics, six were made by the oblispolkom chairman, one by the obkom secretary in charge of agriculture, and four by the obkom first secretary. The chairman of the Sovnarkhoz made one report on industrial matters, as did the obkom secretary in charge of industry, while the first secretary spoke three times on this topic. Four of the eight reports on ideological questions were given by the obkom secretary in charge of ideology, and one was read by the city Party secretary in charge of ideology. The assistant head of the agitprop otdel of the CC CPSU made a co-report at the latter plenum. At the July, 1957 plenum, which discussed the "anti-Party group," the major report was undertaken by the obkom first secretary. In 1960, two raikom first secretaries gave co-reports to a plenum discussing ideological work in their respective districts. The obkom first secretary and the secretary in charge of cadres and lower Party organs made two major reports each on work with cadres.

The oblispolkom chairman appears from this evidence to take the lead in routine agricultural plenums, with the obkom first secretary making the report when a Central Committee plenum or decree demands that special emphasis be placed on some particular agricultural problem. Thus, at all but one of the annual May plenums devoted to agriculture, the major report was delivered by the oblispolkom chairman. However, in July, 1954, less than two months

---

[56] The list of speakers in organizational plenums was never published in *Stalingradskaia Pravda* during the period under study.

[57] This information and that following in this section relating to speakers at obkom plenums is gathered from reports on the plenums and other items identifying individual speakers published in *Stalingradskaia Pravda,* 1954–1960.

after the last agricultural plenum, the obkom first secretary gave the
major report at a plenum concerned with implementing the decision
adopted by a Central Committee plenum on June 27, 1954.[58] Again,
in December, 1956, after a very difficult agricultural year during
which the obkom bureau adopted and published in the oblast press
at least eight harsh decisions concerning specific failures in live-
stock production in the oblast, the obkom first secretary presented
the major report at an obkom plenum discussing this topic. It is
perhaps significant that the first secretary, Zhegalin, who had just
been appointed to head the Stalingrad Party organization in December, 1955, devoted his primary attention during this year (1956)
to improving agricultural production. On two other occasions the
obkom first secretary delivered the major address to agricultural
plenums. Both times these were so-called "enlarged plenums"; that
is, in addition to the committee members, nearly all local officials
connected with agriculture were invited. At the first of these, in
June, 1958, a co-report was also made by the head of the Agricultural otdel for the RSFSR of the CC CPSU. The second enlarged
plenum, on January 8, 1960, discussed the implementation of the
Central Committee resolution adopted on December 25, 1959.[59]

From 1956 through 1958, the first secretary seems to have taken
the primary responsibility for plenum reports on industrial questions, having made three of four such speeches during this period. In
the one exception, on October 19, 1957, this responsibility was delegated to the obkom secretary in charge of industry and construction.
In this case, however, the subject, improving housing construction,
was of relatively secondary significance. Only in 1959, did the chairman of the Sovnarkhoz participate in an obkom plenum as a major
speaker. Since no additional plenums were devoted to industry
during the period under study, it is not possible to determine
whether any trend was developing at this time toward giving the
Sovnarkhoz primary responsibility for reports on industrial matters
at obkom plenums. However, it is worth noting that at the obkom
conferences of January, 1959, and January, 1960, the major addresses, giving primary emphasis to industrial questions, were delivered by the obkom first secretary. The participation of the

[58] *KPSS v Rezoliutsiiakh* . . . , IV, 9–45.
[59] *Ibid.*, pp. 571–589.

Sovnarkhoz chairman, it seems, is probably simply the result of the obkom secretary requesting the official most directly responsible for the topic under discussion, the construction of enterprises, to make a report on this matter to the plenum. Evidence to this effect is that the official in charge of building the Stalingrad Hydroelectric Station was also asked to report on his work at this plenum, as well as at the May, 1958 session.

Judging from the relatively lower positions of the major speakers, ideological questions appear to be of relatively secondary importance throughout most of the period of this study. In five of seven cases, major reports on this subject were read by Party secretaries in charge of ideological work. In one of these instances, the only time at any Stalingrad obkom plenum covered in this study, the principal speaker was the Stalingrad gorkom secretary in charge of ideology.[60] In October, 1960, two raikom secretaries were given the responsibility for presenting the major co-reports on ideological work. Only in the unusual and politically sensitive circumstances following the June, 1957 CC CPSU plenum, did the obkom first secretary find it necessary to make a major report on a question of ideological work.

The question of work with Party cadres, while obviously given very secondary importance by the Stalingrad obkom prior to 1958, seems to have been given considerable significance in 1959 and 1960. After severe criticism at the 20th Party Congress for not admitting enough new members to the Party, the principal report on this topic at the May, 1956 plenum was assigned to the obkom secretary in charge of cadres and lower Party organs. Again, in 1958, when the obkom had been strongly attacked for not discussing the problem of selecting, training, and promoting Party cadres for four years, the major speech was made by the same obkom secretary, in spite of the presence at the plenum of a Central Committee official. Yet, in both the 1959 and 1960, instances when the obkom discussed problems of work with Party cadres, the obkom first secretary delivered the principal address. Apparently after the criticisms of 1956 and 1958, the first secretary felt this subject important enough to demand his personal attention.

The overall pattern that emerges here indicates that the major

60 The plenum referred to was held on May 29, 1959.

reports on both routine matters and those considered of somewhat secondary significance are delegated to either second-level Party officials, the chairman of the oblispolkom, or, as in one instance, to the chairman of the Sovnarkhoz. While these latter two officials do not come from groups directly subordinated to the Party, there is little reason to believe that they could make policy proposals at obkom plenary sessions that differ in any important respect from those advocated by the Party secretaries. Since two obkom secretaries, including the first secretary, are also members of the oblispolkom, there can be little doubt that any proposals made by the oblispolkom chairman would have received the prior endorsement of the Party officials. It is further significant that no major speeches were presented to obkom plenums by industrial officials until after the 1957 reorganization had placed the Sovnarkhoz chairman in a position vis-à-vis the obkom secretaries not unlike that of the oblispolkom chairman, in terms of policy formation.[61] On this basis, it must be concluded that participation in the deliberative process, in the form of major addresses to obkom plenary sessions—on even relatively minor questions—is open only to Party officials and those who can be relied upon to make proposals fully in line with positions approved by the Party secretaries.

Moreover, when particularly important matters are brought up before the Party committee, the first secretary takes the presentation of the major addresses upon himself. Thus, when a plenum discussed the proposed industrial reorganization in 1957, when the circumstances surrounding a topic were particularly sensitive politically —as in June, 1957—or when the situation was perceived as threatening the position of the first secretary—as in the agricultural crisis preceding the December, 1956 plenum[62]—then the obkom first secretary permitted no one but himself to give the principal report.

The major addresses are followed by a series of shorter reports. Table 11 analyzes the participants in discussions on agricultural questions at plenums of the Stalingrad obkom by occupation.[63]

---

[61] For a discussion of the competence of the obkom in matters of industrial policy, see Chapter 6, pp. 106–119.

[62] See Chapter 6, pp. 101–106.

[63] The lists of speakers in the discussion at the July, 1954 and the December, 1956 agricultural plenums are not available to this writer.

Table 11: Participants in Discussions on Agricultural Questions at Stalingrad Obkom Plenums

| PLENUM MONTH/YEAR | PARTY SECRETARIES | | | GOVERNMENT OFFICIALS | | MANAGERIAL OFFICIALS | CULTURAL-EDUCATIONAL OFFICIALS | FARM OFFICIALS[a] | WORKERS AND PEASANTS | TOTAL |
|---|---|---|---|---|---|---|---|---|---|---|
| | RAIKOM | GORKOM | OBKOM | MINISTRY OR SOVNARKHOS | SOVIET | | | | | |
| 5/54 | 9 | — | 1 | 3 | 4 | — | 1 | 4 | — | 22 |
| 6/56 | 8 | — | 2 | 1 | 2 | — | — | — | — | 13 |
| 3/57 | 4 | — | 1 | 1 | 6 | — | 1 | 3 | — | 16 |
| 6/57 | 6 | — | 1 | 1 | 4 | — | — | — | 1 | 13 |
| 2/58 | 5 | — | 1 | 2 | 2 | — | 2 | — | — | 12 |
| 6/58 | 6 | 1 | — | 2 | 2 | — | — | 2 | — | 13 |
| 11/59 | 3 | — | 1 | 3 | — | 1 | 2 | — | — | 10 |
| 1/60 | 1 | — | 1[b] | — | 1 | 1 | — | 13 | 8 | 25 |
| 5/60 | 8 | — | — | — | 1 | — | 1 | 1 | — | 11 |

SOURCES: *Stalingradskaia Pravda*, 1954–1960.

[a] Farm Officials include directors of state farms and Machine Tractor Stations, as well as chairmen of collective farms and agricultural specialists working on farms.

[b] The speaker here was the first secretary of the Stalingrad Oblast Komsomol Committee.

The total number of such participants varied from a high of 25 at the enlarged plenum of January, 1960, to a low of ten at the November, 1959 session. Normally, the number of participants was limited to 12 or 13.

The direct responsibility of raion Party committee secretaries for successes or failures in the execution of the agricultural program is reflected in the fact that they formed the largest single group of speakers at five of the nine agricultural plenums, while in one instance they equaled the number of speakers from the ministries. In only one case, the enlarged plenum of January, 1960, did the raikom secretaries form the smallest group of speakers.

At six plenums, when he did not present the major report, the obkom first secretary made the concluding speech. Since both obkom first secretaries during this period followed this procedure, it may be assumed to be the general practice in such cases.[64] In June, 1959, the obkom secretary in charge of agriculture also participated in the discussions. The only city Party secretary to speak in the debates on an agricultural question was the Stalingrad gorkom first secretary, who spoke at the enlarged plenum of June, 1958. At the second enlarged plenum during this period, in January, 1960, no city or oblast Party committee secretaries took part in the discussions, but rather only the first secretary of the oblast Komsomol Committee participated in the debates. While no obkom secretary spoke on agricultural matters at the May, 1960 plenum, the first secretary did make an address at the conclusion of the second question of the day concerning the training of youth.[65]

At every plenum discussing agriculture, up to November, 1959, at least one ministry official took part in the discussions. These included such persons as a "fully-empowered" representative on the Ministry of Procurement, the first vice-chairman of the Council of Ministers of the RSFSR, and an official of the RSFSR Ministry of Agriculture. These officials presented the positions and demands of the central authorities to the obkom plenums. Other ministry per-

[64] This same practice has been followed in the Central Committee in at least three cases in recent years, when Khrushchev gave no initial report, but made the concluding speech. See *Plenum Tsentral'nogo Komiteta Kommunisticheskoi Partii Sovetskogo Soiuza, Stenographicneskii otchel* for 24–29 June, 1959; 22–25 December, 1959; and 10–18 January, 1961. At the December, 1958 plenum, Khrushchev not only made the initial report, but gave a concluding speech as well. See *Ibid.*, 15–19 December, 1958.

[65] *Stalingradskaia Pravda*, May 28, 1960.

sonnel participating in obkom plenum discussions included the heads of sovkhoz trusts, offices for cattle fodder and vegetable seeds.

Aside from the chairmen of the oblispolkom and the raiispolkoms,[66] and their vice-chairmen in charge of agriculture, other participants from the Soviet organs include the heads of the oblast agricultural administration, the oblast planning office, and the oblast administration for construction on the kolkhozes.

As may be expected, few persons from the managerial or cultural categories took part in the discussions of agricultural problems. The two managers who did speak were directly concerned with agriculture—the head of a meat-packing plant and the director of the Stalingrad Tractor Factory. The few cultural-educational officials to participate were all professors at the Stalingrad agricultural institute.

The local farm administrators and specialists were called upon to speak in plenum discussions only from time to time. While four such persons took part in 1954, three in March, 1957, and two in June, 1958, none participated in the three other agricultural plenums in this period. The largest group of farm officials ever to speak at a plenum of the Stalingrad obkom did so at the enlarged plenum of January, 1960. Yet, only one farm director spoke at the annual agricultural plenum in May of the same year, and almost none of the participants in this category are members of the obkom. They appear to be called upon to take part in an obkom plenum as an example to others of either exceptionally fine work or utterly incompetent performance.[67] This also holds true for the few rank and file peasants and workers asked to speak at obkom plenums, except that these people are nearly always "Heroes of Socialist Labor," who are used to provide examples of levels of achievement that others should strive to equal.[68]

A somewhat different pattern of participation is observed in the discussions on industrial questions at plenary sessions of the Stalingrad obkom. Table 12 shows the distribution of speakers by occupation. Overall, fewer persons took part in the discus-

[66] Raiispolkom is the Russian abbreviation for district Soviet executive committee, the executive board of the local government body.

[67] For example, see *Stalingradskaia Pravda*, May 22, 1954; March 10, 1957; and January 8, 1960.

[68] *Ibid.*, See especially, January 8, 1960.

Table 12: Participants in Discussions on Industrial Questions at Stalingrad Obkom Plenums

| PLENUM MONTH/YEAR | PARTY SECRETARIES | | | | GOVERNMENT OFFICIALS | | MANAGERIAL OFFICIALS | CULTURAL-EDUCATIONAL OFFICIALS | TRADE-UNION OFFICIALS | OTHER | TOTAL |
|---|---|---|---|---|---|---|---|---|---|---|---|
| | PPO[a] | RAIKOM | GORKOM | OBKOM | MINISTRY OR SOVNARKHOZ | SOVIET | | | | | |
| 4/57 | — | 2 | 1 | — | 2 | 2 | 1 | — | 1 | 2 | 11 |
| 5/58 | 1 | 1 | 1 | — | 2 | — | — | — | — | 2 | 7 |
| 5/58 | — | 3 | 1 | 1 | 2 | 2 | 1 | 1 | 1 | 1[b] | 12 |
| 11/59[c] | 2 | — | — | 1 | 6 | — | 6 | — | 1 | — | 16 |

SOURCE: *Stalingradskaia Pravda*, 1957–1959. The topics discussed at each of the above plenums are as follows: 4/57—Khrushchev's theses for the reorganization of industrial administration; 5/58—On the development of the chemical industry and the production of synthetic materials; 5/58—On the course of the construction of the Stalingrad Hydroelectric Station; 11/59—On speeding up the construction of enterprises in the oblast.

a PPO is an abbreviation for primary Party organization.

b This item refers to the first secretary of the Stalingrad oblast Komsomol committee.

c Data are not available for the September, 1956 and the October, 1957 plenums.

sions on industrial questions than on agricultural matters, the highest number in the former being 16 and the lowest, seven, with 11 and 12 persons speaking in the other two plenums respectively.

Whereas the raikom secretaries definitely occupied the dominant place in the discussions on agricultural problems, no single group held a comparable position in the debates on industrial matters, except at the November, 1959 session on speeding up the construction of enterprises. At this plenum, industrial and ministry officials accounted for 12 of the 16 participants. In the other three cases the speakers were fairly evenly divided between Party secretaries, and ministry, managerial, and Soviet officials. Other speakers included a scattering of lesser personages.

At the same time, there is a noticeable division between those whose primary concern is the formation of industrial policy and those whose first duty is its direct execution. Generally, the Party officials fall into the former category, and the ministry and managerial personnel, into the latter. The only obkom secretary to participate in these discussions was Chmutov, the second secretary in charge of industry. The principal Party official to take part in the debates at the April, 1957 plenum and in the discussion of the first question at the May, 1958 session was the first secretary of the Stalingrad city Party committee, whose primary area of responsibility is supervision of the industrial complex within the city of Stalingrad.[69] While the Party secretaries may also take on themselves important functions in carrying out policy, especially in terms of overseeing, guiding, and prodding its direct executors, the fact of their membership in the Party committee bureau assures them important roles in policy formation.

When we examine the lists of government and managerial officials who spoke on industrial questions, it becomes evident that these persons occupy, for the most part, purely administrative positions. Thus, the director of the office of the chief administration of metal supply and the director of the oblast office of the chief administration of timber supply were the only two ministry officials to speak at the April, 1957 plenum.[70] They were joined by two Soviet officials—a vice-chairman of the oblispolkom and the chief of

69 *Ibid.*, April 11, 1957, confirms this point.
70 *Ibid.*

the oblast administration of labor reserves.[71] The only industrial manager to speak was the director of the Kamyshin textile *kombinat*.

In the discussion on the development of the chemical industry at the May, 1958 session, the two Sovnarkhoz officials who participated were the chief of the oil and gas industries administration and the assistant chief of the administration of metallurgical and chemical industries. Other speakers at this plenum include the secretary of the oil refinery Party organization, the head of the agitation and propaganda otdel of the Party obkom, and the secretary of the Party committee for the district in which the refinery is located.[72]

Similarly, in the debates on the course of construction of the Stalingrad Hydroelectric Station, the only ministry officials to speak were the assistant chief of the Trans-Volga Railroad and the vice-minister of the RSFSR river fleet. The director of the hydroelectric station, the chairman of a raiispolkom, and the chairman of the oblispolkom were the managerial and Soviet officials who took part in this discussion.[73]

This same pattern is evident in the discussions on speeding up the construction of enterprises at the November, 1959 plenum, when all six Sovnarkhoz officials who spoke were concerned with some aspect of construction. One of these, for example, was the head of Administration Number One of the Chief Administration for Electrical Construction (*glavelektromontazh*).[74] Likewise, the six managerial officials who spoke were directors of either recently completed enterprises or projects still under construction.[75] None of these construction trusts or enterprises, however, was of sufficient importance to assure its chief or director very high potential influence on policy formation. Rather, these ministerial, Soviet, and managerial officials were expected to devote their plenum contributions, for the most part, to assessing progress made in implementing policies formulated by others, as opposed to suggesting new

[71] Since the oblispolkom vice-chairman was formerly the first secretary of the Stalingrad gorkom, and since he was still a member of the obkom bureau, his position should not be regarded as simply administrative.

[72] *Stalingradskaia Pravda*, May 15, 1958.

[73] *Ibid.*, November 13, 1959. Since the chairman of the oblispolkom is a member of the obkom bureau he must be considered a policy-maker as well as an administrator.

[74] *Ibid.*

[75] *Ibid.*

courses of action. At the same time, it is significant that the Party leaders consistently call upon these ministerial, Soviet, and managerial officials for reports on industrial problems at obkom plenums. In contrast to the situation in agriculture where it is the local Party officials who, first of all, must answer for work in this sphere to the oblast Party committee plenums, it is the economic administrators who must bear the primary responsibility before the Party committee for results in industrial production.

Unfortunately, data is available on speakers at only three of the seven plenums that discussed problems of ideological work during the period of this study. However, the available information shows again the pattern of calling upon the lower level administrators to account for shortcomings in the execution of policies formulated by others. Table 13 outlines the distribution by occupation of participants in the discussions on ideological questions at plenums of the Stalingrad obkom.

The number of speakers on ideological questions varied from 23 in December, 1954, to 16 in March, 1957, to only eight in May, 1960. The large number of raikom secretaries who spoke on improving ideological work in the oblast Party organization is consistent with their direct responsibility for such questions, as enunciated in the Party Rules.[76] That fewer Party secretaries took part in the discussion when it concerned improving ideological work among the general population and that only two such officials spoke on problems of indoctrinating children may indicate that the lower secretaries' responsibility for the administration of ideological training programs is limited primarily to those involving Party members.

In each of these three plenums, the first secretary limited his participation to making a concluding speech, leaving the major address to the obkom secretary in charge of ideology. The only other obkom officials to take part in these discussions were the chairman of the obkom Party commission[77] and the head of the obkom otdel of schools and higher educational institutions. The contribution to the debates by the city Party committee officials in both 1954 and 1957 was presented by the secretary in charge of

[76] *Programma i Ustav KPSS*, art. 42(b).

[77] The obkom Party commission is responsible for enforcing Party discipline and also hearing appeals from decisions of lower bodies on exclusions from the Party and Party reprimands. See *Programma i Ustav KPSS*, art. 40.

*Table 13: Participants in Discussions on Ideological Questions at Stalingrad Obkom Plenums*

| PLENUM MONTH/YEAR | PARTY SECRETARIES | | | | GOVERNMENT OFFICIALS | | CULTURAL-EDUCATIONAL OFFICIALS | VLKSM[a] OFFICIALS | POLICE OFFICIALS OR PROCURATOR | OTHER | TOTAL |
|---|---|---|---|---|---|---|---|---|---|---|---|
| | PPO | RAIKOM | GORKOM | OBKOM | MINISTRY OR SOVNARKHOZ | SOVIET | | | | | |
| 12/54 | 1 | 8 | 1 | 1 | — | 4 | 5 | — | 1[b] | 2 | 23 |
| 3/57 | — | 3 | 2 | — | — | 3 | 6 | 1 | 1 | — | 16 |
| 5/60 | — | 1 | — | 1 | — | 5 | — | 1 | — | — | 8 |

SOURCE: *Stalingradskaia Pravda*, 1954–1960. Data are not available for the July, 1957; May, 1959; March, 1960; or October, 1960 plenums where ideological questions were discussed. The topics discussed at each of the plenums for which data are available are as follows: 12/54—Measures for improving ideological work in the oblast Party organization; 3/57—On strengthening political work among the population; and 5/60—On measures for improving the training of children.

[a] VLKSM is a Russian abbreviation for the Komsomol.

[b] This item refers to the head of the oblast administration of the *KGB*.

ideology, although in the latter case he was joined by the first secretary of the Kamyshin gorkom.

The list of speakers in the debates at the December, 1954 plenum reflects the wide variety of organizations engaged in ideological indoctrination. Thus, the participants from the Soviet organs included the vice-chairman of the oblispolkom in charge of ideological work, the chiefs of the city and oblast administrations of culture, and the assistant chief of the oblast administration of agriculture. The cultural and educational officials were represented by the director of the Gor'ky Drama Theater, the chairman of the oblast trade-union council, the secretary of the Stalingrad division of the Society for the Dissemination of Political and Scientific Knowledge,[78] the editor of the Komsomol newspaper, *Molodoi Leninets,* and the assistant editor of *Stalingradskaia Pravda.*[79] The tutorial role of the Soviet police is exemplified by the participation of the head of the oblast division of the Committee of State Security *(KGB)* in the plenum on political indoctrination.

When the March, 1957 plenum examined the question of strengthening political work among the whole population, the bulk of the speakers were either Soviet or cultural and educational officials, with only three raikom secretaries taking part. Three Soviet officials—the chief of the oblast administration of culture, the chief of the oblast administration of communications, and the head of the oblast administration of internal affairs,[80]—contributed to the discussion. Also participating in the debates were the oblast prosecutor, the heads of the departments of the Fundamentals of Marxism-Leninism of both the Stalingrad Medical Institute and the Pedagogical Institute, a trade-union official, the chairman of the oblast committee of DOSAAF,[81] the secretary of the oblast Komsomol committee, the chief editor of *Stalingradskaia Pravda,* and, again, the head of the oblast division of the mass-propaganda society.

[78] This is a national organization that carries out a continuous program of mass political indoctrination.

[79] Apparently the assistant editor bears a special responsibility for questions of ideology.

[80] This is another term for the *MVD* or local police attached to the oblast Soviet executive committee.

[81] DOSAAF is the abbreviated name for the voluntary society for cooperation with the armed forces. It gives young people training in military techniques, but also has the important function of political indoctrination.

In the discussion on improving the training of children at the May, 1960 plenum, nearly all the participants were directly connected with the administration of the educational system. The five Soviet officials who spoke included the vice-chairman of the oblispolkom in charge of ideology, the chairman of the city Soviet executive committee, the head of the oblast Soviet executive committee otdel of education, and the heads of two raion Soviet otdels of education. Others who took part included the secretary of the oblast Komsomol committee, and the secretary of a Party raikom.

Once again, whereas the major addresses at plenums were made by bureau members who thus possess a relatively high degree of potential influence on policy-making, most of the discussants occupy positions that would appear to limit them to largely administrative roles.

As Table 14 shows, the number of participants in the discussions on cadres questions varied from ten in May, 1956, to 13 in both the February, 1958 and the March, 1960 sessions. Since the Party Rules assign the Party committees the direct responsibility for the selection, assignment, and training of leading cadres for all sections of Soviet society,[82] it follows that the Party secretaries would comprise the bulk of speakers on this topic. However, except for one concluding speech by the first secretary,[83] the secretary in charge of cadres was the only obkom official to participate in these three plenums, and he delivered the major addresses. Otherwise, the Party secretaries who took part were all from the city, district, or, in three instances, the primary Party organizations.

The one speaker, other than Party secretaries, at the May, 1956 plenum was the secretary of the oblast Komsomol committee. His participation in each of the other two discussions on work with cadres, in spite of the fact that this position was occupied by a different individual at the time of each plenum,[84] is indicative of the Komsomol's role as a training ground for Party cadres.

The director of the electrical network construction administration and the first vice-chairman of the Sovnarkhoz were the two economic administrators who spoke at the March, 1960 plenum. They were undoubtedly called upon to account for the "highly im-

[82] *Programma i Ustav KPSS*, art. 42(d).
[83] On February 21, 1958.
[84] See *Stalingradskaia Pravda*, June 1, 1956; February 21, 1958; and March 26, 1960.

Table 14: Participants in Discussions on Cadres Questions at Stalingrad Obkom Plenums

| PLENUM MONTH/YEAR | PARTY SECRETARIES | | | | GOVERNMENT OFFICIALS | | | CULTURAL-EDUCATIONAL OFFICIALS | VLKSM OFFICIALS | OTHER | TOTAL |
|---|---|---|---|---|---|---|---|---|---|---|---|
| | PPO | RAIKOM | GORKOM | OBKOM | MINISTRY OR SOVNARKHOZ | SOVIET | MAN-AGERIAL OFFICIALS | | | | |
| 5/56 | — | 7 | 2 | — | — | — | — | — | 1 | — | 10 |
| 2/58 | 2 | 3 | 1 | 1 | — | 2 | 1 | 1 | 1 | 1 | 13 |
| 3/60 | 1 | 2 | 4 | — | 2 | 2 | — | 1 | 1 | — | 13 |

SOURCE: *Stalingradskaia Pravda*, 1956, 1960. Data are not available for the March, 1959 plenum on improving the work of the primary Party organizations in Stalingrad oblast. The topics discussed at each of the above plenums are as follows: 5/56—On the growth of the Stalingrad oblast Party organization; 2/58—On work with cadres in the oblast Party organization; 3/60—On the selection, assignment, and training of cadres in the oblast Party organization.

proper" attitudes of some Sovnarkhoz officials.[85] Only under these unusual circumstances were such officials brought into the discussion of work with cadres.

The Soviet officials who participated in the 1958 plenum were the chief of the oblast water system administration and the chairman of a raiispolkom, while the chairman of the oblispolkom and the head of another raiispolkom took part in the 1960 session. Three officials engaged in training cadres made contributions to the debates at various plenums. The head of the department of Marxism-Leninism of the Agricultural Institute and the secretary of the Party organization at the Stalingrad oblast Higher Party School spoke at the 1958 session, and the director of an engineering institute did so in 1960.

From this analysis it becomes clear that speakers are chosen for the discussions at obkom plenums not so much on the basis of the contributions they may make to a thorough, all-round elucidation of a particular problem area, or because of the proposals they may make as to the most suitable policy to adopt to deal with the question at hand, but rather on the basis of who should be called upon to account for shortcomings in the execution of previously formulated policies, or on the basis of who will be assigned the direct responsibility for fulfilling new decisions. Whereas, the major addresses are always given by those who appear to occupy policy-making positions, participation in the discussions is limited, for the most part, to lower level administrators.

Official Soviet writing professes that one of the principal purposes of plenary sessions is to give the committee members the opportunity to "criticize shortcomings in the work of the bureau, the secretaries, and the staff."[86] However, that this purpose is not everywhere realized was attested in 1954 by *Pravda Ukrainy:* "In a number of places plenary sessions have not yet become true forums for developing criticism and self-criticism and for disclosing shortcomings."[87] The reason given for this difficulty was that not only were many guests invited to plenary sessions, but also that

---

[85] At the oblast Party conference in January, 1960, it was revealed that the obkom bureau had expelled from the Party several Sovnarkhoz officials, recently transferred from Moscow, for trying in every way to return to the capital. See *Stalingradskaia Pravda*, January 27, 1960.

[86] *Pravda Ukrainy*, June 2, 1954, p. 1.

[87] *Ibid.*

most speakers were there by invitation. "Obviously," *Pravda Ukrainy* concluded, "such a practice leads to a situation whereby plenary sessions are turned into general mass meetings and cease to furnish leadership."[88]

That statement refers particularly to the so-called enlarged plenums. To some of these are invited up to 500 persons connected in some way with the problem to be discussed.[89] Three such plenums were held by the Stalingrad obkom—in May, 1954; June, 1958; and January, 1960.[90] All of these enlarged plenums discussed agricultural topics. The guests at the June, 1958 session included the chairmen of kolkhozes and raiispolkoms, directors of sovkhozes, RTS',[91] and MTS', quality inspectors of the ministry of agriculture, raikom secretaries, secretaries of kolkhoz and sovkhoz Party organizations, and agricultural specialists.[92] In addition to these officials the enlarged plenum of January, 1960, included the first secretaries of gorkoms, secretaries of raion Komsomol committees, scholars, leading workers, and managerial personnel from industrial enterprises and construction projects, and responsible Party workers.[93] While warning that such forms as enlarged plenums must be used skillfully and intelligently since "a plenum is a plenum and must not be turned into an ordinary *aktiv* meeting," *Partiinaia Zhizn'*, in a 1962 article, concluded that such sessions are useful since "after the plenum its participants become local organizers for the fulfillment of the adopted decisions."[94] These enlarged plenums provide an especially convincing example of the essentially tutorial function of Party committee plenums.

If participation by noncommittee members were limited simply to listening to the speeches or presenting an occasional report to the enlarged plenums, the complaint that sessions are frequently not true forums for criticism could not be taken too se-

[88] *Ibid.*
[89] "Collectivity of Leadership and Personal Responsibility," *Partiinaia Zhizn'*, No. 12 (1962), p. 19.
[90] See Chapter 5, p. 55.
[91] An RTS is a Machine Tractor Station that after the joint resolution of the Central Committee of the CPSU and the RSFSR Council of Ministers of April 18, 1958, was turned into a Repair Tractor Station. For the text of the decree, see *SPR* (1959 ed.), pp. 293–311.
[92] *Stalingradskaia Pravda*, June 28, 1958.
[93] *Ibid.*, January 8, 1960.
[94] "Collectivity of Leadership and Personal Responsibility," *Partiinaia Zhizn'*, No. 12 (1962), p. 19.

*Table 15: Participants in Stalingrad Obkom Plenums 1954–1960*

| DATE | TOPIC | FULL MEMBERS | CANDIDATES | GUESTS |
|---|---|---|---|---|
| 5/54 | *Agriculture* | 6 | 2 | 17 |
| 12/54 | *Ideology* | 12 | 2 | 9 |
| 5/56 | *Agriculture* | 9 | 1 | 4 |
| 5/56 | *Cadres* | 3 | 4 | 3 |
| 3/57 | *Ideology* | 4 | 2 | 10 |
| 3/57 | *Agriculture* | 7 | 4 | 5 |
| 4/57 | *Industry* | 4 | — | 7 |
| 7/57 | *Agriculture* | 7 | 1 | 5 |
| 2/58 | *Agriculture* | 6 | 1 | 5 |
| 2/58 | *Cadres* | 9 | — | 4 |
| 5/58 | *Industry* | 3 | 1 | 2 |
| 5/58 | *Industry (Const.)* | 5 | 1 | 6 |
| 6/58 | *Agriculture* | 9 | — | 4 |
| 11/59 | *Industry* | 2 | 1 | 13 |
| 11/59 | *Agriculture* | 5 | 1 | 4 |
| 1/60 | *Agriculture* | 6 | — | 20 |
| 3/60 | *Cadres* | 10 | 1 | 2 |
| 5/60 | *Agriculture* | 5 | 2 | 4 |
| 5/60 | *Ideology* | 3 | 1 | 5 |
| | *Total* | 115 | 25 | 129 |

SOURCE: These figures are compiled from data on participation in obkom plenums and lists of obkom members published in *Stalingradskaia Pravda*, 1954–1960.

riously. In actuality, as can be seen in Table 15, 129 out of 269 contributions to the discussion at 19 plenary sessions of the Stalingrad obkom from 1954 through 1960 were made by persons who were not members of the Party committee.[95] In seven plenums the number of guest speakers actually exceeded the number of full members who took part, while equalling the latter in one instance. In this light, if the above-quoted statements to the effect that large numbers of guest speakers appearing frequently at obkom plenums make serious discussion difficult if not impossible are true, very serious doubt must be cast on any assertions that serious policy debate and discussion take place at Party committee plenary sessions.

If, then, guest speakers do act as a limiting influence on serious debate and discussion, it is important to determine who are the full committee members who participated in obkom plenum discus-

[95] Table 15 shows the number of obkom members, candidate members and guests respectively who spoke in each plenum in this period.

sions, for the thoroughness and comprehensiveness of discussion must depend in large part on the diversity of occupational viewpoints represented by the committee members who speak at the plenums. If one group overwhelms all other participants, discussions and decisions are very likely to be one-sided and lacking in objectivity, while criticism is apt to be formal and perfunctory.[96] Yet, the record of participation by committee members in plenary sessions of the Stalingrad obkom shows clearly the dominant position of one group—the professional Party secretaries. Seventy-six of the 115 speeches by full committee members were made by the Party secretaries, including 50 by raikom, 11 by gorkom, 14 by obkom, and one by primary Party organization secretaries. Of the remaining 39 speeches, ten were given by Soviet, 11 by ministry or Sovnarkhoz, two by managerial, two by educational-cultural, and nine by trade-union, Komsomol, military, and legal officials, while only five contributions were made by rank and file peasants and workers who were members of the obkom.

At plenary sessions of the Stalingrad obkom it was quite unusual for a person to speak more than once in the discussions. At the 19 sessions under study 194 persons made a total of 259 contributions to the plenum debates. Of these, 147 persons[97] were limited to a single speech, 24 participated twice, ten individuals made three speeches, and nine officials spoke four or more times.[98] All of the persons who took part in just one plenum fall into three fairly equal sized groups. The first group of 55 persons includes the heads of organizations and institutions that are oblast or city-wide in scope or importance. Within this group 25 were members or candidate members of the obkom, gorkom, or both, while 30, members of neither Party committee, were invited guests. The second group embraces 46 persons from the level of assistant chiefs of oblast or city-wide organizations or institutions, and officials from the raion level. This group divides evenly between 23 members and candidate members of the oblast and city Party committees, and 23 invited

---

[96] These points are the themes of many articles in the Soviet press and Party journals on collective leadership. See for example, "The Principle of Collective Leadership," *VPR*, pp. 49–55; and, "Collectivity is the Highest Principle of Party Leadership," *Pravda*, May 25, 1956, p. 2.

[97] This figure does not include the four officials from the central organs, each of whom also spoke only once.

[98] *Stalingradskaia Pravda*, 1954–1960.

guests, members of neither committee. In the third group of 46 persons are those participants with positions below the district level, such as secretaries of primary Party organizations, and rank and file workers. Among this group, only 11 were members or candidate members of the obkom or gorkom, while 35 were persons, members of neither committee, who spoke by invitation.

The 24 persons who participated two times in the discussions at oblast Party committee plenums divide among the three groups with nine, 13, and two speakers in each group respectively. All of these individuals, with the exception of one, a kolkhoz chairman, were members of the obkom. The first group—heads of organizations of oblast-wide significance—includes I. T. Grishin, obkom first secretary from 1950 to 1955; [99] A. A. Vdovin, chairman of the oblast trade-union council from 1954 to June, 1958; S. I. Sadovskii, first secretary of the oblast Komsomol committee from 1958 to at least 1960;[100] B. G. Shirokov, chairman of the oblast planning commission from 1957 to 1959; and P. A. Pankrat'ev, director of the Kamyshin cotton textile *kombinat* from 1957 to at least 1959;[101] as well as the second secretary of the obkom[102] and three gorkom secretaries. The second group of 13 persons—assistant heads of oblast organizations or heads of raion level institutions—includes ten first secretaries of district Party committees, one chairman of a raiispolkom, the fourth vice-chairman of the oblispolkom, and the assistant director of the Stalingrad Agricultural Institute. In the third group are two kolkhoz chairmen, one of whom was a member of the obkom.

Among the ten persons who spoke three times in obkom plenums, three fall within the first group, and seven fit into the second, leaving none in the third. Only one of these ten, a minor ministry official,[103] was not a member of the obkom. The first group included N. A. Nepokupnoi, the obkom third secretary; K. S. Nekrasov, the first vice-chairman of the oblispolkom from March,

99 It should be noted that the figures on participation include only two plenums held during Grishin's tenure and thus give an incomplete picture of his participation record.

100 At the end of the period under study, Sadovskii was still in this position.

101 The last reference to this position in *Stalingradskaia Pravda* is November 13, 1959.

102 The obkom secretaries are included in the first group since their membership on the obkom bureau and the obkom secretariat gives them a degree of potential influence on decision-making at least equaling that of the heads of other oblast organizations represented on the bureau.

103 The chief of the goods-transport administration of the chief administration for oil supply (*glavneft'sbyt'*).

1957, to June, 1958, and chairman of the oblast trade-union council since that time; and O. I. Rozhkov, first secretary of the oblast Komsomol committee from June, 1956, to April, 1958. In the second group are four first secretaries of raion Party committees, the chairman of a raiispolkom, and the head of a department at the Stalingrad Agricultural Institute.

In addition to three first secretaries of Party raikoms, the five persons who spoke four times in the discussions at obkom plenums include S. A. Krasnov, who between 1954 and 1960 held such positions as a "fully-empowered" representative of the ministry of procurement, the chief of the oblast administration of state farms, the director of a meat trust, and the assistant chief of the Sovnarkhoz administration of the food and light industries, and I. V. Larin, the chief of the oblast administration of agriculture.

The three persons who participated five times in obkom plenum debates are I. S. Pankin, the chairman of the oblispolkom; L. S. Kulichenko, the first secretary of the Stalingrad gorkom; and I. A. Logunov, first secretary of the Novo-Nikolaevskii raikom.

I. K. Zhegalin, the obkom first secretary from late 1955 to 1961, is the one person who spoke six times in the discussions at obkom plenums.

While the number of guest speakers either equaled or exceeded the number of committee members from each of the three groups who participated in the discussions at only one plenum, there were just two invited guests among the 34 persons who took part in two or more plenary sessions. Moreover, while all those who spoke at only one session divided fairly evenly into the three hierarchic groupings, among those who spoke in two or more sessions only two persons come within the lowest grouping with the remainder splitting nearly evenly between the two higher level groupings. Thus, repeated participation in obkom plenums was limited, almost exclusively, to members of the Party committee who headed either oblast or raion level organizations. However, even among those who were able to speak more than once at plenum discussions a wide diversity of viewpoints is lacking. With 26 of the 34 individuals who took part in more than one plenum professional Party secretaries from the raion, city, and oblast Party committees, the dominant position of the Party officials is only too obvious.

The overall record of the Stalingrad oblast Party committee's plenary sessions shows that it does not serve as a deliberative body where the collective experience is formulated into policy decisions on the basis of thorough and comprehensive discussion of problem areas from diverse points of view, but rather, it acts essentially as a forum for assessing progress made by the various administrative personnel in fulfilling current programs and for announcing, detailing, and approving new policies devised either by the central organs, the Party committee bureau, or some combination of the two. Plenary sessions provide a channel through which those in places of authority and responsibility throughout the oblast can be informed of the Party's position on major questions, under the guise of open discussion. The point of view of the Party officials is assured acceptance by the rules governing discussion within the Party, and by the dominant position of the Party secretaries in both the organization and carrying out of Party committee plenary sessions.

Having shown that policy decisions are not made in the oblast Party committee plenary sessions, we must not underestimate the significance of these sessions, however, for the decision-making process within the oblast Party organization. Through giving an account of the reasons for success or failure in his work at an obkom plenum and by hearing similar reports from others, the local administrator is made, hopefully, to feel more responsible for his work, and thus gains additional motivation for putting more energy into his tasks. Perhaps just as important, the organized discussion at obkom plenums should give him a clearer conception of just what his most important task at the moment is: whether to make certain that the farms under his supervision plant and harvest enough silage to feed the cattle during the winter, or to press forward with the construction of the new oil refinery. In short, it sets him specific priorities for the coming period. The local official for his part may make positive contributions by bringing to the attention of both the Party secretaries and local officials either shortcomings that hinder progress, or new methods that may make easier the solution of pressing problems. If the plenary sessions effectively fulfill these tutorial functions, then the obkom bureau, rather than having to devote considerable energy to adopting disciplinary and other measures to secure compliance with its decisions, may find more time to approach the formation of major policies in a careful and thoughtful manner. It is in this sense that the plenary sessions must be regarded as having a significant place in the decision-making process within the oblast Party committee.

Throughout the discussion of the oblast Party conference and the oblast Party committee plenums the most important decisions were seen as those made by the obkom secretaries or the obkom bureau. Chapter 6 examines the process of decision-making in the obkom bureau.

# SIX

# The Oblast Party
# Committee Bureau

🔲🔲

### FUNCTION

The Party Rules adopted at the 19th Party Congress in 1952, provide for the election in the local Party committees of an executive body, or bureau, consisting of not more than 11 members, including three secretaries.[1] The fundamental duty of the bureau is to ensure that the decisions of the higher Party organs are fulfilled. The bureau is given broad powers to enable it to carry out this responsibility. The most significant of these is the right to issue "instructions on the most important problems of economic, cultural, and inner-Party work . . . ."[2] Although the range of questions on which the bureau issues orders in practice has varied considerably, especially in the realm of economic problems,[3] the obkom bureau must

[1] Hazard, p. 239. The Rules adopted at the 22nd Congress provide for the election of a bureau but do not specify a maximum size, nor a maximum number of secretaries. See *Programma i Ustav KPSS*, art. 45.

[2] "On Preparations for Meetings of the Party Committee Bureau," *Partiinaia Zhizn'*, No. 6 (1958), p. 37.

[3] For a detailed analysis of the role of the obkom bureau in industrial decision-making see the dissertation by Jerry F. Hough, "The Role of the Local Party Organs in Soviet Industrial Decision-Making" (unpublished Ph.D. dissertation, Department of Government, Harvard University).

be regarded as the central policy-making body within the oblast. This position is strengthened by the bureau's authority to select, confirm, and remove a definite group of leading personnel in all major organizations and institutions of the oblast. As explained by a leading Party theoretician:

> Leadership from one center is necessary for the organized distribution of Party forces. The Party could not direct the work of Soviet, economic, and social organizations, could not direct all sides of the state, economic, and cultural life of the country if it did not have the possibility of placing cadres in accordance with political and economic tasks. It is impossible to direct the country without the placement of cadres.[4]

We have already seen the role of the obkom bureau in the organization and carrying out of the Party committee conferences and obkom plenums. In this chapter we shall examine the organization of the bureau of the Stalingrad oblast Party committee, the questions it decided, and the process of decision-making in bureau meetings.

COMPOSITION

The Party committee bureau is elected at the first plenum following the Party conference. During the period under study four bureau elections took place—in February, 1954; January, 1956; December, 1957; and January, 1960.

Although the Party Rules authorized the election of a bureau of 11 members, the bureau of the Stalingrad obkom elected after the 9th oblast Party conference in 1954 consisted of only nine full members and three candidate members. This bureau included the following full members: three oblast Party committee secretaries: I. T. Grishin, the first secretary; L. S. Kulichenko, the second secretary; and N. I. Chmutov, the third secretary; the chairman of the oblast Soviet executive committee, I. S. Pankin; the first secretary of the Stalingrad city Party committee, K. S. Nekrasov; the head of the agricultural otdel of the obkom, N. A. Nepokupnoi; the chairman of the oblast trade-union council, A. A. Vdovin; the chief of the oblast administration of the *KGB*, I. A.

---

4 Slepov, p. 18.

Mel'nikov; and N. D. Antonov who was never identified but may have been the oblast military commander.[5] The three candidate members elected in 1954 included the first secretary of the oblast Komsomol committee, V. T. Bogatyrev; the head of the agitation and propaganda otdel of the obkom, I. M. Vovchenko; and the head of the obkom otdel of Party, trade-union, and Komsomol organs, N. I. Gusev.

Several features of the composition of the obkom bureau elected in February, 1954, deserve comment. With five of the nine full members either Party secretaries or heads of Party committee otdels, the Party officials are assured a majority of votes in the bureau. Moreover, of the 12 identified members and candidates all, except possibly the chief of the *KGB*, are heads of organizations that come under the close control of the oblast Party committee.

The Party Rules give the oblast Party committee the right to "guide the activities of the oblast . . . Soviet and public organizations through the Party groups within them."[6] In Stalingrad oblast, Party control of the oblast Soviet and trade-union organizations was strengthened by the membership of two obkom secretaries on the oblispolkom, and the membership of the obkom secretary in charge of Party, trade-union, and Komsomol organs on the presidium of the oblast trade-union council.[7] Day to day supervision over the work of the trade-union and Komsomol organs was maintained by the obkom otdel for Party, trade-union, and Komsomol organs. So, with the possible exception of the head of the *KGB* and perhaps the unidentified bureau member, the bureau elected in 1954, is composed entirely of Party or Party-oriented officials.

The diminution of the Party's role in industrial matters in the last years of Stalin's life and the first period following his death is reflected in the membership of the Stalingrad obkom bureau. Not even I. F. Sinitsyn, the director of the Stalingrad

[5] This information is derived from the list of such members published in *Stalingradskaia Pravda*, February 13, 1954, and from other items identifying the positions held by specific individuals published in the same source during 1954.

[6] *Programma i Ustav KPSS*, art. 48.

[7] This was true at least for the only time such information was published. See *Stalingradskaia Pravda*, March 10, 1957, for a listing of the oblispolkom membership; and see *ibid.*, June 3, 1958, for a listing of the trade-union council presidium membership.

Tractor Factory—probably the most important single enterprise in the oblast—was given a place on the bureau in 1954. Moreover, the director of the largest construction project in the oblast, the Stalingrad Hydroelectric Station, was not even elected a member of the obkom. Perhaps even more significantly, N. I. Chmutov, the obkom secretary who was referred to as "in charge of industry and construction," was given the place as third secretary behind L. S. Kulichenko, the secretary in charge of Party, Soviet, trade-union, and Komsomol organs.[8]

Within a month and a half after the 9th oblast Party conference, an organizational plenum was held at which certain changes were made in the composition of the obkom bureau. N. A. Nepokupnoi, bureau member and until this time head of the obkom agricultural otdel, and V. S. Krasavin were elected obkom secretaries, bringing to five the total number of obkom secretaries.[9] Krasavin's responsibilities centered around questions of ideological work, and Nepokupnoi was made secretary in charge of agriculture.[10] Krasavin and P. N. Sergeev, the chief of the oblast agricultural administration, were both made full members of the bureau at this time. This brought the total number of full members to 11, the maximum permitted under the Party Rules.

With five obkom secretaries on a bureau of only 11 voting members, the dominant role of the Party officials was now made even more secure. Evidence to the effect that one purpose of a large number of secretaries on the bureau is precisely to ensure their superiority over all other groups, or even to enable them to replace the bureau, was given by no less an authority than Khrushchev himself at the 19th Party Congress in his speech on proposed changes in the Party Rules. While supporting the formation of secretariats within the oblast Party committees, "in the interests of more effective examination of current questions," he nevertheless felt compelled to suggest that "in order to prevent the secretariats from supplanting the bureaus, the number of secretaries should

---

[8] *Ibid.*, February 12, 1954. This secretary is also referred to as "in charge of cadres." This latter designation is used in this book.

[9] *Ibid.*, March 27, 1954.

[10] The responsibilities of Krasavin and Nepokupnoi are inferred from their activities. Krasavin gave major speeches on ideological work on May 19, 1954, and July 19, 1954. Nepokupnoi regularly made major addresses on agriculture problems beginning on May 25, 1954.

be reduced to three and the secretariats should be directed to report the decisions adopted by them to the bureau of the oblast Party committee . . . ."[11]

In late December, 1955, at an organizational plenum of the Stalingrad obkom, I. T. Grishin, after five years as first secretary, was relieved of his duties in connection with his transfer to diplomatic work.[12] At the same plenum, Ivan Kuzmich Zhegalin, who had served for the previous six years as first secretary of the Grozny obkom, was elected first secretary of the Stalingrad oblast Party committee.

Following the election of the new first secretary certain changes were made in the obkom bureau at the conclusion of the 10th oblast Party conference, in January, 1956. While positive proof is lacking, it appears that the first secretary brought with him a certain D. P. Zhuravlev, who was elected obkom secretary in charge of ideology in place of Krasavin, who appears to have left the oblast at this time.[13]

Undoubtedly the most important change in the bureau's composition at this time was the election of I. F. Sinitsyn, the director of the Stalingrad Tractor Factory, as a full member.[14] Although the only bureau member from an organization not under close control of the obkom, except possibly for the chief of the oblast administration of the *KGB*,[15] Sinitsyn's election to the bureau is a sign of the reassertion of the Party's role in matters of industrial

[11] *Pravda*, October 13, 1952.

[12] *Stalingradskaia Pravda*, December 20, 1955. At this time Grishin became ambassador to Czechoslovakia. It is sometimes contended that assignment to a diplomatic post in eastern Europe is a "demotion" for first secretaries of important obkoms. The evidence in this case seems to indicate that the move involved no decline in status for Grishin, since after five years in the diplomatic post he became a Deputy Minister for Foreign Trade involved in many important trade missions to the Middle East, eastern Europe, and southeast Asia. See *Who's Who in the USSR 1965/1966*, Andrew I. Lebed, Heinrich E. Schultz, and Stephen S. Taylor, eds. (New York: Scarecrow Press, 1966), p. 291.

[13] Whereas every other member of the bureau elected in 1956 was a member of either the obkom or gorkom in 1954, there is no mention made of Zhuravlev in *Stalingradskaia Pravda* prior to the 10th conference, in 1956. On the other hand, no mention was made of Krasavin after 1955. If he had been simply demoted, he would probably have remained a member of the obkom or gorkom. On this basis it seems logical to conclude that the former came into the oblast only in 1956 and the latter left it at that time. Since a new first secretary also was elected about this time, it is surmised that perhaps Zhuravlev was brought to Stalingrad by the new obkom leader.

[14] *Stalingradskaia Pravda*, January 20, 1956.

[15] Unfortunately the Stalingrad press contained little material on Party control of the *KGB* at the oblast level, but it is quite probable that measures to assert such control were taken in this period. See *Vneocherednoi XXI S'ezd KPSS*, stenograficheskii otchet (Moscow: Politizdat, 1959) II, 249–254.

policy. It is significant that in the period under study the first plenum to discuss questions of industry was held in this same year, 1956.[16]

P. N. Sergeev, the chief of the oblast administration of agriculture was not re-elected to the bureau in 1956. He was replaced on that body by his immediate superior, P. P. Eliseev, the vice-chairman of the oblispolkom in charge of agriculture.[17] Other changes in the bureau at this time included the removal of Antonov and Vovchenko.[18]

From the 10th to the 11th Party conference, then, the obkom bureau consisted of five secretaries, the chairman of the oblispolkom, the first secretary of the Stalingrad gorkom, the chief of the oblast administration of the *KGB*, the director of the Stalingrad Tractor Factory, the vice-chairman of the oblispolkom in charge of agriculture, and the chairman of the oblast trade-union council presidium as full members, and the head of the obkom otdel of Party organs, and the first secretary of the oblast Komsomol committee as candidate members.[19]

In the early part of 1957, still eight or nine months prior to the 11th Party conference, several shifts and changes occurred among the oblast leadership group. A listing of candidates for election to the oblast Soviet, published on February 5, 1957, included the name G. S. Stytsenko, and identified him as the chief of the oblast administration of the *KGB*,[20] thus indicating that sometime prior to this date the former chief, Mel'nikov, either had been removed or transferred. On March 9th of the same year, an organizational plenum of the obkom removed Kulichenko from his position as second secretary of the obkom in connection with his election as first secretary of the Stalingrad city Party committee.[21] That same day it was announced that an organizational plenum of the gorkom had released Nekrasov from his duties "in connection

16 See Chapter 5, p. 60.

17 *Stalingradskaia Pravda*, January 20, 1956.

18 *Ibid.* By this time Vovchenko was no longer listed as holding any position in the Party apparat or as a member of the Party committee.

19 *Ibid.* The order given above is the order given in the press. Since the names of the persons holding these positions were not listed in alphabetical order, this listing may be taken as some indication of the relative importance of the various bureau members. *Conquest* provides a sound argument in support of this assumption. See, *Conquest*, pp. 61–65.

20 *Ibid.*, February 5, 1957.

21 *Ibid.*, March 9, 1957.

with his transfer to other work."[22] On the following day the oblast newspaper stated that N. S. Nekrasov had been appointed first vice-chairman of the oblispolkom.[23] At the March obkom plenum, N. I. Gusev, then head of the Party organs otdel of the obkom and a bureau member, was elected an obkom secretary to replace Kulichenko. Judging by his previous position, and by his activities after his election as obkom secretary, it seems clear that Gusev assumed the responsibilities of supervising the Party, Soviet, trade-union, and Komsomol organizations formerly exercised by Kulichenko.[24] The obkom bureau elected in December, 1957, reflected these changes.

In the newly elected bureau, Zhegalin remained first secretary. Chmutov, the secretary in charge of industry, was promoted from third to second secretary. This undoubtedly reflects the increasingly important position of industrial questions in the life of the Stalingrad obkom bureau after the industrial reorganization, announced at the February, 1957 Central Committee plenum.[25] The secretary in charge of Party organs was reduced from second to third secretary. Nepokupnoi remained as the fourth secretary in charge of agriculture, and Zhuravlev continued as fifth secretary with the responsibility for supervising ideological work.[26]

Several changes were also made at this time among the other bureau members, both in the positions and personnel represented.[27] The most interesting change was the replacement of Eliseev, the oblispolkom vice-chairman in charge of agriculture, by Nekrasov, the first vice-chairman of the oblispolkom whose responsibilities involved supervising the work of industry. This change reflects both the continued influence of the former gorkom first secretary, and the relative priority of industrial over agricultural matters at this time.[28]

[22] *Ibid.*

[23] *Ibid.*, March 10, 1957.

[24] Gusev gave a major speech on "work with cadres in the oblast Party organization," to an obkom plenum on February 21, 1958. On June 3, 1958, he was elected a member of the oblast trade-union council presidium.

[25] For the text of the resolution, see *SPR* (1957 ed.), pp. 112–120.

[26] *Stalingradskaia Pravda*, December 27, 1957, and other articles identifying the positions held by particular individuals.

[27] It is worthwhile noting that whereas the obkom secretaries continued to be listed according to rank, the other full and candidate members were now listed in strict alphabetical order.

[28] *Stalingradskaia Pravda*, December 27, 1957.

Although I. F. Sinitsyn remained a bureau member, it was in his new capacity as chairman of the Stalingrad oblast Council for the National Economy (Sovnarkhoz), rather than in his former position as director of the Stalingrad Tractor Factory.[29] Kulichenko also remained on the bureau, but this time in his capacity as first secretary of the Stalingrad gorkom. The only other change among the full members of the bureau was the election of Stytsenko in place of Mel'nikov. Vdovin and Pankin retained their bureau membership as chairman of the oblast trade-union council and chairman of the oblispolkom respectively.[30]

Among the former candidate bureau members, Gusev became an obkom secretary and full bureau member, but Bogatyrev was replaced as first secretary of the oblast Komsomol committee by O. I. Rozhkov, on June 1, 1956.[31] Bogatyrev was elected a candidate member of the bureau in December, 1957. For the first time during the period of this study the editor of the oblast Party and Soviet newspaper, *Stalingradskaia Pravda*, was elected a candidate member of the obkom bureau. Also for the first time, the commander of the Stalingrad oblast military garrison became a candidate bureau member in 1957, bringing to three the number of candidates.

It is perhaps a sign of the degree to which Khrushchev had succeeded in filling the obkom bureau with persons loyal to him and his policies that not one person was removed from the bureau in the aftermath of the anti-Khrushchev events of June, 1957, in the central Committee Presidium. As we have shown, all of the changes to occur in that year were brought about in February and March, except for the promotion of Sinitsyn in June, and the replacement on the bureau of Eliseev by Nekrasov. While this latter change could have been connected with the June events, it seems more plausible to attribute it to changes in the relative priority of industry and agriculture.

In the period between the 11th and 12th oblast Party conferences several important personnel changes occurred. On May 18, 1958, it was announced that A. A. Vdovin had been removed from the obkom bureau "in connection with his retirement" as

---

29 *Ibid.* On June 13, 1957, it was announced that Sinitsyn had been removed as director of the Stalingrad Tractor Factory and confirmed as chairman of the Sovnarkhoz.
30 *Ibid.*
31 *Ibid.*, June 1, 1956 .

chairman of the oblast trade-union council presidium,[32] a position
he had held since at least 1954.[33] At the age of 59, Vdovin was the
oldest bureau member. The next oldest was the first secretary at
52. The ages of the other bureau members were all between 45
and 51, except for the first secretary of the oblast Komsomol
committee, Rozhkov, who was only 30. The average for all bureau
members and candidates in 1958, was 47.5 years.[34] In this light it
is perfectly possible to conclude that Vdovin was retired because
of his age. That no criticism of Vdovin or of his work was made
public at this time gives this reasoning added plausibility. However, one piece of evidence remains disturbing. Why was he replaced
by Nekrasov, who had served only one year and three months
as first vice-chairman of the oblispolkom? Unfortunately one can
only conjecture in the absence of any firm information. It may
have been that the first secretary sought the removal of an older,
less flexible person in favor of a younger person (Nekrasov was
51 at this time) whose promotion would tie him more closely to
the first secretary.

The person selected to replace Nekrasov as first vice-chairman
of the oblispolkom was V. T. Bogatyrev who, as first secretary of
the oblast Komsomol committee, had been a member of the obkom
bureau in 1956. Shortly after his first election to the bureau,
Bogatyrev was transferred from his position with the Komsomol
to the post of first secretary of the Kotel'nikovskii raion Party
committee. In this position he retained his membership on the
obkom bureau until March 10, 1957, when he was removed "at his
own request."[35] By December of the same year, he had been
advanced to the first-secretaryship of one of the most important
district Party committees of the city of Stalingrad—the Tractor
Factory raikom.[36] Six months later, at only 32 years of age, Bogatyrev was selected to replace Nekrasov on the oblispolkom.[37] On
February 28, 1959, he was reelected to the obkom bureau as a

32 *Ibid.*, May 16, 1958.

33 The first reference to Vdovin in the period of this study mentions him as chairman
of the oblast trade-union council. See *ibid.*, February 12, 1954.

34 *Ibid.*, February 5, 1957. The listing of candidates for election to the oblast Soviet provided the date of birth of each candidate. The above figures were calculated from this
information.

35 *Ibid.*, March 10, 1957.

36 *Ibid.*, December 8, 1960.

37 *Ibid.*, June 3, 1958.

candidate member.[38] The candidate status of the oblispolkom first vice-chairman should not be interpreted as any diminution of the importance attributed to industry by the obkom bureau but should be attributed, rather, to the relative youth of Bogatyrev.

In March, 1959, when Andriushchenko, the oblast military commander, was transferred to work outside the oblast, he was replaced by S. K. Kurkotkin,[39] who was elected a candidate member of the obkom bureau in January, 1960.[40]

Rozhkov, after nearly two years as a candidate bureau member and first secretary of the oblast Komsomol committee, was transferred to Party work.[41] S. I. Sadovskii, the second secretary of the oblast Komsomol committee, was selected as its first secretary, and in January, 1960, he was made a candidate member of the obkom bureau.[42]

The obkom bureau elected in January, 1960, contained the same five secretaries as the previous bureau, with the difference that Gusev, the secretary in charge of cadres, was now listed as fifth secretary instead of third as in 1957. Nepokupnoi now became third secretary in charge of agriculture, and Zhuravlev fourth secretary in charge of ideological work.[43] The other full members were Pankin, the oblispolkom chairman; Kulichenko, the gorkom first secretary; Nekrasov, the chairman of the oblast trade-union council; Stytsenko, chief of the oblast administration of the *KGB;* and Mon'ko, the editor of *Stalingradskaia Pravda.*[44] The candidate members, none of whom were bureau members in 1957, included Kurkotkin, the oblast military commander; Sadovskii, the oblast Komsomol committee first secretary; and Bogatyrev, the first vice-chairman of the oblispolkom.[45]

The latter part of 1960 and the first month of 1961, saw several important changes in the bureau of the Stalingrad oblast Party committee. After nearly five years as first secretary of the Stalingrad obkom, Zhegalin was transferred out of Party work and given

[38] *Ibid.,* February 28, 1959.
[39] *Ibid.,* March 28, 1959.
[40] *Ibid.,* January 28, 1960.
[41] *Ibid.,* April 27, 1958.
[42] *Ibid.,* January 28, 1960.
[43] *Ibid.*
[44] *Ibid.*
[45] *Ibid.*

an assignment as ambassador to Rumania.[46] At this same plenum, with the participation of V. M. Churaev—a member of the Central Committee Bureau for the RSFSR and head of the CC CPSU otdel of Party organs for union-republics—the committee members elected a new first secretary, A. M. Shkol'nikov.[47]

Another organizational plenum of the Stalingrad obkom was held January 31, 1961. This plenum relieved I. S. Pankin of his duties, in connection with his transfer to work outside the oblast. The plenum also freed Chmutov from his obligations as second secretary of the obkom in connection with his election as chairman of the oblast Soviet executive committee. Kulichenko was promoted from first secretary of the gorkom to second secretary of the obkom, while Cherednichenko was elected to the bureau in connection with his promotion from second to first secretary of the Stalingrad city Party committee.[48]

A high degree of stability in the positions represented on the Stalingrad obkom bureau is evident from this study. From March 27, 1954, to at least January 31, 1961, the bureau included five obkom secretaries, the chairman of the oblast trade-union council, and the chief of the oblast administration of the *KGB* as full members, and the first secretary of the oblast Komsomol committee as a candidate member. With the exception of 1954, either the director of the most important enterprise in the oblast, or the chairman of the Sovnarkhoz was always elected to the bureau.

Other positions appear to have been included more or less at the discretion of the obkom first secretary, or by a decision of the Central Committee. While the heads of three obkom otdels— Party organs, agitprop, and agriculture—were included on the bureau in 1954, only one of these, the head of the Party organs otdel, remained in 1956. Not until 1957 was either the oblast military commander or the editor of *Stalingradskaia Pravda,* given a place on the bureau. Although only a candidate at first, the military commander was promoted to full membership in May, 1957.[49] The

---

[46] *Ibid.,* November 27, 1960, and *Who's Who in the USSR 1961/1962,* p. 889.

[47] *Stalingradskaia Pravda,* November 27, 1960.

[48] *Ibid.,* January 31, 1961.

[49] *Ibid.,* May 16, 1958. It should be noted that the admission of a military official to the obkom bureau came only after Khrushchev announced the reestablishment of firm Party control over the armed forces at the October, 1957 Central Committee plenum. For a text of the resolution, see *SPR* (1959 ed.), pp. 133–136.

editor was not so advanced until 1960. The second vice-chairman of the oblispolkom was honored with a place on the bureau only once, in 1956, but the first vice-chairman was included in 1957 as a full member, and in 1960 as a candidate. These latter appear to have been either included or dropped depending on the relative priorities of agricultural and industrial questions in the bureau's work.

COMPETENCE

The materials in *Stalingradskaia Pravda* yield no precise data on the frequency with which bureau meetings were held; however, other materials provide some useful indicators. From his study of the Smolensk archives, Merle Fainsod found that the bureau of the Smolensk obkom during 1936 met in formal session "approximately every eight or nine days."[50] Shortly after Stalin's death, reports began to appear in the press criticizing individual obkoms for not holding plenary sessions with sufficient frequency. The Lower Amur oblast Party committee was criticized in 1953, for not holding any bureau sessions between May 20 and July 7, leaving its functions to be handled by the secretariat.[51] *Partiinaia Zhizn'* reported in 1954, that "there are Party committees where bureau sessions are held once a month or even more seldom." Moreover, other Party committees were seriously discussing whether it was even necessary to hold bureau meetings. In Dagestan, *Partiinaia Zhizn'* continued, things had come to the point where the bureau did not even discuss "the most important and principled questions in the life of the Party organization," but rather left these problems to "the personal decision of the obkom secretary."[52] By 1955, the situation appears to have reached the other extreme. Referring to a raikom bureau, *Partiinaia Zhizn'* now complained that "in 1953 the bureau met 28 times, in 1954, 60." In January, 1955, the raikom bureau met nine times.[53]

[50] Fainsod, *Smolensk Under Soviet Rule* (Cambridge: Harvard University Press, 1958), p. 68.

[51] *Pravda*, September 4, 1953, p. 2.

[52] "Collective Leadership and the Training of Cadres," *Partiinaia Zhizn'*, No. 9 (1954), p. 15.

[53] "Let's Make Fuller Use of the Potentials of Kolkhozes," *Partiinaia Zhizn'*, No. 4 (1958), p. 24.

As part of a drive to cut down on the number of meetings, the bureau of the Khar'kov obkom passed a resolution in 1957, setting aside certain days during which neither bureau sessions nor other meetings were to be held. However, it was reported that this decision was violated by the obkom itself, when it held bureau meetings on any day of the week.[54] To the degree that these comments reflect practices that were widespread it would appear that for the first few years after Stalin's death bureau sessions were held infrequently, with most major questions being decided by the obkom secretaries. Once the bureaus began to hold regular sessions, the press of problems with which they had to deal forced them, willy-nilly, to meet very frequently and for many hours at a time.[55]

While the agendas of the bureau meetings are never published, from references to particular questions decided by the Stalingrad obkom bureau it is evident that their decisions encompassed a very wide range of activities—from approval of plans for spring sowing, to decrees on improving lecture propaganda in the oblast; from hearing the report of a secretary on carrying out preparations for a Supreme Soviet election, to removing from their posts and expelling several Sovnarkhoz officials from the Party. The decisions adopted by the bureau range from matters of major significance, such as the proposal for the creation of the Stalingrad Sovnarkhoz, to such petty questions as confirming the list of speakers for a meeting of Party activists.

Although the available data give an incomplete picture, it appears that the great majority of decisions adopted by the Stalingrad obkom bureau are concerned with securing fulfillment of current, short-term goals for industrial and agricultural production. The bureau is apparently constantly diverted from working out and executing perspective, long-range plans by the press of immediate tasks. This problem was described at the 1956 oblast Party conference by a raikom secretary:

> The Party obkom and right along with it the Party raikoms examine questions of agriculture in a campaign-like manner. Suppose it is the beginning of the harvest campaign. One after the other,

54 "A Few Questions About the Work of the Party Apparat," *Partiinaia Zhizn'*, No. 4 (1958), p. 24.

55 *Ibid*. This article states that bureau sessions frequently lasted from 10 A.M. until evening.

representatives come to the raion and demand the fulfillment of obligations before the state, putting other questions to the side. But the trouble is that, usually, the entire cycle of agricultural work is carried out in this manner: the sowing of winter crops, plowing, preparation of feeds, the preparation of seeds, etc. The campaign approach to the leadership of agriculture has left its imprint on the work of the bureau of the oblast Party committee itself. The sessions of the bureau discuss, predominantly, questions connected with the current campaigns.[56]

In the spring of 1956, a series of bureau decisions on agricultural problems was published in *Stalingradskaia Pravda*. These decisions give a vivid illustration of both the "campaign nature" of bureau activity, and the degree to which the bureau tries to regulate the details of agricultural production. In order to put this series of decisions into perspective it is necessary to note a few developments from the summer and fall of 1955. In the July, 1955 issue of *Partiinaia Zhizn'*, I. T. Grishin, then first secretary of the Stalingrad obkom, wrote that "we are still using the institution of *upolnomochenny*." "Let's say that *upolnomochenny* are not sent for the sowing of sunflowers, then only about 40 per cent of them would be sown in the square-bunch method, while if *upolnomochenny* are sent for the planting of corn, then there would not be one hectare planted in rows, all would be planted in the square-bunch method." Grishin concluded that, "while criticizing it at meetings, we still agree to the sending of *upolnomochenny*."[57]

At the May, 1956 obkom plenum, A. M. Puzanov, a member of the Bureau of the CC CPSU for the RSFSR, revealed that the previous autumn, when the plan for fall planting was not being fulfilled for lack of seed, these *upolnomochenny*, on the instructions of the obkom bureau, had ordered the kolkhozes and sovkhozes to use their seed and grain reserves to meet the current plan. This meant that there would inevitably be a seed shortage in the spring. Perhaps Grishin was aware at that time that he was about to be promoted to a diplomatic post and so would stop at nothing to

---

56 *Stalingradskaia Pravda*, January 19, 1956. The charge of *kapaneishchina*, or campaigning, appeared with some frequency in the Stalingrad press, tending to confirm the finding of Inkeles that "storming" is endemic to the Soviet system. See, Inkeles *et al.*, *How the Soviet System Works* (Cambridge: Harvard University Press, 1956).

57 "Object-Lesson Instruction of Leading Cadres," *Partiinaia Zhizn'*, No. 14 (1955), p. 11. *Upolnomochenny* are "fully-empowered" representatives, with full authority to give orders within a specific area of activity.

achieve the successful completion of his last agricultural campaign. At any rate, in December, his promotion came through, and Zhegalin was saddled with this problem. Since Zhegalin had had previous experience as a successful obkom first secretary—from 1949 until late 1955 as first secretary of the Grozny obkom[58]—and considering that he suffered no untoward consequences as a result of his handling of this crisis, the methods used must be considered within the range acceptable to the Central Committee.

That the 1956 agricultural season should begin with the above-quoted criticism of a "campaign approach" only to be followed by a whole series of detailed bureau decisions on the current agricultural campaign is perhaps indicative of the conflict between the official prescriptions of Party behavior and the activities of a real obkom bureau faced with an actual threatening situation. If the new first secretary permitted his first agricultural campaign to fail, this would not augur well for the future of his career.

The first published bureau decision was one taken jointly with the oblispolkom on January 25, 1956, "On the results of milk production in the kolkhozes and sovkhozes for the period October-December, 1955." This decision severely criticized individual raikoms and collective farms for failing to fulfill their milk production quotas and threatened dire consequences if the situation did not improve immediately.[59] On the 8th of March, the obkom bureau issued a decision arising directly from the seed shortage created the previous fall, "On the unsatisfactory direction by the Logovskii raikom CPSU and raiispolkom of preparations by the kolkhozes and MTS' of their raion for spring sowing." In this decree the obkom bureau gave direct instructions to both the local Party and Soviet officials on beginning the spring sowing.[60] Three days later, on March 11, the obkom bureau issued another decision relative to seed preparation throughout the oblast, "On the unsatisfactory preparation of seeds for field crops for spring sowing in the kolkhozes of the oblast."[61] The agricultural campaign continued with an oblast conference of leading agricultural workers on the 22nd of March. The major speech was given by the oblispol-

[58] *Who's Who in the USSR 1961/1962*, p. 889.
[59] *Stalingradskaia Pravda*, January 25, 1956.
[60] *Ibid.*, March 8, 1956.
[61] *Ibid.*, March 11, 1956.

kom chairman, Pankin, and the concluding remarks by the first secretary, Zhegalin. This conference adopted an appeal to all agricultural workers of the oblast to plant and harvest a record crop.[62]

In the middle of April, the Bureau of the CC CPSU for the RSFSR held a meeting of secretaries of RSFSR obkoms and krai (regional) Party committees to discuss the carrying out of the spring sowing and the topic "On studying the decisions of the 20th Congress of the CPSU in the Party organizations and the tasks of explaining these decisions to the toilers." It is perhaps indicative of the normalcy of such agricultural crises that Zhegalin was reported as speaking not on the first but on the second question, which was undoubtedly concerned with how to explain the de-Stalinization speech, made by Khrushchev the previous month, to the local Party cadres.[63]

Toward the end of April, the obkom bureau again found it necessary to adopt and publish a decision on failures in fulfilling the spring sowing plan. This decision, "On shortcomings in the organization of work for spring sowing in the kolkhozes of the Gorodishchenskii Machine Tractor Station," is worth quoting at some length to illustrate the format and content of obkom bureau decisions.

The first several paragraphs describe the problem and whom the obkom blames for it:

> As a result of verification carried out by the obkom CPSU, it was determined that serious shortcomings were permitted in the first few days of field work in the kolkhozes and sovkhozes of the Gorodishchenskii MTS. The MTS and the kolkhozes began the spring sowing in a disorganized manner. . . .
>
> These serious shortcomings in the organization of the spring sowing work are the result of an insufficiently thorough analysis of the work of the MTS, individual kolkhozes and tractor brigades by the Gorodishchenskii raikom CPSU.[64]

The next section describes the orders issued by the obkom bureau in this decision:

62 *Ibid.*, March 22, 1956.
63 *Ibid.*, April 17, 1956.
64 *Ibid.*, April 24, 1956.

The bureau of the obkom CPSU called the attention of the bureau of the Gorodishchenskii raikom CPSU and its first secretary, c. Stepanov, to the presence of serious shortcomings in the carrying out of spring field work in the kolkhozes of the Gorodishchenskii MTS. The obkom bureau obliged the Gorodishchenskii raikom CPSU (c. Stepanov),[65] the raiispolkom (c. Admaikin), the MTS director c. Gindin, and the secretary of the Party organization c. Antonov to take immediate measures for the removal of the indicated serious shortcomings in the carrying out of the spring sowing in the kolkhozes of the Gorodishchenskii MTS and to assure completion of the early grain crops and mustard greens in the next five to six days.

The bureau of the obkom CPSU ordered the chief of the oblast administration of agriculture (c. Larin) to inflict a penalty on the agronomists guilty of violating the rules of agro-technology in the sowing of mustard greens in the kolkhoz named after Stalin.

Considering the rapidly increasing soil temperature, the bureau of the obkom CPSU proposed to the MTS and kolkhoz administrations that together with the sowing of the early grain crops they carry out the sowing of corn, using for this the square-bunch seeding machines at their disposal in the first instance.

The concluding paragraph obliges the local Party secretaries to do what one would think was their direct responsibility already:

The bureau of the obkom CPSU obliged the raikom secretary for the MTS zone c. Glub, the secretary of the MTS Party organization, c. Antonov, and the secretaries of the kolkhoz Party organizations to remove the serious shortcomings in the organization of socialist competition of tractor and field brigades for spring sowing, to assess the results of each day's work by individual tractorists, to disseminate widely the experience of leading tractorists, who achieve a high output per work shift, and to remove the organizational and other shortcomings in the operation of the tractors which hinders highly productive work; to organize the regular publication of wall newspapers in the tractor and field brigades, the carrying out of conversations and political agitation among the tractor brigade workers, mobilizing them to the fulfillment of the decisions of the 20th Party Congress, the quickest possible completion of spring sowing, and high quality of field work.[66]

---

[65] The names in parentheses refer to the particular officials in the organizations named who will be held responsible by the obkom for executing the orders given.
[66] *Ibid.*

The all-encompassing authority of the obkom bureau in regard to fulfilling the current agricultural plans is evident in this decision. Without hesitation the bureau issues direct orders to the district Soviet officials and the head of the oblast agricultural administration. Its decision ranges from broad commands to fulfill the sowing plan in five to six days to such details as ordering the regular publication of wall newspapers for the tractorists. The obkom bureau even issued the orders as to when and by what method the corn must be sown.

It must be emphasized, however, that these decisions were taken only when the problem reached what must have been a state of real or impending crisis, threatening the position of the obkom secretary. Since this was the only time of the entire period under study that such decisions were published it should probably be assumed that under more normal circumstances such problems as the petty details of the spring sowing campaign are decided in other organs, particularly in the oblispolkom and the oblast agricultural administration. Some evidence to this effect may be seen in the fact that it was the oblispolkom chairman who usually made the major reports at plenary sessions of the oblast Party committee concerning agriculture.[67]

The problems of the 1956 spring sowing campaign did not end with the adoption of the above-quoted decision. On April 29, the obkom issued a decree, "On shortcomings in the preparation and carrying out of corn sowing."[68] The same day the bureau and oblispolkom adopted and published a joint decision obliging several construction trusts to complete some mechanized chicken farms by July 1, 1956, or face severe penalties.[69]

Twelve days later the obkom called a meeting of the first secretaries of all rural raikoms where, in the major address, the first secretary stressed the urgent need to overfulfill the sowing plans. The seriousness of the situation at this time is evident in that N. I. Beliaev, a Central Committee secretary and vice-chairman of the Central Committee Bureau for the RSFSR, "took part" in this meeting. While, as we have seen, it is fairly common

67 See Chapter 5, pp. 65–66.
68 *Stalingradskaia Pravda,* April 29, 1956.
69 *Ibid.*

for representatives of the Central Committee to participate in obkom plenums, this is the only instance during the period under study when such an official took part in a meeting of raikom secretaries in Stalingrad oblast.[70]

Within six more days the obkom bureau published a decision "On gross violations of agro-technology in spring field work in the kolkhozes of the Solodchinskii-Kondrashovskii MTS zone of the Solodchinskii raion," in which, among other things, it ordered the firing and expulsion from the Party of an MTS director and a chief agronomist, and it issued stern warnings to others.[71] The next day, the obkom and the oblispolkom again issued a joint decree, "On the course of spring sowing in the kolkhozes and sovkhozes of the oblast," declaring as unsatisfactory the course of spring sowing in a number of raions, and ordering the completion of all sowing in four to five days.[72] At the end of May, an obkom plenum, with the participation of a member of the Central Committee Bureau for the RSFSR,[73] assessed the results of the spring sowing, cultivation, and preparations for the harvest and delivery of agricultural products. This plenum marked the end of the sowing and the beginning of the harvest campaign.

According to reports published in its press, the oblast completed the plan for delivery of agricultural products by 100.1 per cent on September 27, 1956.[74] But, while the immediate goal may have been achieved, the methods used to bring this about may have been self-defeating. In 1954, *Partiinaia Zhizn'* strongly criticized those who "think they can accomplish everything through pressure, scolding, and threatening."[75] The following year, the Stalingrad obkom first secretary wrote in the same journal that because of such "incorrect methods of training," the local cadres "do not always display the necessary self-reliance, and at times wait for the *upolnomochenny*," and orders from above.[76] The very use of such pressure methods gives rise to habits that require the

70 *Ibid.*, May 11, 1956.
71 *Ibid.*, May 18, 1956.
72 *Ibid.*, May 18, 1956.
73 *Ibid.*, May 30, 1956.
74 *Ibid.*, September 28, 1956.
75 "Oversimplified Methods of Party Leadership," *Partiinaia Zhizn'*, No. 13 (1954), p. 58.
76 "Object-Lesson Instruction of Leading Cadres," *Partiinaia Zhizn'*, No. 14 (1955), p. 18.

continued application of threats and orders for the achievement of results.

Although few decisions of the obkom bureau concerning problems of industry were published in *Stalingradskaia Pravda,* it is possible to define the general outlines of the bureau's competence in industrial questions through an examination of materials from the Party journals and press. This analysis will help to place in proper perspective the few available references to decisions on industrial matters adopted by the Stalingrad obkom bureau.

Prior to the industrial reorganization of 1957, the oblast Party organizations occupied a position of relative impotence in regard to questions of industrial policy. The general position of the Party organs vis-à-vis the ministerial hierarchy was aptly described by a Central Committee official:

> It is well known that the local Party organs carry full responsibility for the work of industrial enterprises, and that, *of course, this does not lessen the responsibility of the ministries.* The gorkom or the obkom has the possibility and the responsibility to direct the enterprises *in accordance with the state plans, with the directives of the Party and government,* to objectively delve into the affairs of the enterprises, and to take measures for the improvement of work.[77] (Italics mine.)

The crucial phrase in this statement is "in accordance with the state plans, with the directives of the Party[78] and government." In general, the Party committees could take decisions designed to help fulfill the production plans of enterprises, or to fulfill orders of the Party or government organs, but the major responsibility for the crucial decisions, on which plan fulfillment might depend, remained in the hands of the ministries and their subdivisions. This was confirmed by the secretary of the Tula obkom in 1957, when he wrote that "questions of material-technical supply, planning, finances, and other questions were decided in the ministries, glavks, and trusts, and the local Party organs most often had to deal with already prepared decisions."[79]

[77] Victor Churaev, "Let's Strengthen Organizational Work for a Further Upsurge of Industry," *Partiinaia Zhizn'*, No. 15 (1955), p. 10.

[78] The "Party" in this sense refers to the Central Committee, and does not include the local organs.

[79] V. Mochalov, "Let's Revive the Initiative of the Economic Cadres," *Partiinaia Zhizn'*, No. 6 (1957), p. 36.

The only way a Party committee could solve the many problems faced by industrial enterprises is to urge the appropriate ministry or department to adopt such and such a decision. While stating that the workers from ministries do come to the Party committee and "try to work together" with them to "achieve definite results," *Partiinaia Zhizn'*, in 1955, complained that some ministry workers "avoid the local Party organs." These are people who do only what is "required" of them, and "if instructions to the effect that one should counsel with the Party organization and consider its opinions do not exist, then they act accordingly."[80] The clear implication of this is that the authority of the local Party committees is dependent upon explicit instructions from either the Central Committee or the higher ministerial organs to the effect that the local ministry officials should seek the help and advice of the local Party committees. Under such conditions it is little wonder that *Partiinaia Zhizn'* reported, "unfortunately many local Party organs concern themselves with questions of economics, and in particular questions of industry, only superficially, conceive their role to be only the hearing of reports of economic managers, pointing out shortcomings, and taking general, mostly useless, decisions."[81]

It was not the intention of the higher Party authorities, however, that the local Party organs should have no jurisdiction over industrial matters. At the same time that it criticized the local committees for devoting so little attention to industry, the Party press outlined several areas on which the attention of the Party committees should be focused. Many of these measures appeared in the period directly following the July, 1955 Central Committee plenum.[82]

In a lead editorial devoted to the results of the July plenum, *Partiinaia Zhizn'* exhorted the Party organizations to exercise "strictest control" over the fulfillment by the ministries and departments of the measures adopted by the plenum "for guaranteeing the broad specialization of enterprises and cooperation in industry."[83] A later article, however, made clear that this "control" would have to be quite limited since questions of specialization

---

[80] "Against Departmental Narrowness in the Solution of Economic Problems," *Partiinaia Zhizn'*, No. 3 (1955), p. 60.

[81] "Economic and Political Work are Indivisible," *Partiinaia Zhizn'*, No. 10 (1955), p. 5.

[82] For the text of the resolution adopted at this plenum, see *KPSS v Rezoliutsiiakh...*, IV, 90–111.

[83] "The July Plenum of the CC CPSU," *Partiinaia Zhizn'*, No. 13 (1955), p. 6.

and cooperation still "are decided by the planning organs and the ministries in the center."[84] It is in "adjustment of cooperation," rather, that the obkom has "an especially great" role. In particular, in reviewing the plans submitted by the various enterprises as part of the Sixth Five Year Plan, the obkom should make adjustments that will end "useless transshipments and evidence of a *kustar* approach."[85] Other areas of responsibility in industry assigned to the local Party committees by the July plenum include supervision and adjustment of the organization and work norms of labor, putting the pay scales in order, and helping to improve the working and living conditions of the workers.[86]

The July plenum especially emphasized the role of the local Party committees in organizing "the introduction into production of the latest achievements of science and technology."[87] In practice this responsibility amounted to summarizing the suggestions of innovators, and working out a plan for the introduction of the best of these into production.[88] At times this also meant pushing the adoption of new machinery or processes devised by the so-called "creative organizations"—the construction bureaus, technological departments, factory laboratories, project organizations, and scientific-research institutions.[89] Even in the solution of these questions the obkom bureau was severely limited in the means at its disposal to ensure compliance with its decisions. The difficulty was, as pointed out by the first secretary of the Gor'ky obkom, that "in many enterprises the plan for the introduction of new technology and the improvement of the technology of production has not yet become the same kind of immutable plan as the plan for the output of goods." "If one or another shop underfulfills the production plan, then the director, the chief engineer, and the secretary of the Party committee go to investigate, but if the plan for the introduction of technological measures is broken, this is no cause for concern."[90]

---

[84] "Current Leadership and the Solution of Economic Problems," *Partiinaia Zhizn'*, No. 20 (1955), p. 26.

[85] *Ibid.*

[86] "The July Plenum of the CC CPSU," *Partiinaia Zhizn'*, No. 13 (1955), p. 7.

[87] *KPSS v Rezoliutsiiakh. . .*, IV, 108.

[88] "Technical Progress and Organizational Work," *Partiinaia Zhizn'*, No. 2 (1956), pp. 9–10.

[89] "A Few Questions of the Leadership of Industry," *Partiinaia Zhizn'*, No. 19 (1956), p. 11.

[90] *Ibid.*

At the 20th Party Congress, Khrushchev gave the oblast Party leaders added reason to devote attention to problems of industry when he declared that "the work of a Party official should be judged primarily by those results attained in the development of the economy for which he is responsible."[91] Removal from their positions was threatened for those officials who "refuse to understand" this new demand. Khrushchev even went so far as to propose that the earnings of Party officials be made to depend in part on the fulfillment of industrial plans.[92]

Judging by this new importance attached to Party supervision of industry, it is perhaps not coincidental that the first mention of a decision of the Stalingrad obkom bureau on an industrial problem was made at a meeting of city Party committee activists shortly after the 20th Congress. At this meeting it was announced that the RSFSR Council of Ministers, in February, 1956, had doubled the amount available for housing construction in the oblast by providing an additional 10 million rubles for that and 3 million rubles for the construction of hospital space. On the 13th of March, the USSR Council of Ministers granted an additional 35 million rubles for the improvement of the Stalingrad communal economy.[93] Considering these additional grants the obkom bureau adopted a decision ordering the inclusion of these funds in the work plan of *Stalingradstroi*, and ordered the raising of its plan for the initiation of new housing construction from the previous 6,500 to 13,500 square meters of housing space. In addition, the obkom ordered the city construction organizations to complete their yearly plans by December 25; i.e., to complete and open for occupancy 142,000 square meters of housing space and 50 buildings designated for cultural-communal and administrative purposes.[94]

At this same meeting, another bureau decision was also revealed, again dealing with problems of the local economy. Sometime during March or April, 1956, the bureau had discussed the course of construction of the city water system. In its decision on this matter, the obkom bureau gave an unsatisfactory evaluation to the activity of the gorkom secretary in charge of industry and

91 *Pravda*, February 15, 1956, p. 5.
92 *Ibid.* It is worth noting that this proposal was never adopted so far as is known.
93 *Stalingradskaia Pravda*, April 19, 1956.
94 *Ibid.*

construction and to the vice-chairman of the gorispolkom "for not taking decisive measures to improve the supplying of water to the population."[95]

It should be noted that both these decisions concern problems of local construction work carried out by enterprises, such as *Stalingradstroi*, that are subordinate to the oblast and city Soviet executive committees. The first decision merely implemented the previous orders of higher bodies, the Councils of Ministers. Perhaps most significantly, neither of these bureau decisions gave any orders to the directors of enterprises subordinated to the central ministries. This quite limited evidence seems to indicate that the oblast Party committee at this time was limited to the solution of industrial problems of only secondary significance, while the central ministries and their local subdivisions retained the authority to decide major industrial questions, particularly those relating to heavy industry.

A few months after the publication of these bureau decisions several articles appeared in the central Party organs which both confirmed the limited role of the obkom in industrial decision-making and signaled the obkom bureau that it must begin immediately to devote more attention to industrial problems. *Pravda*, on September 5, 1956, under the title, "The Stalingrad Gorkom Has Weakened the Leadership of Industry," lashed out at the city Party committee bureau, and indirectly at the obkom bureau, for not concerning itself in a purposeful manner with industry, for not deciding the basic problems hindering the steady and rhythmic work of enterprises and their technological advancement. The blame for this situation was laid on the second secretary of the city Party committee. For failing to devote enough attention to problems of industry, he was fired and removed from the gorkom.[96] The obkom, as explained by *Partiinaia Zhizn'* in reference to a similar situation in Kurgansk oblast, must share the guilt for not "using its influence to tell the gorkom what concrete measures it would be necessary to carry out for the liquidation of shortcomings."[97] This same journal, in a lead editorial, reiterated the criticism of the Stalingrad gorkom and obkom, citing them for giving

95 *Ibid.*
96 *Pravda,* September 5, 1956, p. 1.
97 "Closer to People, To Production," *Partiinaia Zhizn',* No. 24 (1955), p. 27.

"little attention . . . to the introduction of new technology, to the organization of production and labor, to setting in order the business of work norms and pay scales."[98]

These articles indicate that the Stalingrad gorkom and obkom were not, in fact, responding adequately to the resolution of the July, 1955 Central Committee plenum defining the limited sphere of industrial problems for which the Party committees would be held responsible. The firing of a second secretary, rather than, say, the gorkom first secretary or even the obkom secretary in charge of industry, is probably best understood as a rather strong hint to the obkom bureau that it had better "pay attention" to those problems of industrial production specified at the July plenum. The absence of references to any new areas of obkom responsibility indicates that it was not intended at this time to expand the obkom bureau's authority over industrial matters.

While the Central Committee sought to limit the intervention of the obkom to those areas, some oblast Party committees engaged in the solution of problems outside of their specified competence. In general, many Party committees found that "the function of the directing organ of the economic region, willy-nilly, came to be fulfilled by the Party organs."[99] Frequently, the Party committees had to act as the integrating and coordinating organ for the industry in their oblast. Very often, "specific economic questions" had to be decided with the interference of the Party organs because of the lack of ties among the many centralized ministries and glavks.[100] Unfortunately, because of the lack of any evidence on this point, no judgment can be made on the extent to which the bureau of the Stalingrad obkom found it necessary to act as the overall coordinator of industrial production in the oblast, at least for the period prior to the industrial reorganization.

The turning point in the competence of the obkom bureau in industrial questions came at the Central Committee plenum of February, 1957, with the announcement of the abolition of many

98 "Let's Direct Industry Persistently and Thoroughly," *Partiinaia Zhizn'*, No. 20 (1956), p. 5.

99 "On the Role of Instructors and Work with Them," *Partiinaia Zhizn'*, No. 6 (1957), p. 62.

100 *Ibid.* It is the central contention of the dissertation by Jerry Hough that this was the main function of the Party committees both before and after the industrial reorganization. See Hough.

ministries and the creation of Councils of the National Economy.[101] From the very start, the bureau of the Stalingrad obkom assumed the dominant position vis-à-vis the Sovnarkhoz. In announcing the creation of the Stalingrad Sovnarkhoz to an obkom plenum the first secretary, Zhegalin, made clear the new role of the obkom bureau:

> Proceeding from the resolution of the February plenum of the CC CPSU and the Theses of comrade Khrushchev's report . . . the bureau of the obkom CPSU together with the Party, economic, and trade-union organizations, worked out the proposal for the reorganization of the structure of the administration. . . .[102]

The ministries, as such, are not even mentioned, while reference is made to the participation of economic organizations only after the obkom bureau and other Party organs. A similar order is preserved in the listing of individuals who made some contribution to working out the proposed reorganization:

> More than 1000 workers, Party, Soviet, economic, and trade-union officials, and specialists of all branches of the economy took part in working out the new structure of the Sovnarkhoz for our oblast.[103]

Articles in the Party journals provide additional evidence of the increased authority of the obkom bureau in these new circumstances. In its lead editorial for February, 1957, *Partiinaia Zhizn'* emphasized that "the Party organs are called upon to head all work in the preparations for the reorganization . . . ."[104] A letter published in a later issue commented that if earlier there was a "significant division" between inner-Party and economic work, this distinction was now "brought almost to an end."[105] By mid-1958, it appears, many obkoms became used to their new position. This is evident in that no longer can they send the "usual note" to the ministry or the Council of Ministers when economic difficulties arise. Rather, the Party committees themselves must examine the reasons for the problems and "together with the Sovnarkhoz" take "im-

101 For the text of the resolution, see *KPSS v Resoliutsiiakh* . . . , IV, 255–262.
102 *Stalingradskaia Pravda*, April 12, 1957.
103 *Ibid.*
104 "For a Further Improvement in the Leadership of Industry and Construction," *Partiinaia Zhizn'*, No. 4 (1957), p. 6.
105 "Letters and Correspondence," *Partiinaia Zhizn'*, No. 22 (1957), p. 48.

mediate measures" for their solution. For the obkom now "there is no one to put the blame on, no one to turn to."[106]

In the early part of 1959, it was reported that some obkoms were going too far by taking on themselves the entire solution of many economic questions. While criticizing the obkom for "replacing" the Sovnarkhoz, *Partiinaia Zhizn'* did not question the right of the obkom to decide the major questions of the leadership of the economy. Rather it explained the obkom's overriding of the Sovnarkhoz by saying that the obkom had in mind "the perfectly good intention of moving matters along quickly."[107] The only difficulty with this approach was that, with the obkom deciding everything, the economic administrators "factually kept aloof from matters and limited their role to simply signaling the obkom about difficulties that have arisen, thinking: once the obkom has been informed, then let it 'have the headaches,' let it remove the troubles."[108]

While there is no evidence to indicate that the obkoms actually appointed the members of the Council of the National Economy, it is significant that in at least two instances it was the obkom first secretary who announced the head of the Sovnarkhoz and the list of officials to sit on the Council. At the April plenum, Zhegalin indicated that the director of the Stalingrad Tractor Factory had been confirmed as head of the Stalingrad Sovnarkhoz.[109] In an article for the April issue of *Partiinaia Zhizn'* G. Denisov, the first secretary of the Saratov oblast Party committee, stated that the Sovnarkhoz in his oblast would consist of the chairman of the Council, and two or three assistants, and the directors and officials of the largest trusts, *kombinats,* and departments subordinate to the Sovnarkhoz, totaling between 11 and 15 members.[110]

Although none of the obkom secretaries are formal members of the Sovnarkhoz, so far as is known, there is evidence that some do participate in Sovnarkhoz meetings. The first secretary of the

---

106 "The True Path to the Further Development of the National Economy," *Partiinaia Zhizn'*, No. 14 (1958), p. 5.

107 "The Local Soviet and Economic Organs Face New Tasks," *Partiinaia Zhizn'*, No. 1 (1959), p. 11.

108 *Ibid.*

109 *Stalingradskaia Pravda*, April 12, 1957.

110 "The True Path to the Further Improvement of Matters," *Partiinaia Zhizn'*, No. 1 (1959), p. 27.

Bashkir obkom, for example, stated that "the secretaries and otdel heads of the CPSU obkom participate at many meetings of the Council of the National Economy, helping it correctly to approach the solution of this or that question."[111] The clear implication of this statement is that the obkom secretary is now the teacher, and the Sovnarkhoz chairman the pupil in need of guidance with instruction along every step of the way.

The subordinate position of the Sovnarkhoz chairman vis-à-vis the obkom first secretary since the reorganization of industry is also brought out in Kochetov's novel, *Secretar' Obkoma.* When the Central Committee calls a meeting to assess the results achieved in industry during the previous six months, it is the obkom first secretary who goes to make the report. Upon his return, the Sovnarkhoz chairman comes to the secretary's office to discuss the outcome of the meeting and the oblast's new tasks.[112]

A particularly poignant illustration of the obkom's increased authority in industrial questions is provided by a joint decree issued by the Kemerovo obkom and Sovnarkhoz, in January, 1958: "On measures for strengthening the output and shipment of coal from the mines of the *Kuzbassugol'* in the first quarter of 1958."[113] In discussing this decision, *Partiinaia Zhizn'* points out that on the surface it appears to be a perfectly normal resolution, indicating specific problems in the mines and measures for removing them. In its essence, however, this decree "contradicts the Leninist principle of Party direction of the economy." The Party is not supposed to rule by means of administrative decrees but through persuasion, through "Party-organizational and mass-political work." Since the obkom obviously is aware of these principles, it may be asked, why was it necessary for the bureau to take a decision jointly with the Sovnarkhoz? The answer given to this question by the editor is very significant:

> If the comrades of the Kemerovo obkom think that the signature of the obkom secretary to a decree increases the authority of the Sovnarkhoz, then they are thoroughly mistaken. The truth is

111 "The Local Soviet and Economic Organs Face New Tasks," *Partiinaia Zhizn'*, No. 1 (1959), p. 10.
112 Kochetov, p. 99.
113 "About One Resolution of the Kemerovo CPSU Obkom and the Sovnarkhoz," *Partiinaia Zhizn'*, No. 3 (1958), p. 37.

just the opposite: it creates the impression that the obkom does not consider the Sovnarkhoz as an organ with enough authority to independently decide economic questions.[114]

In the first part of the above explanation the obkom seeks to lend some of its weight to the Sovnarkhoz to bolster the latter's authority, while in the second part of the explanation it is the obkom, as the higher body, who decides whether the Sovnarkhoz has enough authority to decide a particular problem on its own. Regardless of which of these considerations motivated the obkom it seems clear that both the obkom and the editor assume the superior authority of the former.

When we examine some of the specific questions relating to industry decided by, or with the participation of the obkom bureau it becomes evident that the competence of the obkom, as extended after the industrial reorganization, assured it a voice in all major industrial decisions within the oblast.

G. Perov, the first vice-chairman of the USSR State Planning Commission, writing in *Partiinaia Zhizn'* about a year after the creation of the Sovnarkhozes, stated that the "obkom's . . . thoroughly, and in a business-like manner examine the project plans that have been worked out by the Sovnarkhozes and planning organs, and intently look after their fulfillment . . . ."[115] While certain aspects of the plans may be influenced by the obkom, it should be pointed out that the latitude permitted either the Sovnarkhoz or the obkom in working out and adjusting the yearly and perspective plans is quite limited, as the first secretary of the Kherson obkom makes clear:

> . . . the necessary detailization of the plans for local regions, for some reason, is preserved and is made into law in the central planning organs. The Sovnarkhoz is severely limited by the control figures for capital investments, which are worked out in final form and confirmed by *Gosplan* for branches, and for above-limit construction. It is left to the local authorities to put the figures into the form of a plan. This binds local initiative.[116]

Within these limitations, some obkom bureaus have made decisions on important planning problems. One obkom, together

[114] *Ibid.*
[115] "The Sovnarkhozes After One Year," *Partiinaia Zhizn'*, No. 14 (1958), p. 15.
[116] "For Better Use of Capital Investments," *Partiinaia Zhizn'*, No. 20 (1959), p. 23.

with the Sovnarkhoz, examined the technical level of output of a number of enterprises and drew up detailed measures for the replacement of old machines. The obkom bureau also supervised the compilation of technical plans for the reconstruction of existing enterprises.[117]

After the June, 1959 Central Committee plenum on speeding up technical progress in industry and construction,[118] the first secretary of the Zaporozhe obkom commented that the obkom directed the work on the "solution of the fundamental problems of the technical reequipping of industry," including such problems as raising the productivity of labor, reconstruction and expansion of existing enterprises and aggregates, modernization of equipment, the introduction of new technology, the mechanization and automation of production, etc.[119] Specifically, the Zaporozhe obkom bureau "heard and discussed" the report of the Sovnarkhoz chairman "on the course of fulfillment of measures for the introduction of new techniques and advanced technology in the industrial enterprises of the oblast." The bureau also "examined and confirmed" the measures of the Sovnarkhoz for fulfillment of the decisions adopted at the June Central Committee plenum. For reports on these same questions the obkom called in a gorkom secretary, the chief of the Sovnarkhoz machine-building otdel, the director of a transformer factory, etc.[120]

When problems arise that cannot be decided at the oblast level, the obkom jointly with the Sovnarkhoz may raise them with the appropriate central authorities. Such an instance was reported in Stalingrad. After the May, 1958 Central Committee resolution on the further development of the chemical industry,[121] the Stalingrad first secretary announced that "not long ago" the obkom, together with the Sovnarkhoz, and a great number of specialists, had worked out a detailed plan for the more "rational" use of the oblast's resources, with special emphasis on increasing the output of the chemical industry in the oblast. After approval by the obkom

117 Let's Improve the Practice of Party Leadership of the Economy," *Partiinaia Zhizn'*, No. 8 (1960), p. 27.

118 For the text of the Central Committee resolution, see *KPSS v Rezoliutsiiakh* . . . , IV, 531–570.

119 K. Skriabin, *Novoe v Rabote Partorganizatsii po Rukovodstvu Promyshlennost'iu* (Kiev: Gospolitizdat UKSSR, 1960), p. 14.

120 *Ibid.*

121 For the text of the Central Committee resolution, see *KPSS v Rezoliutsiiakh* . . . , IV, 325–331.

bureau and the Sovnarkhoz, the proposals were sent to the Central Committee and the USSR Council of Ministers. Zhegalin told an obkom plenum that many of the proposals had already been accepted.[122]

It is significant that instances of the obkom devoting particular attention to major industrial problems appear to correspond with Central Committee plenum decisions on these same questions. This together with the highly centralized planning system and the fact that the obkom found it necessary to appeal to the central Party and government organs for the solution of many major problems indicates the rather close control of the center over the obkom's exercise of its prerogatives in the realm of industrial decision-making.

Apparently these central controls are not altogether without their justification. Especially in the first period after the industrial reorganization, instances of "localist tendencies," particularly in the use of capital investment funds and in inter-regional deliveries, gave rise to severe criticism of the local Party and Sovnarkhoz officials.[123] These practices were summed up by *Pravda* in September, 1958, as follows:

> Unfortunately, there are Party workers who not infrequently promote anti-state practices. Not having themselves delved into the heart of the matter, they begin to support incorrect suggestions of industrial officials and in some cases even force such officials to carry out work not included in the plan in order to suit local interests.[124]

To counter such occurrences and to warn against their repetition in the future, the Presidium of the Supreme Soviet of the USSR issued a special decree in June, 1958, according to which all those guilty of failure to fulfill orders for other economic regions and orders for social needs are to be looked upon as "gross violators of state discipline" and subject to disciplinary, material, and criminal responsibility.[125]

If the local Party committees were sometimes criticized prior

---

[122] *Stalingradskaia Pravda*, May 17, 1958.
[123] See for example, *Pravda*, May 19, 1958.
[124] *Ibid.*, September 1, 1958.
[125] Reported in "The True Path to the Further Development of the National Economy," *Partiinaia Zhizn'*, No. 7 (1958), p. 4.

to the industrial reorganization for acting as "distributive institutions,"[126] that is, offices for the distribution of scarce supplies, even in the period after 1957 the obkom frequently found itself forced to fulfill this same function. Writing in *Partiinaia Zhizn'*, the first secretary of the Stalingrad obkom revealed his frustration with this problem:

> At the conferences, gatherings, and meetings some economic managers devote their whole speeches to demands for this or that material, to requests for the creation of softer circumstances for them or their enterprises, to decide this or that question. No one is saying that questions of material supply, in particular some raw materials, semifabricates, are not often in a difficult condition in our oblast. But it is also evident that some managers try to hide their own poor work behind these facts.[127]

We have seen that if prior to the industrial reorganization the competence of the obkom bureau to deal with problems of industry was limited to questions of secondary importance, then after 1957, the obkom acquired the dominant position in industrial decision-making in the oblast. Its competence extended to most of the major questions of industrial production, within the limitations imposed by the central authorities on all local decision-making bodies.

The selection and distribution of leading cadres is a third major area of obkom bureau decision-making responsibility. A leading Party theoretician sees this as the crucial power without which "the Party could not direct the work of the Soviet, economic, and social organizations, could not direct all aspects of the administrative, cultural, and economic life of the country."[128]

The cadres are defined as the "basic permanent reserve of qualified workers" of Party, Soviet, economic, trade-union, Komsomol, and all other organizations, leading figures in science and culture, military officers in the armed forces, and workers of the "mass professions" throughout Soviet society.[129] Such people number in the "tens of millions."[130] Each raikom, gorkom, and obkom con-

---

126 "The City Party Committee and Industrial Enterprises," *Partiinaia Zhizn'*, No. 22 (1956), p. 25.
127 "Raise Work with Cadres to the Level of the New Tasks," *Partiinaia Zhizn'*, No. 13 (1958), p. 10.
128 Slepov, p. 18.
129 *VPS*, p. 317.
130 *Ibid.*

centrates its attention on a definite group of these officials, whom it "directly selects and personally confirms."[131] This group comprises what is known in Soviet terminology as the *nomenklatura* of the Party organ; it encompasses the "basic, decisive sectors of leadership in the raion, city, or oblast."[132]

Figures on the number of positions included in the *nomenklatura* of the Stalingrad oblast Party committee never were published. However, an estimate may be possible. In 1950, Louis Nemzer reported that the *nomenklatura* of some obkoms included "as many as 2,600 types of positions," while raikoms were responsible for "some 700 job categories."[133] At the February, 1958 obkom plenum the obkom secretary in charge of cadres stated that the *nomenklatura* of the Leninskii raikom included 203 positions.[134] If we assume the same ratio between the size of the raikom and obkom *nomenklaturii* reported by Nemzer, then the Stalingrad obkom would select and confirm persons for about 1000 positions. In view of the extreme degree of centralization during the last years of Stalin's life, and the subsequent appearance of statements to the effect that *nomenklaturii* should not be allowed to become too large, since this would result in only formal confirmation of positions,[135] it appears reasonable to assume that some diminution probably did occur in the size of the obkom's *nomenklatura* by 1958. In any case, the size and composition of the *nomenklatura* is not immovable. Depending upon the tasks and priorities of the given moment the Party committees can review and adjust the lists of persons appointed and confirmed by them. [136]

An examination of the lists of persons and positions included in a Party committee's *nomenklatura* would show what areas of industry and agriculture are considered "decisive" for the particular moment, the size of the leadership group, and the education, experience, age, and sex of the leading officials.[137] This and other information, including an analysis of each individual's "political maturity,"

[131] *Ibid.*, p. 336.
[132] *Ibid.*
[133] Louis Nemzer, "The Kremlin's Professional Staff," *American Political Science Review*, 44 (January, 1950), 65.
[134] *Stalingradskaia Pravda*, February 22, 1958.
[135] *VPS*, p. 336.
[136] *Ibid.*
[137] *Ibid.*

is used as the basis for making appointments to positions on the Party *nomenklatura*.[138]

Aside from the basic *nomenklatura*, there exists in the Party committees the so-called registration *nomenklatura*.[139] Persons included in the registration *nomenklatura* are not subject to confirmation by the Party committee, but the committee is supposed to keep an eye on them as a "reserve for promotion."[140] Positions included on this registration *nomenklatura* are probably mostly at the assistant chief level, for it is at this level that the Party committees are told to seek their "reserve for filling out the leading cadres."[141]

In the period from 1953 to about 1956, the Stalingrad obkom devoted considerable attention to selecting and confirming agricultural cadres. After the Central Committee plenum of September, 1953,[142] the obkom assumed the responsibility for selecting and confirming the new raikom secretaries for MTS zones, and for improving the quality of agricultural cadres in general. By the end of 1954, the Stalingrad obkom had completed the reorganization of the raion Party apparat with the creation of 143 zonal Party groups. All 143 secretaries for MTS zones, and 166 instructors to work under them, were "nominated and confirmed" by the Stalingrad obkom. The obkom also replaced 22 of 39 raion Party committee first secretaries.[143] In addition, the obkom made considerable efforts to improve the quality of agricultural specialists. To do this it extended its *nomenklatura* to include a whole range of such personnel. Shortly after the September Central Committee plenum the Stalingrad obkom selected and sent to the MTS 1,263 specialists, including 62 persons as directors, 108 as chief engineers, 69 as chief agronomists, and 203 as live-stock specialists and veterinarians.[144]

While much was said initially about the "great improvements" that the obkom had brought about in the quality of agricultural

138 *Ibid.*
139 *Ibid.*
140 *Ibid.*
141 *Ibid.*
142 For the text of the Central Committee resolution, see *KPSS v Rezoliutsiiakh* . . . , III, 610–653.
143 *Iz Istorii Stalingradskoi Partiinoi Organizatsii* (Stalingrad: Stalingradizdat, 1959), p. 260.
144 *Stalingradskaia Pravda*, January 20, 1956.

cadres, by 1956, the obkom came under criticism for selecting as secretaries for MTS zones many persons who were not even agricultural specialists.[145]

Apparently the obkom did not relinquish its control over the appointment of kolkhoz chairmen even after the abandonment of the system of raikom secretaries for MTS zones in September, 1957.[146] Speaking at the February, 1958 obkom plenum, the first secretary of the Zhdanov raikom stated explicity that "the *nomenklatura* of the obkom includes all kolkhoz chairmen, directors of MTS and sovkhozes. . . ."[147] The obkom at this time also appointed or confirmed raikom secretaries, the heads of raikom otdels, and the chairmen of raion Soviet executive committees.[148]

While it is not possible to say with certainty just which appointments require the confirmation of the obkom bureau, and which are handled by the secretariat alone, it appears that the bureau of the Stalingrad obkom concerns itself primarily with the raikom first secretaries and the chairmen of raiispolkoms, leaving to the cadres secretary and the otdels the selection of other agricultural personnel. In a speech to the February, 1958 plenum, the obkom secretary in charge of cadres referred specifically to the obkom bureau as selecting and confirming raikom first secretaries and the chairmen of raiispolkoms.[149] At the same time, a raiispolkom chairman criticized the obkom otdel of Party organs, the obkom agriculture otdel, and the oblast administration of agriculture for not giving enough attention to the selection of kolkhoz chairmen, implying that these otdels have the major voice in appointing such personnel.[150]

By 1960, the obkom appears to have delegated the responsibility for selecting kolkhoz chairmen to the raion Party committees. In his speech to the March plenum the first secretary observed that the obkom in its recent work with cadres "had devoted particular attention to strengthening the raion level of Party and Soviet workers."[151] At the same plenum the first secretary criticized the

[145] *Ibid.*, January 18, 1956.
[146] *SPR* (1959 ed.), pp. 545–546.
[147] *Stalingradskaia Pravda*, February 22, 1958.
[148] *Ibid.*
[149] *Ibid.*
[150] *Ibid.*
[151] *Ibid.*, March 26, 1960.

raikoms for "taking an incorrect attitude to the selection of kol-khoz chairmen who cannot cope with their responsibilities."[152]

The competence of the obkom bureau over the appointment and removal of industrial cadres is much less inclusive than its authority over agricultural personnel. The assignments made directly by the obkom bureau appear to be restricted to the highest level officials. An official of the Leningrad city Party committee reported that with the creation of the Sovnarkhoz, the *nomenklatura* of the gorkom was expanded to include "a large circle of economic officials heading the council and its branch administrations."[153] In Stalingrad, the obkom itself appears to have taken the lead in selecting officials for the Sovnarkhoz. Describing the work done by the obkom after the industrial reorganization, the obkom secretary in charge of cadres stated that "a great deal of work was carried out in assigning cadres to the Sovnarkhoz, and a series of measures was taken to strengthen the cadres of many industrial enterprises and construction projects."[154]

There is some evidence that the obkom bureau does not normally participate directly in the appointment or removal of heads of trusts and some enterprises, but rather delegates this authority to its industrial otdels and the Sovnarkhoz administrations. Thus, in 1958, when the gorkom sought the removal of the head of a construction trust for failure to fulfill its plans for industrial and housing construction, it applied to the Sovnarkhoz construction administration and the construction otdel of the obkom "for a decision on this question."[155] Only after two vice-chairmen of the Sovnarkhoz had prevented the solution of this problem did the gorkom raise it before the obkom bureau where, "over the protests" of the Sovnarkhoz vice-chairmen, the industrial manager was removed.[156] The implications of this example are that the Sovnarkhoz and obkom otdels share the initial responsibility for deciding, subject to the approval of a Sovnarkhoz vice-chairman, appointments and removals of at least some trust and enterprise managers. However, the obkom bureau retains the authority to intervene if these lower

152 *Ibid.*
153 *VPS*, p. 336.
154 *Stalingradskaia Pravda*, February 22, 1958.
155 *Ibid.*, March 26, 1960.
156 *Ibid.*

officials cannot make a decision or if the bureau disagrees with it. This delegation of responsibility is confirmed by other information from Stalingrad.

In 1956, a raikom and the Stalingrad gorkom were criticized for waiting a long time before raising the question of the removal of an incompetent steel mill director before the "appropriate authorities." Only after things in the plant had reached a difficult stage was the director removed by a decision of the obkom bureau.[157] At an obkom plenum in 1958, the director of a meat trust criticized some of the Sovnarkhoz officials who had been transferred to Stalingrad from Moscow. The speaker observed that these people felt themselves "guests, people who had come for only a short while," and who, therefore, felt no need to apply themselves seriously to their assigned work. Finally, two years later, the obkom first secretary announced at the oblast Party conference that "many communists" in the Sovnarkhoz had assumed an "undisciplined and non-Party attitude to matters, trying in every way to return to Moscow." As a result, the obkom bureau had taken a decision to remove from their posts and expel from the Party the chief of the Sovnarkhoz administration of material-technical supply, and the chief of a production department.[158] In conclusion, the first secretary pointed out that this situation had arisen because the gorkom and the obkom otdels had not properly fulfilled their functions in relation to industrial cadres.[159] The two-year delay between the first public criticism of these Sovnarkhoz officials and the final intervention of the obkom seems to indicate that the bureau decided to take appropriate measures only as a last resort after the subordinate otdels either failed or refused to fulfill their direct obligations.

While the role of the obkom bureau in the appointment of higher level industrial officials remains not entirely clear, there is definite evidence that the obkom delegates the whole responsibility for the selection and removal of lower level industrial cadres to the Sovnarkhoz. Speaking before an obkom plenum, the secretary of the Zhdanov raikom criticized the obkom for including in its *nomenklatura* such lowly agricultural officials as kolkhoz chairmen, while

[157] *Ibid.*, January 18, 1956.
[158] *Ibid.*, January 27, 1960.
[159] *Ibid.*

leaving such officials of the oil industry as the director of an office of oil drilling and the chiefs of construction administrations entirely within the *nomenklatura* of the Sovnarkhoz otdel of cadres.[160] "The entire responsibility" for the selection and assignment of these officials, continued the raikom secretary, "is placed on the administrations of the Sovnarkhoz and trusts."[161] Even here, however, the obkom bureau maintains the right of supervision and policy formation in relation to industrial cadres. Thus, at an obkom plenum in 1960, the obkom first secretary revealed that the previous December the obkom bureau had reviewed the process of cadres selection in the Sovnarkhoz. As a result of its investigation the obkom bureau obliged the Sovnarkhoz to "raise the personal responsibility of vice-chairmen, chiefs of administrations and departments, and managers of enterprises and construction projects for the selection, assignment, and training of cadres."[162]

Aside from the cadres for the local Party, agricultural, and industrial organizations, the obkom selects personnel for the oblast Soviet, trade-union, Komsomol, and other mass organizations. While the list of positions in the oblast Soviet filled by obkom bureau appointments is known with some exactness, the number of positions in the other organizations appointed or confirmed by the obkom bureau is less clear. At the 1960 oblast Party conference, the obkom first secretary stated that the obkom had given constant attention to "strengthening the organizational role" of the executive committee of the oblast Soviet, its otdels and administrations. To this end, "the Party organs carried out significant measures to strengthen the Soviet organs with qualified cadres."[163] Similarly, speaking at the March, 1960 obkom plenum, the first secretary of the Kamyshin gorkom stated that the city Party committee had "strengthened the otdels of the executive committee of the city Soviet of Working Peoples' Deputies with skilled and energetic cadres."[164] On the basis of these statements, and judging by the overall role of the obkom bureau in the selection of cadres, it would appear reasonable to assume that the obkom bureau at

160 *Ibid.*, February 22, 1958.
161 *Ibid.*
162 *Ibid.*, March 26, 1960.
163 *Ibid.*, January 27, 1960.
164 *Ibid.*, March 26, 1960.

least confirms and may select outright the members of the oblispolkom.[165] In Stalingrad this would include the heads of the nine otdels and twelve administrations as well as the chairman and four vice-chairmen of the Soviet executive committee. It is doubtful whether the obkom first and second secretaries, who also serve as members of the oblispolkom, require bureau confirmation in this latter capacity.[166]

With regard to the trade-union, Komsomol, and other mass organizations the role of the obkom bureau is more difficult to ascertain. The Party Rules make it quite certain that the Party committees are to take an active part in the leadership of these organizations and in selecting their personnel.[167] Speaking at an obkom plenum in 1958, the secretary in charge of cadres observed that "the obkom has taken significant steps to improve the cadres of the trade-union and Komsomol organs."[168] Since the obkom secretary is a member of the oblast trade-union council presidium,[169] it is probable that he has a major voice in the selection of the other ten members of that body, with the appointment of the chairman and trade-union council secretary doubtless made by the obkom bureau itself.

It is known that the Stalingrad obkom "took significant steps" to select more qualified cadres for the trade organizations and cooperatives, the courts and procuracy, and also for local industry.[170] In the case of these appointments it appears likely that the bureau limits its role to confirmation of the heads of the most important organizations, delegating the responsibility for other appointments to the obkom otdel for administrative and trade-financial organs.[171]

[165] This assumption would be in line with Fainsod's findings on the practice in Smolensk oblast in the 1930's when the obkom's *nomenklatura* included the heads and deputy heads of all oblispolkom departments and administrations, as well as the section chiefs within these. See Fainsod, *Smolensk Under Soviet Rule*, p. 99.

[166] The list of members and positions on the Stalingrad oblast Soviet executive committee is from *Stalingradskaia Pravda*, March 3, 1957. This is the only time during the period 1954–1961 that such a list was published in the oblast press.

[167] See *Programma i Ustav KPSS*, art. 42, secs. (v) and (g) which charge the obkom with the "leadership" of these organizations and with the "selection and assignment of leading cadres."

[168] *Stalingradskaia Pravda*, February 22, 1958.

[169] *Ibid.*, June 3, 1958; and *ibid.*, April 15, 1960.

[170] *Ibid.*, February 22, 1958.

[171] In Smolensk, in 1936, the Soviet-trade otdel, the rough equivalent of the present administrative, trade-financial otdel, handled appointments to 742 such positions, though its role was limited mostly to approval of appointments initiated by the various government departments. See Fainsod, *Smolensk Under Soviet Rule*, p. 65.

The power of the obkom bureau to appoint and remove a large number of leading personnel in every major organization within the oblast serves as a powerful tool for assuring compliance with its decisions on all spheres of activity within the oblast. Normally, this power appears to be used only when other measures fail. So long as the industrial production plan is being met, so long as an agricultural district remains "prosperous," the ruling officials are not likely to be touched. In fact, the first secretary of the Stalingrad obkom stated that some cadres in such circumstances "remain without attention for years," because the bureau and the otdels work only as "First-Aid teams."[172] At other times, even when certain officials have consistently failed in past assignments, they are constantly reappointed to other responsible positions.[173] However, when an important administrative reorganization occurs, there may be a considerable turnover in leading cadres with the obkom devoting considerable time and effort to the selection of new and capable personnel. This appears to have been the case especially during the reorganization of the rural raikoms after the September, 1953 Central Committee plenum and following the industrial reorganization of 1957.

On the other hand, many cases have been reported in the Soviet press where obkom secretaries and bureaus have used their power of cadres selection to create what is known, in Soviet terminology, as a "family circle," with many of the characteristics of a political machine.[174] While it is probable that each of the first secretaries of the Stalingrad obkom sought to fill the bureau and other leading positions with persons with whom they could establish good working relationships, there is no real evidence to indicate that either of them tried to turn the obkom into his personal political machine.

DECISION-MAKING STYLE

Information is all too scarce on the style of decision-making in the bureau of the oblast Party committee itself, but there are enough

[172] "Object-Lesson Training of Leading Party Cadres," *Partiinaia Zhizn'*, No. 14 (1955), p. 17.

[173] *Stalingradskaia Pravda*, February 22, 1958.

[174] For an analysis of the oblast Party committee as a political machine, see my essay, "The Obkom Under Khrushchev—A Study in Machine Politics" (unpublished Certificate essay, Russian and East European Institute, Indiana University, 1962).

128 POLITICAL POWER IN THE SOVIET UNION

clues to trace in outline the processes involved. Meetings are probably held about once every eight or nine days, as was noted above;[175] and if Kochetov's novel reflects actual practice, bureau meetings are probably held in the office of the first secretary.[176] In order to conduct business, a quorum must be present.[177] In the case of Stalingrad this means that a meeting can be held properly with the participation of only six members; for instance, with only the five obkom secretaries and the gorkom secretary, or the oblispolkom chairman, present.

It seems quite apparent that at the time of Stalin's death bureau meetings frequently were held without a quorum or were simply skipped altogether.[178] In the latter case decisions were adopted largely by the so-called questionnaire method in which the project decision is circulated around to the bureau members, who read and sign it. At other times, decisions were adopted by the secretariat in the name of the bureau. In this case there was nothing for the bureau members to do but to "familiarize themselves with the text of a resolution that had been adopted without their knowledge or assistance."[179] Since criticisms of these methods largely ceased to appear after 1954, it can be assumed with some certainty that this problem was largely overcome by that time.

The discussion of each major question at bureau sessions appears to be organized around a report. Usually these are composed by the obkom otdels. Thus, if a question deals with the unsatisfactory work of a raikom, the Party organs otdel would probably make an investigation on the spot and draw up the report for the bureau.[180] Similarly, if a question concerns the work of an enterprise, the obkom industrial otdel, perhaps together with the factory director, may conduct a study of the problems and prepare a report on the question.[181] These reports should be circulated to the bureau members prior to the meeting so that they may "work out their own opinions."[182] When the bureau members have not had the op-

[175] See Chapter 6, 99–100.
[176] Kochetov, p. 166.
[177] *Pravda*, September 4, 1953, p. 2.
[178] See for instance, *Pravda*, April 16, 1953, p. 2; and *ibid.*, May 11, 1953, p. 2.
[179] *Ibid.*
[180] *Stalingradskaia Pravda*, March 26, 1960.
[181] *Ibid.*, December 12, 1957.
[182] "A Bureau Meeting is in Progress," *Partiinaia Zhizn'*, No. 1 (1958), p. 25.

portunity to make a thorough study of the matters under consideration, discussion tends to become dragged out, major issues remain unclarified, and if a decision is adopted, it is likely to be ineffectual.[183] In actual practice, however, it seems probable that on the major questions each of the bureau members does receive reports for his study prior to the bureau session. On the other hand, it appears that on most routine matters, such as confirming many appointments, decisions are made without lengthy preliminary investigations.

The discussion of major topics is usually initiated by a reporter and a co-reporter who point out the issues involved in the question under discussion and present the project resolution.[184] In addition to these reporters it frequently occurs that a large number of other officials are invited to contribute to the bureau discussions. In *Secretar' Obkoma*, a bureau meeting was described in which 20 persons participated. [185] At a bureau meeting in Stalingrad 46 persons participated in the discussion of 17 questions.[186]

Although in the first few years after Stalin's death there were many reports that little real criticism and discussion occurred at bureau meetings,[187] it appears probable that fairly open and full discussion now takes place in many Party committee bureau sessions. In relation to the Central Committee Presidium, Fainsod points out that while Khrushchev was the supreme authority within that body, he nevertheless appears to have desired and encouraged frank and open discussion prior to the adoption of decisions.[188] Emphasis in the Party press on the need for collective discussion "to expose shortcomings, to devise suggestions about the problem at hand, and to determine the organizations and persons responsible for the fulfillment of the contemplated measures,"[189] indicates that this is the desired approach for the obkom also.

In his novel, *Secretar' Obkoma*, V. Kochetov points up the crucial role of the first secretary not only in regulating the amount

[183] "On Preparations for Meetings of a Party Committee Bureau," *Partiinaia Zhizn'*, No. 6 (1958), p. 37.

[184] *Ibid.*

[185] Kochetov, p. 166.

[186] *Stalingradskaia Pravda*, March 10, 1954.

[187] See for instance, *Pravda*, September 4, 1953, p. 2; and *ibid.*, April 16, 1953, p. 2.

[188] Fainsod, *How Russia is Ruled* (2nd ed.), p. 338.

[189] *VPR*, p. 51.

and kind of discussion but in all aspects of bureau decision-making from the make-up of the agenda to the wording of the decisions. When Denisov, the first secretary of the Stargorod obkom, visits Artamonov, the first secretary of the neighboring Vysokogorod obkom, he finds the latter engaged in a bureau meeting. Denisov is surprised by the high-handed manner in which Artamonov runs his bureau. At first, Artamonov suggests that he'll "turn over the reins of government to the second secretary," so that the two leaders can have time for a little chat. When Denisov protests that he doesn't want to interrupt the bureau's work, Artamonov invites him to sit in on the session. Returning to the bureau, the first secretary procedes to run the whole show. He explains that a certain raikom secretary has failed to fulfill his agricultural delivery plan, although all other raions have completed theirs. Turning to the bureau members Artamonov asks: "Have I formulated the question correctly?" "Yes, correctly!" comes the reply from a few voices. Having thus concluded the discussion, the first secretary turns to the resolution:

> "Well then, what proposals do I hear?" Artamonov turned his glance to the participants in the bureau. All remained silent. "Then I have a few observations. . . ." He stood up, went to the window, and having put his right hand into the opening of his blue jacket looked at the street. "Well then, write, as follows . . ."

After dictating the descriptive part of the resolution to the stenographer, he proceeds with the specific points:

> "Point one! Proceeding from the above, the secretary of the Lobanovskii raikom CPSU, comrade Kruglikov, Vladimir Ivanovich, is hereby given a strict warning with the inclusion of this on his personal record. Are there any objections?
> No!
> Then it is unanimous. Second point. The chairman of the raion Soviet of Workingmen's Deputies, comrade Sosinin, Dmitry Grigor'evich, is hereby given a warning. Any objections?
> No!
> It is unanimous. Point three . . ."
> Vasilii Antonovich [Denisov] and Sergeev [the chairman of the Stargorod oblispolkom] exchanged furtive glances: So this is

why they used to joke about us as the "chief talkers" in the oblast.[190]

That this is not an example simply of genuine unanimity and efficiency in a matter on which all agree is made clear shortly after this incident when Denisov is talking with Artamonov:

> Vasilii Antonovich listened to him, observed him; he remembered the faces of the bureau members, unanimously approving Artamonov's every word; he remembered their rapidly nodding heads. But there were also those who sat silently, gloomily looking at the table and straight ahead. Vasilii Antonovich was familiar with persons in such a state. They either had not yet clarified everything to their satisfaction, or doubted something, or in general disagreed with this or that solution of a problem.[191]

Continuing his line of thought, Denisov describes the way he feels bureau members should be brought into the discussions:

> He knew that, even if they remain quiet, one must definitely bring them out, one must know how to create conditions so that they will speak out, so that they will express their doubts and objections. Otherwise the question may be decided incompletely, one-sidedly, or even completely incorrectly. Most of all one must be careful of those who look you in the mouth, grab at your every word, and noisily and hurriedly approve everything you say. These are thoughtless, untrustworthy people. With them it is easy to pronounce a decision, but then it's difficult to fulfill it.[192]

Both the description of the incorrect way to run the bureau and the observations on the proper organization of discussion bring out the central position of the first secretary. The first secretary does hold the "reins of government," and in a real sense he is the "chief talker." It is with good reason that article after article in the Party journals stresses the responsibility of the first secretary to "unite the Party bureau, to assure friendly, collective work."[193] Unfortunately it is impossible to determine the frequency with

[190] Kochetov, p. 166.

[191] *Ibid.*

[192] *Ibid.*

[193] "A Bureau Meeting is in Progress," *Partiinaia Zhizn'*, No. 1 (1958), p. 25. Other articles stressing this point include: *VPR*, esp. p. 50; and "The Division of Responsibilities Between Members of the Bureau of a Primary Party Organization," *Partiinaia Zhizn'*, No. 20 (1956), pp. 67–70.

which full and free discussion actually occurs in sessions of the obkom bureau. However, it is probably safe to assume that normal practice is, in most cases, somewhere between complete regulation and entirely open discussion.

Aside from the attitude of the first secretary, another factor that may hinder thorough discussion of all questions before the bureau is simply the number of problems the bureau must handle. One raikom bureau in Alma-Ata oblast, for instance, was reported to have examined up to 200 or more questions in a year. Commenting on this situation, *Partiinaia Zhizn'* stated that "it is perfectly obvious that any kind of serious preparation of such a quantity of questions is more than the apparat of the raikom can handle. . . ."[194] The problem of an overloaded agenda has also been a persistent feature of obkom bureau activity. Fainsod describes the bureau of the Smolensk obkom as being so overburdened with problems for its decision that most topics on the agenda went "untouched." Mainly, the obkom could find time to deal only with those immediate problems "whose urgency could not be denied."[195] And, as late as 1962, seeking some way to limit the number of questions the bureau must decide, *Partiinaia Zhizn'* proposed that "there ought to be a rule for Party committees to take decisions only in necessary cases, when something actually must be decided."[196]

After the discussion is concluded the draft or project decision is brought up for a vote. While the draft may be drawn up directly at the bureau session, as in the instance cited from Kochetov's novel, it appears to be the usual practice for the project resolution to be written by the same officials who undertake the original investigation and make up the background reports.[197]

A resolution is considered adopted if it receives the votes of a majority of bureau members present and voting.[198] If agreement

194 "On Preparations for a Meeting of a Party Committee Bureau," *Partiinaia Zhizn'*, No. 6 (1958), p. 38.

195 Fainsod, *Smolensk Under Soviet Rule*, p. 69.

196 "Let's Improve Organizational-Party Work," *Partiinaia Zhizn'*, No. 3 (1962), p. 8.

197 Some articles referring to this as the normal procedure include the following: "On Preparations for a Meeting of a Party Committee Bureau," *Partiinaia Zhizn'*, No. 6 (1958), pp. 3–11; "A Bureau Meeting is in Progress," *Partiinaia Zhizn'*, No. 1 (1958), pp. 24–25; and *Pravda*, September 4, 1953, p. 2.

198 "Answers to Reader's Questions: Can a Bureau Member Make Proposals at a Party Meeting that Differ from Bureau Decisions?" *Partiinaia Zhizn'*, No. 1 (1956), p. 65.

cannot be reached on the project decision, it may be rejected and sent back to the otdel that prepared it with instructions to reexamine the question and come up with a new proposal, or a special group of bureau members may be assigned to look into the problem.[199]

Several conclusions emerge from this analysis of decision-making within the obkom bureau. The most obvious of these relates to the position of the first secretary within the bureau. On him more than anyone else depends the degree of influence that any other bureau member, or for that matter any official within the oblast, will have on the formation of policy within the obkom. If he is open-minded and gregarious, he may welcome the expression of divergent opinions or even the promotion of ideas at variance with his own. On the other hand, depending upon his psychological make-up, he may restrict discussion to the simple mouthing of approval for his own proposals. In other words, while many of the important organizations in the oblast may be assured *formal* access to decision-making within the bureau by the membership of their chief on that body, the *effectiveness* of such access is almost entirely dependent upon one man—the first secretary. Unfortunately, before any final conclusions can be drawn regarding the degree to which individual bureau members, or the groups they represent, do in fact influence the content of bureau decisions, much more information must become available on the actual course of deliberation on specific policy problems.

199 "Organizing the Fulfillment of a Decision," *Partiinaia Zhizn'*, No. 11 (1955), p. 5.

# SEVEN

# The First Secretaries

[7:7]

The crucial role played by the first secretary in setting the style of obkom policy making—in determining the kinds of information that are considered, in limiting or extending the range of acceptable proposals, and in selecting whose voices will be given the most weight—suggests the importance of an analysis of the backgrounds of obkom first secretaries. A secretary with an engineering education, followed by senior managerial positions prior to entering Party work will most certainly differ in his approach to industrial problems from a secretary trained in pedagogical institutions whose previous career consisted primarily of Komsomol work. It might be predicted in this case, for example, that the opinions and outlook of managers would receive a more sympathetic ear from the former than the latter. In fact, the data from Stalingrad,[1] appear to confirm this proposition. If observed on a national scale this finding might indicate increased actual influence of managers.

In addition to providing a more systematic basis for drawing

[1] See Chapter 5, pp. 71–75 and Chapter 9, pp. 199–214.

conclusions on patterns of influence within the oblast, comparative analysis of the social backgrounds and career patterns of first secretaries may make possible identification of characteristics most closely associated with a long or short tenure and with promotion or demotion. It may be hypothesized, for instance, that those who enter full-time Party work before reaching 35 years of age are more likely to have a long tenure as first secretary than those who enter at a later age. Similarly, it may be found that those who serve for less than four years as head of an obkom are significantly more likely to be promoted or transferred to a job of similar status than those whose total tenure as first secretary is of longer duration.

While scholars have long been interested in these and similar questions, the great paucity of data on the social backgrounds of the Soviet elite in general and of Party officials in particular has discouraged systematic inquiry in this area.[2] Fortunately, recent developments have brought about a very significant increase in both the quantity and quality of information available on Party officials. Particularly since the late 1950's there has been a rapid improvement in the reporting of biographical information in Soviet sources. Although still requiring diligent and painstaking surveying of a wide variety of Soviet publications, it has now become possible to describe in extensive detail the career patterns of a very large percentage of those who have held the post of obkom first secretary over the past 16 years.[3] In addition to sources available in the West, the Soviet regional press also reports the biographies of first secretaries in detail on the occasion of their election to the Republic or USSR Supreme Soviet.

[2] The only large-scale, intensive study of the middle-level elite published to date is the early work by John A. Armstrong, *The Soviet Bureaucratic Elite* (New York: Praeger, 1959). Several other major elite studies are now in preparation, however, utilizing the more complete data now available. These include studies by Seweryn Bailer at Columbia University and by George Fisher. For useful recent articles see especially John A. Armstrong, "Party Bifurcation and Elite Interests," *Soviet Studies*, No. 4 (April, 1966), pp. 417–430; and Jerry Hough, "The Soviet Elite: Groups and Individuals," *Problems of Communism* (January-February, 1967), pp. 28–35.

[3] The most valuable compilations of data on Soviet personnel are the following: *Who's Who in the USSR 1965/1966*, Andrew I. Lebed, Heinrich E. Schulz, and Stephen S. Taylor, eds. (New York: Scarecrow Press, 1966); *Who's Who in the USSR 1961/1962*, Heinrich E. Schulz and Stephen S. Taylor, eds. (New York: Scarecrow Press, 1962); *Biographic Directory of the USSR*, Wladimir S. Merzalow, ed. (New York: Scarecrow Press, 1958). The first source mentioned contains by far the most extensive biographic data on Party officials ever available to Western scholars. For added accuracy, and particularly to make the data used in this study complete through June, 1966, the following Soviet sources were utilized: *Pravda*, 1950–1966; *Sovetskaia Rossiia*, 1950–1966; and *Bol'shaia Sovetskaia Entsiklopedia*, Yezhzgodnik, 1956–1964.

BACKGROUND

Although only three individuals held the post of first secretary of the Stalingrad obkom during the period of this study, a description of their backgrounds will provide a setting for the analysis of the career patterns of a large group of first secretaries. In many ways the careers of these three men are illustrative of the more significant background characteristics of regional Party leaders.

Ivan Timofeevich Grishin, first secretary of the Stalingrad obkom from 1948 to December, 1955, was born in 1911 of peasant parents in the village of Khvoroshchevka, Riazan oblast. By the age of 15 he had begun to work as a blacksmith in various Moscow enterprises, such as "Electrozavod," and "Electrostal'." Grishin showed an early interest in politics. At 19 he joined the Komsomol and in 1931, at 23 he joined the Communist Party. Since becoming a member of the Komsomol, Grishin has been actively engaged in Party or Party-directed activity, first with a trade-union organization and then a factory Party committee. Shortly after joining the Party he was elected chairman of the Party construction committee and then secretary of the Party cell at the Electrostal' factory.

When Grishin was drafted into the Red Army in 1933, he continued to participate actively in Party and Komsomol work, first as secretary of the regimental Party organization, and later as secretary of the regimental Komsomol bureau. After two years of military service, Grishin returned to Electrostal' where he worked as the Party organizer in the rolling shop. From 1937 to 1939 Ivan Timofeevich was engaged in directing Komsomol work, holding successively the following positions: secretary of the Noginsk city Komsomol committee, secretary of the Riazan oblast Komsomol committee, and then head of the department of leading Komsomol organs in the Komsomol Central Committee in Moscow.[4]

Ivan Kuzmich Zhegalin, who served as first secretary of the Stalingrad obkom from December, 1956 to January, 1961, was born in 1906 in the village of Senodsk, Saratov oblast, the son of a railroad worker. Zhegalin began to work at the age of 14 as a manual laborer. However, unlike Grishin, Zhegalin was able to obtain a

4 *Stalingradskaia Pravda*, February 19, 1954.

secondary education. In 1925, apparently recognizing his technical abilities, the Komsomol sent him to the Amkhabad Transportation Technicum. Although most of his activities were probably related to obtaining a technical education, Zhegalin must have demonstrated some interest in political affairs during his school years for after his first year of schooling, in 1926, he was admitted to the Party. Upon completing his schooling he worked in the rapidly expanding railroad industry where he rose from a locomotive machinist, to assistant chief of a railroad depot, and later to assistant chief of a district division of the Samara-Zlatoustovskii railroad.

In 1933, at the end of the First Five Year Plan, Zhegalin was transferred to managerial work in heavy industry. While holding the position of Chief Engineer at the Kirov factory in Orenburg, Zhegalin completed a Mechanical Engineering degree at the Ufa Industrial Institute of Economists. From 1936 to 1939, during the most intense period of the purges, Zhegalin served as Director of the Kirov factory.[5]

Aleksei Mikhailovich Shkol'nikov, first secretary in Stalingrad from 1961 to December, 1965, was born of Great Russian parents in 1914. At 19 he completed his secondary education, graduating from an industrial technicum. Later he received a partial higher education by completing three correspondence courses at an industrial academy. Upon completing his secondary education Shkol'nikov spent ten years in various industrial positions, serving consecutively as a shift foreman, a senior craftsman, a section manager, then as chief power engineer in a factory in Perm oblast. Shkol'nikov's political interests and activities were developed somewhat later than were the interests of the two previous first secretaries; however, in 1940, at 26, he became a member of the Communist Party.[6]

The early careers of these three secretaries illustrate well the gradual shifts in Party recruitment of potential leaders. Grishin represents those of little formal education beyond primary school. He was "adopted" by the Party at a very early age and his whole life has been devoted to Party activities. His involvement with

5 *Ibid.*, February 18, 1958.
6 *Who's Who in the USSR 1965/1966*, p. 761.

Party functions, whether he was formally employed by a factory or even called into military service, distinguishes him as a professional Party *apparatchik*.

Zhegalin occupies a somewhat intermediate position. Lacking education beyond primary school, he too showed an early interest in political affairs; however rather than "adopting" him and bringing him into full-time Party work immediately, the Party sent him to school and then into industry. Although he served in a senior managerial position for a relatively short time, this experience doubtless left its imprint on his later Party activity. Shkol'nikov differs from Zhegalin in that he completed his education and worked in industry for some time before joining the Party. However, his entry into full-time Party work at 29 after ten years in rather junior managerial positions probably means that his subsequent long career in Party work had the greater impact on the formation of his decision-making style in the obkom. In short, his early career pattern would seem to characterize him neither as a full-fledged Party *apparatchik* nor as an industrial manager turned Party official.

Regardless of early career differences, all three men displayed the kinds of skills in their Party careers necessary to rise to the leadership of an oblast and into positions of major responsibility in the central leadership. In May, 1939, Ivan Timofeevich Grishin was called to full-time Party work in the Central Committee. For two years he served as vice-chairman of the Party Control Commission, responsible for enforcing Party discipline and supervising the execution of Party decisions.[7] Early in 1941 Grishin was sent to Novosibirsk oblast as the "fully-empowered" representative of this commission. On the eve of World War Two Grishin was elected chairman of the Novosibirsk oblast Soviet executive committee (oblispolkom). In this position he was active in the reestablishment of evacuated enterprises, in the resettling of evacuees, and also in the mobilization of the population for the war effort. As a result of his work during the war, Grishin was awarded the Order of Lenin and the order of the Red Banner of Labor. After the war Grishin was sent to the Higher Party School, completing the course in 1948.[8] After a nine-month period as second secretary,

---

[7] For a description of the role of the Party Control Commission see Fainsod, *How Russia is Ruled* (2nd ed.), pp. 195, 221–222.

[8] See Chapter 7, pp. 160–162 for an extended discussion of the Higher Party School.

in December, 1948, Grishin was elected first secretary of the Stalingrad oblast Party committee. In 1952 he was elected to the Party Central Committee, a position he maintained until 1961.[9]

Like Grishin, Zhegalin was assigned to full-time Party work in 1939, helping to fill the gaps in the Party apparatus left by the Great Purge. First he worked as an instructor in the Orenburg obkom, then as head of the obkom oil department. After two years in the obkom apparatus he was elected an obkom secretary. In 1946, Zhegalin was assigned to work in Turkmenistan as first secretary of the Krasnovodskii obkom and gorkom simultaneously. After one year he was called to work for a brief period in the Party Central Committee. Following this experience, Zhegalin was transferred to the Rostov oblast Party organization as its third, and subsequently second secretary. During this period Zhegalin completed a two-year correspondence course at the Higher Party School. His first opportunity to direct a large region came in 1949 when he was appointed first secretary of the Grozny obkom. In 1955, in the midst of an agricultural crisis, Zhegalin was given the major assignment of first secretary of the Stalingrad obkom. From 1952 to 1966 Zhegalin was a member of the Party Central Committee.[10]

Aleksei Shkol'nikov entered full-time Party work in 1943, three years after joining its ranks. He worked first as a department head, then secretary of the Perm obkom. Following the war, Shkol'nikov spent two years as the representative of the Party Control Commission, first in Vladimir, then in Voronezh oblasts. In 1947 he was elected second secretary of the Kaluga obkom, a post he held until entering the Higher Party School in 1949. Upon completing his Party education Shkol'nikov served for three years as first secretary of the Tambov obkom. In 1955 he was transferred to the first secretaryship of the Voronezh obkom. After five years in Voronezh, Shkol'nikov was sent to head the Stalingrad oblast Party organization. During the period of bifurcation of the Party, from November, 1962 to November, 1964, he was first secretary of the Stalingrad rural obkom, returning to his former position after the Party reverted to its traditional structure.[11]

9 *Stalingradskaia Pravda*, February 19, 1954.

10 *Stalingradskaia Pravda*, February 18, 1958.

11 For a description of the bifurcation of the Party structure and an analysis of its significance, see Fainsod, *How Russia is Ruled* (2nd ed.), esp. pp. 203–205.

A period of successful service directing the affairs of Stalingrad oblast brought further promotions to each of the men who
held the first secretaryship during this study. After a total of eight
years as first secretary, Grishin was appointed ambassador to
Czechoslovakia, a post he held for five years. In 1960 he became
Deputy Minister of Foreign Trade, receiving his second Red
Banner of Labor award for work in this capacity in 1961.[12] Zhegalin,
following six years as first secretary in each of two oblasts received
an appointment as ambassador to Rumania, a position he continues
to occupy.[13] To this date Shkol'nikov probably has been the most
successful of the three; early in 1966 he was appointed first vice-
chairman of the Russian Republic Council of Ministers.[14]

While the careers of the three men who headed the Stalingrad
Party organization during the period of this study are illuminating
and suggestive of hypotheses regarding general trends, in order
to establish actual trends in the career patterns of obkom first secretaries it is necessary to analyze as large a sample as possible. Until
recently the scarcity of data made it impossible to systematically
examine the careers of any but a small sample of Ukrainian first
secretaries, and this for the period up to 1956 only.[15] As a result
of recent developments that have brought a very significant increase
in both the quantity and quality of information available on Party
officials[16] some systematic analysis of the backgrounds of a large
proportion of all who served as regional first secretaries in recent
years is now possible.

The period chosen for analysis is from 1950 to June, 1966.
This time span has been selected as corresponding closely to the
period covered by the analysis of Stalingrad while at the same
time adding a sufficient number of years to show trends with
clarity. Included in the study are nearly all those who at any time
during this period held the post of first secretary in any of the

[12] *Who's Who in the USSR 1965/1966*, pp. 291–292.

[13] *Ibid.*, p. 761.

[14] *Pravda*, June 15, 1966.

[15] This pioneering work was Armstrong's, *The Soviet Bureaucratic Elite*.

[16] These developments include an apparent change in Soviet policy, and, about 1959, the
quality and quantity of biographic material published in public sources was vastly increased. This increase was aided by the systematic and highly competent gathering and
compilation of these data by the Institute for the Study of the USSR, Munich, Germany.
The results of these developments can be seen by comparing the 1961/1962 and the 1965/
1966 editions of the *Who's Who in the USSR*.

*Table 16: The Sample*

| REPUBLIC | NUMBER OF PARTY ORGANS | TOTAL MAN-YEARS | | PER CENT COVERED | |
|---|---|---|---|---|---|
| | | 1950–66 | 1954–66 | 1950–66 | 1954–66 |
| RSFSR Obkoms | 50 | 850 | 650 | 84.0 | 96.8 |
| RSFSR Kraikoms | 6 | 102 | 78 | 89.3 | 93.6 |
| RSFSR Aut. Obkoms | 3 | 51 | 39 | 53.0 | 69.3 |
| RSFSR Aut. Rep. Obkoms | 16 | 272 | 208 | 88.7 | 95.7 |
| Ukrainian Obkoms | 25 | 425 | 325 | 79.6 | 90.2 |
| Belorussian Obkoms | 6 | 102 | 78 | 70.6 | 83.4 |
| Uzbekistani Obkoms | 10 | 170 | 130 | 68.7 | 80.0 |
| Kazakhstani Obkoms | 16 | 255 | 191 | 54.6 | 69.2 |
| Georgian Obkoms | 3 | 51 | 39 | 70.6 | 93.4 |
| Azerbaidzhani Obkoms | 2 | 34 | 26 | 76.5 | 84.7 |
| Kirgizian Obkoms | 1 | 17 | 13 | 71.6 | 92.4 |
| Tadzhikistani Obkoms | 1 | 17 | 13 | 35.3 | 46.2 |
| Republic Central Committees | 14 | 237 | 178 | 78.1 | 88.3 |
| Totals | 153 | 2583 | 1968 | (av.) 78.6 | 89.2 |

following Party organs: (1) oblast Party committee, including obkoms in the RSFSR as well as the Union Republics; (2) krai (regional) Party committee; (3) Republic Central Committee; or (4) obkom in an autonomous republic or autonomous oblast.[17]

Table 16 details the completeness of the sample for type of obkom and each republic as a percentage of the total number of man-years for each of two periods, 1950 to 1966 and 1954 to 1966. The sample is most complete for the Russian republic obkoms and kraikoms, averaging 84.6 per cent when 1950 is taken as the initial year and 96.8 per cent when 1954 is used as the starting point. The average for all other Republics combined is 73.4 per cent for the 1950 to 1966 period and 85.0 per cent for the shorter period. These calculations are based upon knowledge of at least the name and the dates of appointment and removal of first secretaries, and thus can be considered as indicators of maximum

17 Autonomous republic and autonomous oblast Party organs are formed in areas of national minorities concentration. Their functions are essentially the same as obkoms or kraikoms, the former are subordinate to the latter. See, *Programma i Ustav KPSS*, art. 47.

coverage. Nearly complete biographic information is available for approximately 45 per cent of the sample. For the remaining 55 per cent the information varies from simple identification to highly generalized career descriptions. Although coverage is not as complete as may be desirable, when used with caution the available data can at least go a long way toward filling the large gaps in our knowledge of the backgrounds of the leading figures in oblast politics.

EDUCATION

The Soviet elite of today is highly educated. No longer is it composed primarily of individuals like Grishin whose sole education beyond primary school consists of several years at a Party school. Indeed, the educational attainments of the Party elite, as exemplified by the delegates to the most recent 23rd Party Congress are far higher than those of Party members as a whole. Whereas in 1964 only 15 per cent of all Party members had a higher education, and 32.7 per cent had either an incomplete higher or a secondary education, among the Congress delegates 55.5 per cent had a higher and 24.0 per cent had an incomplete higher or a secondary education.[18] While precise information on the educational attainments of all obkom first secretaries is not available, their general educational level appears to be quite high. Evidence from the sample indicates that probably more than 90 per cent of those who held the post of obkom first secretary between 1950 and 1966 had some kind of higher education. Thus, all but two of the 181 first secretaries whose educational background is known possess a higher education.[19] Even if none of those for whom data are unobtainable completed a higher education, this still means that about 40 per cent, as a minimum, have completed a higher education.

The kinds of education found most commonly among those Party officials who have risen to become obkom first secretaries are largely the same as those of the Party elite as a whole. More

[18] "The CPSU in Figures (1961–1964)," *Partiinaia Zhizn'*, No. 10 (1965), p. 11.

[19] Unless otherwise indicated all data on obkom secretaries is derived from analysis of the materials contained in the following sources: *Who's Who in the USSR 1965/1966; Who's Who in the USSR 1961/1962; Biographic Directory of the USSR; Pravda,* 1950–1966; *Sovetskaia Rossiia,* 1960–1966; and *Bol'shaia Sovetskaia Entsiklopediia,* Yezhegodnik, 1956–1964.

*Table 17: Comparison of Educational Backgrounds
of Party Elite and First Secretaries*

| KIND OF EDUCATION | 23RD CONGRESS DELEGATES | | FIRST SECRETARIES | |
|---|---|---|---|---|
| | PER CENT[a] | N | PER CENT | N |
| Engineering-Technical | 45.9 | 1484 | 33.3 | 52 |
| Agricultural and Veterinary | 15.3 | 493 | 23.7 | 37 |
| Pedagogical, Medical, Law | 13.9 | 451 | 11.5 | 18 |
| Party Education | 24.9 | 806 | 31.5 | 49 |
| | 100.0 | 3234 | 100.0 | 156 |

SOURCES: *Pravda*, April 1, 1966; *Who's Who in the USSR 1965/1966* (New York: Scarecrow Press, 1966).

[a] The percentages given refer only to those actually identified or declared to have the indicated educational backgrounds and not to all Congress delegates nor to all first secretaries.

than 86 per cent of obkom first secretaries for whom information is available and more than 65 per cent of all delegates to the 23rd Party Congress possess either an engineering-technical, an agricultural, a pedagogical, or a Party education. An engineering-technical education is the most common among both groups. It is worth noting that although the usual generalizations regarding the primacy of engineering training in the backgrounds of Party officials[20] are supported by this data, the frequency of this background among secretaries is nearly one-third less than for Congress delegates. Conversely, the percentage of secretaries with an agricultural background is about a third greater than for Congress delegates. This undoubtedly reflects the great stress placed on the Party's role in agriculture by Khrushchev.

The high percentage of both groups with a Party education indicates the intensity of the Party's interest in improving the educational qualifications of its present elite while at the same time seeking new recruits for responsible positions who have already obtained a higher education.

It has been suggested by one noted scholar that associations formed during school years may be a significant factor in the formation of those personal connections and affiliations that seem

20 For example, see Frederick C. Barghorn, *Politics in the USSR* (Boston: Little, Brown and Company, 1966), p. 203.

## Table 18: Education by Type of Institution

| TYPE OF INSTITUTION | N | PER CENT |
|---|---|---|
| *Industrial-Technical* | 45 | 24.8 |
| INCLUDING: | | |
| Leningrad Institute of Railroad Engineering | 2 | |
| Urals Industrial Institute | 2 | |
| Moscow Mining Institute | 2 | |
| Dneprodzherzhinsk Metallurgical Institute | 3 | |
| Kharkov Mechanical and Machine-Building Institute | 2 | |
| Bauman Mechanical and Machine-Building Institute | 2 | |
| *Industrial-Technical and Higher Party School* | 7 | 3.8 |
| *Agricultural* | 26 | 14.3 |
| INCLUDING: | | |
| Timiryazev Agricultural Academy | 4 | |
| Azov-Black Sea Agricultural Institute | 3 | |
| Omsk Agricultural Institute | 2 | |
| *Agricultural and Higher Party School* | 11 | 6.0 |
| INCLUDING: | | |
| Gorky Agricultural Institute | 2 | |
| *Higher Party School CC CPSU* | 31 | 17.1 |
| *Pedagogical* | 8 | 4.4 |
| *Pedagogical and Higher Party School* | 8 | 4.4 |
| *Party Organized Education* | 13 | 7.2 |
| *Higher Party School CC CP Ukraine* | 5 | 2.8 |
| *Veterinary* | 5 | 2.8 |
| *Veterinary and Higher Party School* | 1 | 0.6 |
| *Military* | 4 | 2.2 |
| *Aviation* | 3 | 1.6 |
| *Aviation and Higher Party School* | 1 | 0.6 |
| *Economic-Planning* | 3 | 1.6 |
| *Economic-Planning and Higher Party School* | 2 | 1.2 |
| *University* | 3 | 1.6 |
| *University and Higher Party School* | 1 | 0.6 |
| *Secondary* | 2 | 1.2 |
| *Medical* | 1 | 0.6 |
| *Legal and Higher Party School* | 1 | 0.6 |
| *Total* | 181 | 100.0 |

to be so important in determining success in the Soviet system.[21] The data from this study, however, tend to disconfirm this hypothesis. Table 18 shows the distribution by type of educational institution of the 181 obkom first secretaries for whom this information is available. This table also indicates all cases where two or more individuals attended the same institution. Among those with an industrial-technical education in only six instances did two or more persons attend the same school; among those with an agricultural education this happened in only four cases. Even in the most general sense of subsequent feelings of comradeship, the "old school tie" would only be relevant to a total of 24 out of 181 individuals who later became obkom first secretaries. Nevertheless, it may be of some significance that two persons from this group—Aleksei Kirichenko, and Leonid Brezhnev—became members of the Politburo (Presidium). Since both served as Central Committee secretaries each probably had the opportunity of influencing, to some extent, the careers of lower Party officials. This is particularly true of Kirichenko who from December, 1957 to January, 1960, directed organizational and cadres activities in the Secretariat.[22] Although Brezhnev's exact responsibilities are unknown, his close association with Khrushchev during his first period as Central Committee secretary, from 1957 to 1960, appears to make reasonable the assumption that he too could assist the careers of at least some subordinate Party officials.[23]

The careers of those who attended the same schools as Kirichenko and Brezhnev may be worth examining in the light of the "old school tie" hypothesis. Lev Borisovich Yermin and Petr Yemelyanovich Doroshenko both attended the same institution as Kirichenko, the Azov-Black Sea Agricultural Institute. Since Yermin graduated in 1952 while Kirichenko completed his schooling in 1936 these two certainly did not become acquainted in school. In the case of Doroshenko the evidence is unclear. Although the date of his graduation is unknown, considering that he was born in 1907, one year before Kirichenko, and worked as

21 Armstrong, pp. 40, 142–150.
22 Fainsod, *How Russia is Ruled* (2nd ed.), p. 328.
23 *Ibid.*, p. 330.

an agronomist after graduation and before 1940, he may well have attended school with Kirichenko. As late as 1959, at 36 years of age, Yermin was the first secretary of a minor Ukrainian raikom, at the same time that Kirichenko was working as cadres secretary in the Central Committee. In that year, however, Yermin was called to work in the Central Committee apparat; and after two years he was appointed second secretary, and, a very short time later, first secretary of the Penza obkom, an important agricultural oblast in the Russian Republic.[24] In the light of the fact that Kirichenko himself was removed as a Central Committee secretary while Yermin was still in its employ, it must be concluded that the latter's career was not entirely dependent upon Kirichenko, although it may have been assisted by him.

Doroshenko's career appears to be more closely associated with Kirichenko's than Yermin's career was. In 1944, when Kirichenko served as cadres secretary in the Ukraine, Doroshenko was brought from an academic career as director of an agricultural technicum to work as head of an oblast agricultural administration. Shortly after Kirichenko was sent to head the Odessa Party organization, Doroshenko became a secretary in the Kirivograd obkom. Two years after Kirichenko returned to Kiev as second secretary of the Ukrainian Central Committee, Doroshenko was brought there to direct the Ukrainian Central Committee's Agricultural Department. After two more years, when Kirichenko was promoted to full membership in the Presidium of the CC CPSU, Doroshenko moved to Moscow as Head of the Central Committee Agriculture Department for Union Republics. Shortly before Kirichenko's removal, Doroshenko was sent back to the Ukraine as an obkom first secretary. As in the case of Yermin, so Doroshenko's career illustrates the complexity of relationships among the Soviet elite. Apparently Doroshenko either found another spokesman or he rose again on his own merits, for in 1965 he became Ukrainian minister of agriculture. On the basis of these data, the most positive conclusion permissible is that ties arising from school associations are not only infrequent among obkom first secretaries, but probably tenuous at best when they do exist.

Leonid Brezhnev completed his training at the Dneprodzher-

24 *Who's Who in the USSR 1965/1966*, p. 955.

zhinsk Metallurgical Institute in 1935. Georgiy Yenyutin and Nikita Tolubeev are the only two first secretaries who also graduated from this Institute, the former in 1932 and the latter in 1951. Comparative analysis of the career patterns of these men indicate no circumstances under which some assistance from Brezhnev on behalf of the others might be reasonably assumed.[25] On the contrary, although Yenyutin had risen to the position of a Deputy Chairman of the Russian Republic Council of Ministers and Tolubeev had served as first secretary of the Dneprodzherzhinsk obkom by the time Brezhnev became first secretary in 1941, by 1966 both had been dropped from the Central Committee and demoted from their high positions.

While school ties do not appear to be a significant factor in the careers of obkom first secretaries, there is evidence to suggest that personal affiliations arising out of career associations may be important elements in explaining the rise of some individuals.[26] These relationships may have their root either in associations formed during early work experiences or in acquaintances made after entering full-time Party work. In the former case a common home town, or job in the same city may be evidence of personal associations, particularly if supported by other evidence of later career associations. In the latter case, the rapid rise of one individual following the promotion of a second to the same area may indicate the existence of personal affiliations.

A comparison of the career pattern of Leonid Brezhnev with all others in the sample indicates that personal affiliations with Brezhnev may have been a factor in the careers of 11 obkom first secretaries. Leonid Brezhnev was first secretary of the Dnepropetrovsk obkom in the Ukraine from 1947 to 1950. While in this capacity, Aleksey Vatchenko, a former physics and math teacher and graduate of Dnepropetrovsk University, then serving as head of the Dnepropetrovsk city department of education, was called to full-time Party work. After 11 years in various Party positions, and following Brezhnev's appointment as a Central Committee secretary, Vatchenko became first secretary of the Khmelnitsky obkom. The continuance over an extended period of some kind

25 *Ibid.*, pp. 142, 861, 953–954.

26 This point has been made by others; however, it is raised here in terms of its specific significance in the careers of obkom first secretaries. See Armstrong, p. 147.

of personal affiliation is suggested by the appointment of Vatchenko as first secretary of the Dnepropetrovsk obkom in 1965 and his election to full membership in the Central Committee at the 23rd Party Congress. [27]

In 1954 Brezhnev became second, and then first secretary of the Kazakh Central Committee. During his two-year stay in Kazakhstan, he appears to have significantly advanced the careers of eight persons who later became obkom first secretaries. Masymkhan Beysebaev, an agronomist, had held various agricultural managerial positions before becoming first secretary of the Kochetav obkom (Kazakhstan) in 1950. Shortly after Brezhnev's arrival, Beysebaev moved to a major position as Deputy Chairman of the Kazakh Council of Ministers. Evidence that this was more than coincidence is suggested by the appointment of Beysebaev as Chairman of the Kazakh Council of Ministers shortly after Brezhnev became first secretary of the CPSU in 1964. This seems particularly significant considering that, after serving as Chairman for only four months, in 1962 he was demoted to First Deputy Premier, resuming his old position only after Khrushchev's removal.[28]

Rakhim Baygaliev worked in a variety of engineering and managerial positions before 1955. In that year, however, he was brought to Kazakhstan as a Deputy Chairman of the Council of Ministers. In 1963, when Brezhnev resumed his position as a Central Committee Secretary, Baygaliev was appointed a secretary of the Kazakh Central Committee.[29]

Two officials given their first major Party assignments by Brezhnev in the Kazakh Central Committee apparatus later became obkom first secretaries. Before 1955, Aleksey Neklyudov held minor Party posts, serving last as first secretary of the Alma-Ata gorkom. After four years as head of the Kazakh Central Committee's department of Party organs, he became first secretary of the East Kazakh obkom, a position he holds at present. Vasiliy Liventsov's early career is unknown before his appointment as deputy chairman of an oblispolkom in 1951. In 1955, however, he was brought into the Kazakh Central Committee as a depart-

---

[27] *Who's Who in the USSR 1965/1966*, p. 901; *Pravda*, April 9, 1966.
[28] *Ibid.*, p. 112
[29] *Ibid.*, p. 97.

ment head. By 1962 he had become first secretary of the Chimkent obkom (Kazakhstan).[30]

Four men for the first time in their careers became obkom first secretaries in Kazakhstan during Brezhnev's tenure there. In at least two of these cases personal affiliations may have been a factor. Mikhail Roginets began his career in the Ukraine. Between 1945 and 1954 he served as first secretary of the Zhitomir and then Chernigov obkoms. In 1955 he was assigned as first secretary of the Kochetav obkom in Kazakhstan. After an uneven career, as Kazakh minister of Sovkhozes, minister of agriculture, and member of the Kazakh Central Committee's agricultural bureau, he again became minister of agriculture in 1965. Although no direct relationship to Brezhnev is demonstrable here, the facts that both are from the Ukraine, that Roginets moved to Kazakhstan at the time Brezhnev became Republic first secretary, and that the former regained his position of minister of agriculture only in 1965 suggest personal affiliations may have been significant.[31]

Sabir Niyazbekov worked as a department head, secretary, and then second secretary of a Kazakh obkom between 1941 and 1956. Prior to Brezhnev's appointment as a Central Committee secretary Niyazbekov became first secretary of the West Kazakhstan obkom. Brezhnev's influence is suggested in his appointment as chairman of the Presidium of the Kazakh Supreme Soviet and his election to candidate status in the Central Committee in 1966, after ten years as first secretary.[32]

Personal affiliations with Brezhnev may also have been a factor in rescuing a former Moscow obkom first secretary, Ivan Kapitonov, from relative obscurity as first secretary of the Ivanovo obkom by his appointment as head of the Central Committee department of Party organs for the RSFSR in 1964, and his subsequent election as a Central Committee secretary.[33]

While this analysis does suggest, then, that personal affiliations may be a significant factor in the careers of some obkom secretaries, the very tenuousness of these relationships not only makes their study difficult but makes any conclusions based on such study

30 *Ibid.*, p. 496.
31 *Ibid.*, p. 698.
32 *Ibid.*, p. 600.
33 *Ibid.*, p. 339.

*Table 19: Year of Completion of Education by Type of Education*

| TYPE OF EDUCATION | PER CENT | | | | | | | |
|---|---|---|---|---|---|---|---|---|
| | 1925–29 | 1930–34 | 1935–39 | 1940–44 | 1945–49 | 1950–54 | 1954–58 | 1959 |
| *Industrial-Technical* | 23.0 | 26.7 | 32.7 | 44.8 | 13.7 | 6.6 | 1[a] | — |
| *Agricultural* | 15.4 | 40.0 | 25.0 | 10.5 | 13.7 | 13.4 | 2 | — |
| *Pedagogical* | 15.4 | 10.0 | 13.4 | 7.9 | — | 6.6 | 1 | — |
| *Higher Party School* | — | — | 1.9 | 13.2 | 63.6 | 53.4 | 1 | 2 |
| *Party* | 15.4 | 13.3 | 7.7 | 2.6 | 9.0 | 13.4 | 1 | — |
| *Other* | 30.8 | 10.0 | 19.3 | 21.0 | — | 6.6 | — | 1 |
| *Per cent* | 100.0 | 100.0 | 100.0 | 100.0 | 100.0 | 100.0 | | |
| *(N)* | (13) | (30) | (52) | (40) | (22) | (15) | (6) | (3) |

[a] Numerals are used in the last two columns because the numbers involved are too small to make meaningful percentages.

highly suspect. Rather than devote excessive energy to an analysis of such factors it may be more useful to describe the objective characteristics of those who have become obkom first secretaries in order to discern any underlying patterns. It is to such an analysis that we now return.

Table 19 shows the period during which the obkom secretaries in the 1950 to 1960 period completed their education. The figures indicate the percentage distribution of those completing their education in each period by type of education. By far the largest single group of secretaries—52 individuals or nearly 29 per cent of the total sample—completed their education in the latter half of the thirties. The next largest groups consist of those who finished their schooling either during the first half of the thirties or during World War Two. The men who came to occupy the major positions among the middle-level elite in the Khrushchev era, then, came of age from the early years of industrialization and collectivization to the even more strenuous years of the war. While this group obviously was aware of the purges in the late thirties, they probably were too young, for the most part, to have experienced directly the morally debilitating effects of these events. In fact, this generation of future Party officials may well have been more influenced by the positive features of this era than their elders who rose to positions of influence during or as a result of the purges.

Significant variations are evident in the types of education acquired by future secretaries in each period. In the earliest period (1925 to 1929) the education appearing most frequently was either military or economic-planning, followed by industrial-technical. Future obkom secretaries graduating during the First Five-Year Plan most frequently had an agricultural training, but again followed by an industrial-technical one. During the following two periods, however, an industrial-technical education became by far the most common training among the next generation of obkom secretaries. The most important type of education in the periods after 1945 is the Higher Party School within the Central Committee. The role of the Higher Party School is discussed in detail on pp. 160–164. These figures, then, show a gradual trend in recruitment of Party workers away from those with more general education toward technically trained men as the industrialization drive gained momentum.

CAREER PATTERNS

Most of those with a future as an obkom secretary enter the ranks of the Communist Party either during the last years of school or shortly following graduation. Table 20 provides data on the age at which this group entered the Party, and age on entry into full-time Party work.

The overwhelming majority of future Party officials enter the Party at a young age, usually at less than 25. Only 15 of a sample of 208 who later became first secretaries entered after age 30. A significant group joined the Party while still in their teens. Unfortunately, no precise data are available on the age of entry of all Party members. However, extrapolations from data on delegates to the 23rd Party Congress appear to confirm that those who became obkom first secretaries between 1950 and 1966 entered the Party at a considerably younger age than the delegates as a whole. The secretaries joined the Party at an average age of slightly more than 24 years. Among the delegates, 30.4 per cent have a Party tenure of less than ten years, yet only 8 per cent are under 30, whereas 32

Table 20: *Distribution of Obkom Secretaries by Age at Entry into the Party,*
*Age at Entry into Full-time Party Work and*
*the Number of Years of Non-Party Work in Between*

| AGE AT ENTRY INTO PARTY | | | AGE ON ENTERING PARTY WORK | | | YEARS OF NON-PARTY WORK | | |
| --- | --- | --- | --- | --- | --- | --- | --- | --- |
| AGE | N | PER CENT | AGE | N | PER CENT | YEARS | N | PER CENT |
| 16–20 | 30 | 14.5 | 18–23 | 9 | 4.9 | 0–4 | 66 | 37.0 |
| 21–25 | 99 | 47.5 | 24–29 | 68 | 37.5 | 5–8 | 44 | 24.7 |
| 26–30 | 64 | 30.7 | 30–35 | 51 | 28.4 | 9–12 | 32 | 17.9 |
| 31–36 | 15 | 7.3 | 36–41 | 32 | 17.7 | 13–16 | 12 | 6.7 |
| | 208 | 100.0 | 42–47 | 10 | 5.5 | 17–20 | 12 | 6.7 |
| | | | 48–55 | 11 | 6.0 | 21–24 | 8 | 4.7 |
| | | | | 181 | 100.0 | 25–28 | 4 | 2.3 |
| | | | | | | | 178 | 100.0 |

per cent are between 31 and 40.[34] This means that the average age
at which the delegates with a tenure of less than ten years joined
the Party is very probably near 30. Although these latter figures refer to the period of the late fifties and early sixties, while the data
on the secretaries refers to practice during roughly the thirties and
forties, the differential seems sufficiently great to justify the conclusion that future oblast Party secretaries enter the Party at a significantly younger age than the broader segment of the elite represented
at the Party Congress. This conclusion is further reinforced by
the fact that although many of those later to become first secretaries
came of age during the early or mid-thirties large numbers were
forced to wait until the end of the decade to join the Party. From
1933 through 1938 the Party was virtually closed to new members. Yet, fully 39 per cent of the 214 secretaries for whom relevant
information is available joined the Party in the years 1939 and
1940. If it were not for the purges, then, the average age of entry
into the Party would have been considerably lower for this group.

Obtaining a Party membership card meant immediate entry
into the Party apparatus as a full-time official for very few of
those later to become first secretaries. For most, as Table 20 indicates, a period of work outside the Party apparat ranging from one
to 28 years was the more normal course. Although 37 per cent began
a Party career after the relatively short period of less than four
years, more than 46 per cent worked at some other profession from
five to 12 years after joining the Party before being called into Party
work. On the average, however, the future secretaries were engaged
for eight years in non-Party work prior to undertaking a Party
career.

As might be anticipated from the foregoing, and as Table 20
shows, very few among this group entered Party work before 24
years of age. On the other hand, most had entered Party work before their 35th birthday. For the group as a whole, 32 years of age
represents the average age on undertaking a career in the Party apparatus. While the figures in Table 20 point to an early entry into
the Party and embarking on a Party career prior to age 35 as the
most general pattern followed by those who eventually become
first secretaries, the evidence does not permit the conclusion that a
Party career is closed to those who do not enter the apparatus at

[34] *Pravda,* April 1, 1966.

an early age. In fact, the ranks of the Party apparatus at the regional secretarial level appear to be open to those whose principal career has been along quite different lines. Among the 21 who entered Party work past age 41, eight had had managerial careers in agriculture, below the level of Republic Minister, five had held senior managerial positions in industry, four had risen to ministerial rank through the state bureaucracy, two had followed military careers, and one each had been engaged in academic and trade-union work.

Analysis of the careers of all secretaries prior to their entry into full-time Party work reveals that this group is recruited from a variety of occupational categories. When correlated with type of educational background, however, some persistent patterns can be observed. One of the clearest is that of secretaries with an industrial-technical education who did not attend the Higher Party School. Fifteen of the 39 with this educational background began their careers either in an engineering position in an enterprise, or in a junior managerial position in industry, such as a shop foreman, or section chief. After several positions at this level, some moved directly into Party work, while six held senior managerial positions, or ministerial posts at the Republic or All-Union level prior to holding a Party position.

The most common pattern among those with an agricultural education is to begin work as an agronomist on a State or collective farm, or perhaps in a district agricultural department, followed by one or two senior managerial positions in agriculture, such as head of an oblast agricultural department, or chairman of an oblast agricultural board. This was the early career pattern of 13 of the 26 secretaries with an agricultural education. Among the others with this background, five held academic positions, three engaged in Komsomol work, and two held positions at the All-Union or Republic ministerial level relating to agriculture. The early careers of those with an industrial-technical or an agricultural education who later attended the Higher Party School are, for the most part, similar to those for their respective groups, except that nearly half of these latter served as Komsomol officials just prior to entering Party work. The early career of all secretaries with a pedagogical education, including those later attending the Higher Party School, form a somewhat different pattern. Half of the 16 who graduated from pedagogical institutes began their careers in academic positions, usually as primary school teachers. Five others went directly into Komsomol work. While this latter group entered directly into Party positions after holding several Komsomol posts, among the former group one worked as a journalist, a second in the security organs, and a third in the district Soviet apparatus just prior to entering full-time Party work.

Those whose only higher education consists of training at the Higher Party School later in their careers display yet other early occupational patterns. Five of the 19 whose careers have been traced back to secondary school entered directly into Komsomol work; three worked for some time as skilled factory workers prior to entering Party work in such minor posts as secretary of a factory shop organization; the early careers of three others consisted entirely of military service in the ranks, followed by minor positions in either the Party or Soviet apparatus.

Three primary patterns emerge from analysis of the early positions of secretaries with all other educational backgrounds. Nearly all of those with a veterinary, or only a secondary education held low level managerial positions in agriculture. In two cases this was followed by posts in agricultural management at the regional level, while the five others with these backgrounds went directly from their subordinate managerial posts into Party work. A second career pattern followed by those with military, economic-planning, aviation, or medical training consists of a number of posts connected with Komsomol work from the time of graduation until beginning full-time Party work. Although four persons in the sample graduated from military schools only two pursued military careers; these two entered Party work after extended military service. Among the early occupations of the relatively few individuals who did not follow the patterns indicated above are the following: work in the district, city, or oblast apparatus, including the posts of Chairman or Deputy Chairman; various trade-union posts, such as Chairman of the oblast Trade-Union Council; work in the ministerial hierarchy, including the positions of USSR or Republic Minister; several kinds of journalism positions, particularly editor of the oblast Party newspaper; and finally a few individuals entered Party work after holding posts in the security organs.

Although the early positions held by obkom secretaries repre-

Table 21: Average Age at Entry into Party Work
and Average Age at Initial First Secretaryship
by Type of Education

| EDUCATION | AVERAGE AGE AT ENTRY INTO PARTY WORK | | AVERAGE AGE AT INITIAL FIRST SECRETARYSHIP | |
|---|---|---|---|---|
| | N | YEARS | N | YEARS |
| Industrial-Technical | 43 | 34.7 | 43 | 46.0 |
| Industrial-Technical and H.P.S.[a] | 8 | 31.3 | 8 | 41.4 |
| Agricultural | 29 | 36.3 | 29 | 45.9 |
| Agricultural and H.P.S. | 14 | 32.1 | 14 | 45.0 |
| Pedagogical | 10 | 30.9 | 10 | 40.2 |
| Pedagogical and H.P.S. | 7 | 27.8 | 7 | 41.2 |
| H.P.S. alone | 26 | 29.0 | 26 | 44.8 |
| Party[b] | 9 | 29.3 | 9 | 44.0 |
| Other | 9 | 33.2 | 9 | 44.0 |
| | 155 | | 155 | |

[a] H.P.S. refers to the Higher Party School of the CPSU Central Committee.
[b] Party education includes all forms of Party organized instruction except for the central Higher Party School.

sent a large cross section of the numerically significant occupations found among the intelligentsia, there are several major kinds of professions from which no future obkom secretaries have been recruited. Among these are the arts, including literature,[35] practicing lawyers and men of other judicial professions, practicing doctors, and most other fields of natural science. Yet, in terms of the priorities of the Soviet political system, emphasizing industrial and agricultural development backed by extensive propaganda and education, the early career patterns of obkom secretaries do appear to constitute appropriate preparation for future Party leaders. At the same time, to the extent that early career patterns are related to later perceptions of social and political priorities any radical change in elite goals is not to be anticipated.

The age at which future obkom secretaries enter Party work on a full-time basis, and the age at which they first are appointed as chief Party official in an oblast, varies significantly with educational background, as the data in Tables 21 and 22 demonstrate.

[35] Salchak Kalbakkhorekovich Toka may be considered an exception to this statement. A Tuvinian, Toka has been engaged in political work among the Tuvinians since 1929. At the same time, however, he has published a number of essays, and plays. He is at present a board member of the RSFSR Union of Writers. *Who's Who in the USSR 1965/1966*, p. 859.

*Table 22: Age at Entry into Party Work and Age at Initial First Secretaryship by Type of Education*

| EDUCATION | AGE OF ENTRY INTO PARTY WORK PERCENTAGE | | | | | | AGE AT INITIAL FIRST SECRETARYSHIP PERCENTAGE | | | | |
|---|---|---|---|---|---|---|---|---|---|---|---|
| | 21–25 | 26–30 | 31–35 | 36–40 | 41–45 | 46– | 31–35 | 36–40 | 41–45 | 46–50 | 51 AND OVER |
| Industrial-Technical | 5.5 | 16.4 | 28.5 | 26.9 | 27.8 | 53.8 | 20.0 | 22.3 | 16.7 | 26.9 | 52.2 |
| Industrial-Technical and H.P.S. | — | 7.3 | 6.1 | 3.9 | — | — | — | 11.2 | 3.0 | 4.8 | — |
| Agricultural | 11.2 | 9.0 | 12.2 | 23.0 | 38.9 | 23.1 | — | 5.5 | 19.8 | 26.9 | 13.1 |
| Agricultural and H.P.S. | 5.5 | 12.7 | 4.0 | 11.5 | 5.5 | — | — | 2.7 | 7.5 | 12.2 | — |
| Pedagogical | 5.5 | 7.3 | 6.1 | 7.7 | — | — | — | 13.8 | 6.0 | — | — |
| Pedagogical and H.P.S. | 11.2 | 7.3 | 2.0 | — | — | — | 20.0 | — | 7.5 | — | — |
| H.P.S alone | 33.3 | 10.9 | 20.4 | 7.7 | 5.5 | — | — | 13.8 | 16.7 | 17.0 | 13.1 |
| Party | 5.5 | 7.3 | 6.1 | 3.9 | — | — | — | 8.4 | 3.0 | — | 4.3 |
| Other | 22.3 | 21.8 | 14.2 | 15.3 | 22.3 | 23.1 | 60.0 | 22.3 | 19.8 | 12.2 | 17.3 |
| Per cent | 100.0 | 100.0 | 100.0 | 100.0 | 100.0 | 100.0 | 100.0 | 100.0 | 100.0 | 100.0 | 100.0 |
| (N) | (18) | (56) | (49) | (26) | (18) | (13) | (5) | (36) | (66) | (41) | (23) |

Although the average age of entry into Party work for the entire sample is slightly over 32, those with a pedagogical education who later attended the Higher Party School began full-time Party work at the very young age of just under 28, while those with a straight agricultural training did not enter Party work until past 36, on the average. These figures appear to support the hypothesis that a pedagogical education is one of the most direct paths to a career in the Party apparatus. Others entering into Party work at an early age include those who have little formal education beyond a secondary one, but who after entering some form of Party work are sent through special Party organized training courses, either in the regional Party schools, in special seminars and courses organized by the Central Committee, or in the central Higher Party School. The career of Ivan Timofeevich Grishin appears to be quite typical of this group.

Those with an industrial-technical or an agricultural education enter Party work at the oldest age, except for the small group with a military education two of whom entered Party work at more than 50 years of age. To put it differently, those with an industrial-technical or an agricultural education are considerably more likely than those with other kinds of education to have spent sufficient time in an industrial or an agricultural career to have been influenced by the distinctive styles or viewpoints of these occupational groups. The lower age of entry into Party work of those with an industrial-technical or agricultural education who also attended the Higher Party School is doubtless a reflection of the fact that most of these individuals attended only technical secondary schools without completing a higher education prior to entering Party work. Although conclusive data are not available it is probable that these men are drawn into Party work rather early, in spite of their limited qualifications for industrial or agricultural management, on the basis of their high aptitude for Party work.

While there is a considerable difference between the highest and the lowest age at which various educational groups enter Party work, there is far less differential in terms of the age at which an individual first comes to head an oblast Party organization. The largest difference is that between those with a pedagogical education who averaged slightly more than 40 years of age and those with an industrial-technical training who became first secretaries at an average age of 46. The average for all types of education is 44½ years. This means that the normal career pattern of future obkom secretaries includes about eight years non-Party work followed by somewhat more than 12 years in Party posts before acquiring sufficient experience for a trial period as the principal political figure for an entire region.

Rather than the diversity evident in the non-Party careers of future obkom secretaries, once these men enter full-time Party work the patterns of training and testing in Party leadership positions tend to be quite similar. The most common Party career among those with an industrial-technical education begins with the post of secretary of a factory primary Party organization, the basic Party unit, followed by an appointment either as first secretary of a district Party organization (raikom), or a position in the Central Committee apparatus, such as Central Committee representative to a particular factory or construction project. Most frequently this position is followed by a term as first secretary of a city Party committee (gorkom), although other common posts at this juncture include obkom or Republic central committee department head; direct appointment as secretary of an obkom; or, less commonly, assignment as deputy chairman or chairman of regional Soviet executive committee (oblispolkom). For the majority the gateway to a first secretaryship is service as an obkom second secretary, although six of 39[36] with an industrial-technical education did serve as an oblispolkom chairman just prior to their initial first secretaryship.

The patterns of Party work leading to a first secretaryship for those with an agricultural education show even less diversity than in the case of the industrial-technical group. With few exceptions these men begin their Party careers in either the obkom or Republic Central Committee apparatus, usually in the agriculture department. Following this, and just prior to appointment to the top regional post, more than half of this group serves as a chairman of an oblispolkom, while about a third hold the post of obkom second secretary. The careers of those with a pedagogical[37] or only a Higher

[36] This figure includes all of this category for whom the relevant information is available.
[37] As used here this category includes those with a pedagogical education who also attended the Higher Party School.

Party School education differ little from the agricultural group. The principal differences reflect their training. Thus, while working in the obkom apparatus most of those in the former groups hold positions in such departments as agitation and propaganda or Party organs. Thus a pedagogical or Higher Party School education—when it is the only *higher* education received—appears to lead to positions in what are commonly known as the staff agencies.[38] From these staff positions, the majority of this group moves into the post of obkom second secretary, while others work either as chairman of an oblispolkom or, as in the case of four with only a Higher Party School education, to a position in the Central Committee apparat. From these positions, the next step is appointment as first secretary of an obkom.

The role of the Higher Party School has so far been discussed as it relates to the career patterns of those who later became first secretaries. Unlike the other kinds of education, however, Higher Party School training is not usually undertaken until some time after an individual has entered full-time Party work.[39] Table 23 indicates the juncture in their careers when Party secretaries studied at the Higher Party School.

For most obkom secretaries, training at this school comes only after an individual has attained a position of some importance in either the Party or the State bureaucracy. Nearly 60 per cent of the sample held major Party or State posts at the regional, republic, or national level before being admitted to the Higher Party School. These men had doubtless already proven their capabilities and demonstrated their potential for leading Party work at the oblast level. Party education at this point appears to provide the opportunity for already proven men to acquire the higher education that they lack. The necessity for advanced training in their careers derives from what appears to be a Party policy of requiring a higher education of all leading officials, including obkom first secretaries.[40]

Those who held minor posts just prior to entering the Higher Party School were younger than the average of slightly less than

---

[38] Armstrong, p. 72.

[39] For a discussion of the general role of the Higher Party School see Chapter 8, esp. pp. 185–188.

[40] "The Preparation of Party and Soviet Workers," *Partiinaia Zhizn'*, No. 14 (1956), p. 38. See also, *Pravda*, April 1, 1966.

*Table 23: Place of Higher Party School in the Career Patterns of Obkom First Secretaries*

| POSITION | PRIOR TO H.P.S. | | AFTER H.P.S. | |
|---|---|---|---|---|
| | N | PER CENT | N | PER CENT |
| *Regional Party* | 22 | 46.9 | 32 | 68.1 |
| INCLUDING: | | | | |
| Obkom first secretary | 3 | | 6 | |
| Obkom or Republic Central Committee secretary | 8 | | 11 | |
| Obkom or Republic Central Committee apparatus | 5 | | 5 | |
| CPSU Central Committee apparatus | 1 | | 6 | |
| *Local Party* | 5 | 10.6 | 4 | 8.6 |
| INCLUDING: | | | | |
| Gorkom first secretary | 1 | | 1 | |
| Raikom first secretary | 1 | | 1 | |
| *State* | 6 | 12.7 | 6 | 12.8 |
| INCLUDING: | | | | |
| Republic Council of Ministers Chairman | 2 | | 1 | |
| Oblispolkom Chairman or Deputy | 2 | | 5 | |
| Republic Minister | 2 | | 0 | |
| *Economic* | 2 | 4.2 | — | 0 |
| *Komsomol* | 6 | 12.8 | 1 | 2.1 |
| *Military* | 4 | 8.5 | 2 | 4.2 |
| *Journalism* | 0 | | 2 | 4.2 |
| *Student* | 1 | 2.1 | 0 | |
| *Unknown* | 1 | 2.1 | 0 | |
| | 47 | 100.0 | 47 | 100.0 |

37 years for all those attending the school, with four exceptions.[41] These men were 38, 39, and two were 40 respectively. One was a raikom first secretary; the second, a gorkom first secretary; while two held other minor Party posts.[42] An examination of the subsequent careers of this group provides some indication of the particularly high political capabilities these men must have displayed to be called to the Higher Party School from relatively obscure positions. The fact that all but two of the 19 in this group have held positions

[41] This figure refers to age at completion of Higher Party School. Since some of the sample completed a shorter correspondence course, this figure is used to make all the data comparable.

[42] The specific positions held are not known in this case.

of major importance at the oblast level or above since at least the early fifties, usually as first or second secretary of an obkom, or chairman of an oblispolkom, together with the fact that all but one continue at present to hold positions at least at the level of obkom first secretary suggests that these are men of considerable political and administrative talent. Among those who have risen successfully beyond the level of obkom secretary are the following: Kirill Mazurov, candidate member since 1957 and full member since 1965 of the Central Committee Politburo, as well as a First Deputy Chairman of the USSR Council of Ministers; Dmitry Polyansky, a Khrushchev protégé and member of the Politburo who, after the latter's removal, also became a First Deputy Chairman of the USSR Council of Ministers; two Republic first secretaries—Ivan Bodyul in Moldavia and Turakun Usubaliev in Kirghizia—and two Republic Central Committee secretaries—Vasiliy Drozdenko in the Ukraine, and Sergei Pritytsky in Belorussia. The other members of national minorities included in this group have risen to positions of some distinction. Rakhmankul Kurbanov, a Uzbek, after serving ten years as an obkom secretary assumed his present post as Chairman of the Uzbek Council of Ministers in 1961. After seven years as first secretary of other Belorussian obkoms, Ivan Polyakov was appointed first secretary of the Minsk obkom in 1964, and elected to the Belorussian Central Committee Presidium a year later. Semen Islyukov, a Chuvash, among the most highly educated of obkom secretaries, holds the degree of Candidate of Legal Science.[43] He appears to have been selected at an early age for the leadership of his countrymen. Immediately upon completing the Kazan Institute of Law, located across the Volga from the Chuvash Autonomous Republic, Islyukov was sent to the Higher Party School, from which he graduated at 26 years of age. After six years of Party work, he was sent back to school, this time to a postgraduate course in the Central Committee Academy of Social Science. Within a year after receiving his candidate's degree, Islyukov was appointed to his present position as Chuvash obkom first secretary.[44] From this analysis it may be concluded that entry into the Higher Party School at a young age and frequently without a complete higher education is possible only for those of exceptional abilities.

[43] A Candidate's degree in the Soviet Union is the rough equivalent of the American Ph.D.
[44] *Who's Who in the USSR*, p. 320.

There is some evidence that the opportunity for rapid advancement at a young age for the present generation of young Party activists will be more restricted than it was for those now holding positions of influence. In 1956 the Central Committee adopted a resolution altering the conditions for entry into the Higher Party School. For the past decade only those who already possess a higher education have been admitted to the central school. In addition, all candidates for admission must be under 40 years of age.[45] If these restrictions had been applied to the generation that rose to prominence during the fifties and sixties, 37 future secretaries would have been affected by the education requirements and nine by the age limitations. Among those lacking the present educational requirements at the time of their admission to the Higher Party School are Shkol'nikov, former Stalingrad first secretary; Mazurov; Pritytsky; Antonov Kochinian, the present first secretary of the Armenian Central Committee; and Ivan Grushetsky, a secretary of the Ukrainian Central Committee. It is, of course, impossible to determine the actual impact of these restrictions on the next generation. Considering the rapidly rising level of education in the Party as a whole—from 1962 to 1964 the percentage of all Party members with a complete higher education rose from 13.7 to 15.0—and among the elite in particular—at the 22nd Congress in 1961 just over 50 per cent had a complete higher education, while the figure for the 23rd Congress was more than 55 per cent—it is doubtful that the present education and age requirements actually affect the upward mobility of many highly skilled Party workers.[46]

When the data on education for all secretaries are correlated with the year in which each became an obkom first secretary for the first time, some underlying patterns reflecting leadership recruitment policies become evident. Since Table 24 includes only those who held the position of obkom first secretary in the period since 1950, the figures for the last three columns are the most significant. Yet it is interesting that the smallest proportion of those who began their secretarial careers in the late forties and continued into the fifties have an industrial-technical education, while the largest percentage consists of those who completed either

45 *SPR* (1957), pp. 410–413.
46 *Pravda*, April 1, 1966.

*Table 24: Year of Initial First Secretaryship by Type of Education*

| EDUCATION | PERCENTAGE | | | | |
|---|---|---|---|---|---|
| | 1940–45 | 1946–50 | 1951–55 | 1956–60 | 1961–66 |
| *Industrial-Technical* | — | 4.7 | 24.0 | 27.8 | 24.6 |
| *Industrial-Technical and H.P.S.* | — | 9.5 | 5.6 | 3.7 | 6.8 |
| *Agricultural* | — | 9.5 | 12.9 | 18.5 | 24.6 |
| *Agricultural and H.P.S.* | — | — | 9.3 | 5.6 | 7.8 |
| *Pedagogical* | — | — | 1.8 | 5.6 | 9.8 |
| *Pedagogical and H.P.S.* | — | 14.4 | 5.6 | 3.7 | 1.9 |
| *Higher Party School alone* | — | 19.0 | 12.9 | 16.6 | 6.8 |
| *Other* | 100.0 | 42.9 | 27.8 | 18.5 | 17.7 |
| *Total* | 100.0 | 100.0 | 100.0 | 100.0 | 100.0 |
| *(N)* | (4) | (21) | (54) | (54) | (51) |

the Higher Party School or another kind of Party education, included in the "other" category.

In the first period after Stalin's death nearly 30 per cent of those recruited as first secretaries had an industrial-technical background, and over 20 per cent an agricultural education. In this period of gradually increasing concern for technical competence among the regional Party elite the number of those recruited into this group with nontechnical backgrounds considerably decreased. During the period of Khrushchev's rise to preeminence, accompanied by extensive increases in the Party's role in industrial management, there occurred only a slight increase in the percentage of new obkom first secretaries with an industrial-technical background. At the same time, probably reflecting Khrushchev's personal interest and concern with agricultural problems in general and the Virgin Lands program in particular the percentage of new recruits to the post of obkom first secretary with a higher agricultural education showed a considerable increase. At the same time the number of secretaries with only a secondary agricultural education who later attended the Higher Party School declined measurably.

During the period since 1961, which saw serious agricultural crises as well as the reestablishment of the ministerial form of industrial administration, not to mention the removal of Khrushchev himself, further shifts in recruitment patterns occurred. Not only did the percentage of agricultural specialists increase once more, but the number of industrial specialists actually declined. The significant increase in the proportion of secretaries with a pedagogical background may reflect the increasing concern for ideological training shown by the Central Committee in several major decrees during 1962.[47] The further decrease in the per cent of new recruits with only a Higher Party School education is a further indication of the general spread of higher education among the Party elite.

The average age of obkom first secretaries has been gradually increasing over the past decade. This has occurred in the Russian Republic as well as among the first secretaries of Republic central committees, autonomous republics and autonomous oblasts, as shown by Table 25. The average age of all obkom first secretaries has increased from less than 46 in 1955 to more than 52 in 1966. This trend toward a gradual increase in the age of the elite was also noted in Armstrong's study of the Ukrainian elite of an earlier period.[48] The reasons for this occurrence are partially revealed in Table 24, showing that between 1946 and 1955 a whole new generation had entered the ranks of obkom first secretaries as the result of a very substantial turnover during this period. Table 25 details the younger age level of these new recruits. The fact that the average age increased by only six years in the course of a decade suggests on the one hand, the new generation proved itself relatively competent, and on the other hand substantial numbers of new and younger men replaced others of the older generation at more or less regular intervals. Table 26 provides additional evidence on the durability of the generation that rose to the top regional positions after 1950.

TENURE

The average total time spent as obkom first secretary, including service at one or more places in the same capacity, for the 167

47 *SPR* (1963), pp. 429–446.
48 Armstrong, pp. 20–22.

Table 25: Age Distribution of Obkom First Secretaries, 1955–1966

| AGE | RUSSIAN REPUBLIC PERCENTAGE | | | | | UNION-REPUBLICS[a] PERCENTAGE | | | | |
|---|---|---|---|---|---|---|---|---|---|---|
| | 1955 | 1958 | 1961 | 1964 | 1966 | 1955 | 1958 | 1961 | 1964 | 1966 |
| 32–35 | — | — | — | — | — | — | — | 1.2 | — | — |
| 36–39 | — | — | 3.5 | — | — | 12.2 | 1.6 | 1.2 | 2.8 | 2.0 |
| 40–43 | 17.2 | 5.1 | 12.5 | 5.2 | 4.2 | 18.6 | 16.9 | 7.5 | 3.9 | 6.1 |
| 44–47 | 31.4 | 28.2 | 19.8 | 12.0 | 4.0 | 28.5 | 30.5 | 27.9 | 18.4 | 12.3 |
| 48–51 | 31.4 | 28.2 | 37.5 | 31.0 | 20.5 | 26.5 | 25.7 | 31.9 | 28.9 | 20.4 |
| 52–55 | 17.2 | 33.4 | 16.0 | 32.9 | 44.8 | 14.2 | 22.0 | 20.2 | 19.7 | 30.6 |
| 56–59 | 2.8 | 5.1 | 10.7 | 17.2 | 22.5 | — | 3.3 | 7.5 | 19.7 | 12.3 |
| 60– | — | — | — | 1.7 | 4.0 | — | — | 2.5 | 6.6 | 16.3 |
| Totals | 100.0 | 100.0 | 100.0 | 100.0 | 100.0 | 100.0 | 100.0 | 100.0 | 100.0 | 100.0 |
| (N) | (35) | (39) | (56) | (58) | (49) | (49) | (59) | (79) | (76) | (49) |
| Av. Age | 45.9 | 49.3 | 49.2 | 51.5 | 52.8 | 45.6 | 46.8 | 49.0 | 55.6 | 51.4 |

[a] The figures for Union-Republics also include the first secretaries of Autonomous Republics and Autonomous oblasts.

Table 26: Total Tenure of Obkom First Secretaries by Type of Education

| EDUCATION | TOTAL TENURE (*in years*) PERCENTAGE | | | | | | |
|---|---|---|---|---|---|---|---|
| | 1–3 | 4–6 | 7–9 | 10–12 | 13–15 | 16–18 | 19+ |
| *Industrial-Technical* | 48.6 | 26.3 | 17.2 | 14.3 | — | — | — |
| *Industrial-Technical and H.P.S.* | 3.0 | 3.3 | 2.8 | 4.8 | 33.3 | — | — |
| *Agricultural* | 18.2 | 19.7 | 17.2 | 14.3 | — | — | — |
| *Agricultural and H.P.S.* | 3.0 | 9.8 | 5.7 | 9.5 | — | — | — |
| *Pedagogical* | 6.0 | 8.2 | — | 4.8 | — | — | — |
| *Pedagogical and H.P.S.* | 3.0 | 8.2 | 2.8 | — | 16.7 | 20.0 | — |
| *Higher Party School alone* | 3.0 | 6.5 | 22.8 | 33.3 | 16.7 | 20.0 | — |
| *Other* | 15.2 | 18.0 | 31.5 | 19.0 | 33.3 | 60.0 | 100.0 |
| *Total* | 100.0 | 100.0 | 100.0 | 100.0 | 100.0 | 100.0 | 100.0 |
| (N) | (33) | (61) | (35) | (21) | (6) | (5) | (2) |

persons whose age and education are known is 7.8 years. For the 196 men whose education is unknown, however, the average total tenure is considerably shorter, 4.9 years. This yields a combined average of 6.3 years total tenure for all obkom first secretaries since 1950. While these averages provide a general picture of the durability of the post-Stalin generation of obkom first secretaries, significant variations in tenure are evident when the individual data are correlated with education. The most general trend emerging from Table 26 is that the less technical the educational background of an obkom secretary the more likely he is to have a long tenure, if the assumption is accepted that the kinds of education listed become less technical from the industrial-technical through the Higher Party School in the order listed. The average total tenure for each type of education supports this generalization. In ascending order the averages are as follows: industrial-technical, 5.1 years; the same with a Higher Party School training, 6.4 years; agricultural, 5.7, but with Higher Party School, 6.2; pedagogical, 6.2, and when followed by Higher Party School, 7.8 years; and Higher Party School alone, 8.8 years.

Another factor that is highly correlated with the total tenure enjoyed by obkom first secretaries is the age at which this position is first attained. The relationship of age to total tenure is shown in Table 27. Those men who are appointed to head a regional Party organization in their middle or late thirties serve longer, on the average, than those of other age groups. Those who become a first secretary in their early thirties are too few for us to draw mean-

*Table 27: Total Tenure of Obkom First Secretaries by Age at Initial First Secretaryship*

| AGE | TOTAL TENURE (*in years*) PERCENTAGE | | | | | | | TOTAL PER CENT | N | AVERAGE TENURE |
|---|---|---|---|---|---|---|---|---|---|---|
| | 1–3 | 4–6 | 7–9 | 10–12 | 13–15 | 16–18 | 19+ | | | |
| 31–35 | 16.6 | 33.3 | 50.1 | — | — | — | — | 100 | 6 | 6.5 |
| 36–40 | 18.9 | 18.9 | 13.5 | 10.9 | 27.0 | 8.1 | 2.7 | 100 | 37 | 9.9 |
| 41–45 | 9.2 | 29.3 | 32.3 | 16.9 | 7.7 | 3.0 | 1.6 | 100 | 65 | 8.3 |
| 46–50 | 2.7 | 40.5 | 35.1 | 16.3 | 5.4 | — | — | 100 | 37 | 7.4 |
| 51+ | 34.7 | 30.5 | 30.5 | 4.3 | — | — | — | 100 | 23 | 4.9 |

ingful conclusions from, except to note that although three of the six served quite short terms, half did last from seven to nine years as an obkom secretary. Although those who become first secretaries past the age of 40 have a progressively shorter tenure, it is important to note that nearly all of these serve more than three years. If an aspiring Party official does not become an obkom first secretary before the age of 50, his chances of a long tenure are exceedingly small.

While the concept of total tenure is quite useful as an indicator of the "life expectancy" of obkom secretaries, it fails to reveal such important factors as the length served in each individual position, or the number of men who serve more than once as obkom secretary. Tables 28 and 29 fill this gap by showing the distribution of obkom secretaries according to tenure in each first secretaryship.

The average first term tenure of obkom secretaries whose education is known is slightly more than five years; the corresponding figure for those whose training is unknown is just less than four years. The combined average first term tenure for all first secretaries is almost four and one-half years. This is an increase of more than one year above the most nearly comparable figure from Armstrong's study of the Ukrainian elite a decade ago.[49] Once again the data tend to confirm the proposition that the tenure of obkom secretaries, either for total length of service, or for individual position, tends to be highly correlated to the technical level of educational background. The less technical a secretary's training the more likely he is to have an extended tenure as first secretary, in either his first, second, or third secretarial post.

The overwhelming majority of obkom first secretaries hold this post only once during their careers. Slightly less than 36 per cent of those whose educational backgrounds are known were appointed to this position in a second oblast, while just over 25 per cent of those whose training is unknown received a second opportunity. The average tenure of the former group is just above four years, and for the latter somewhat less than four. Only ten per cent of all secretaries occupied this position for a third time; those who did served for an average of three and one-half years.

---

[49] *Ibid.*, pp. 52–53. Armstrong's figure of slightly more than three years is an average for all positions.

*Table 28: Tenure in Years of Obkom First Secretaries by Position and by Education*

| EDUCATION | FIRST POSITION PERCENTAGE | | | SECOND POSITION PERCENTAGE | | | THIRD POSITION[a] | | | FOURTH POSITION[a] |
|---|---|---|---|---|---|---|---|---|---|---|
| | 1–3 | 4–6 | 7+ | 1–3 | 4–6 | 7+ | 1–3 | 4–6 | 7+ | 1–3 |
| Industrial-Technical | 30.0 | 19.8 | 15.3 | 29.0 | 7.4 | — | 2 | — | — | 1 |
| Industrial-Technical and H.P.S. | 5.0 | 6.6 | 4.3 | 3.3 | 3.7 | 2 | — | 1 | 1 | — |
| Agricultural | 16.7 | 18.4 | 13.0 | 9.7 | 22.2 | — | 4 | — | — | 1 |
| Agricultural and H.P.S. | 5.0 | 10.5 | 4.3 | 9.7 | 3.7 | 1 | 2 | 1 | — | — |
| Pedagogical | 6.6 | 5.2 | 2.2 | 6.4 | 3.7 | — | — | — | — | — |
| Pedagogical and H.P.S. | 5.0 | 3.9 | 2.2 | — | 7.4 | — | — | — | — | 2 |
| H.P.S. alone | 8.4 | 17.2 | 17.3 | 19.4 | 22.2 | 1 | 2 | 2 | — | — |
| Other | 23.3 | 18.4 | 41.4 | 22.5 | 29.7 | 2 | 2 | 2 | 2 | 1 |
| Total | 100.0 | 100.0 | 100.0 | 100.0 | 100.0 | | | | | |
| (N) | (60) | (75) | (46) | (31) | (27) | (6) | (12) | (6) | (3) | (5) |

a Numbers are used in these columns because quantities are too small for percentages to be meaningful.

*Table 29: Tenure of Obkom First Secretaries by Positions (Education Unknown)*

| TENURE (in years) | FIRST POSITION | SECOND POSITION | THIRD POSITION[a] | FOURTH POSITION[a] |
|---|---|---|---|---|
| 1–3 | 56.1 | 59.5 | 5 | 3 |
| 4–6 | 32.6 | 28.6 | 5 | — |
| 7+ | 11.3 | 11.9 | 2 | — |
| Per cent | 100.0 | 100.0 | | |
| (N) | (196) | (42) | (12) | (3) |
| Average Tenure | 3.7 | 3.7 | 4.0 | 2.0 |

[a] Numbers are used in these columns because quantities are too small for percentages to be meaningful.

The few persons, less than three per cent of the total, holding a fourth first secretaryship remained in this post an average of one and a half years.

PROMOTION PATTERNS

The reasons for the very high turnover of secretaries after an initial appointment are rather complex. The analysis of the role and responsibilities of the first secretary discussed in Chapter 7 provides part of the answer. The demands made by the center upon the regional Party leaders are exceedingly high. The successful first secretary must be a skilled manager, capable of making decisions that result in concrete economic achievements in both agriculture and industry. At the same time he must display a keen political sense enabling him to establish and maintain relationships with a successful patron while not aligning himself so closely that he is left without allies if his patron should suffer a setback. In addition, the successful obkom secretary must create a sufficiently cohesive network of mutual relationships among the leading officials of the oblast that his inevitable errors and violations of established rules may be kept from the watchful eyes of his superiors. Yet, at the same time, the appearance of meaningful criticism and self-criticism must be maintained to avoid charges of creating a "family-circle."[50] In the face of these demands it should not be at all surprising to find many men removed after a short term because they lacked some of these talents.

Of course, another explanation may be that those who are the best managers, or who are the most highly skilled politicians are promoted to more responsible positions after a relatively brief experience as obkom first secretary, while those of more mediocre abilities are left as obkom first secretaries for a relatively long time. If the first proposition is valid, if those removed after a short time fail to display the requisite abilities, then it would be expected that most of those eliminated after a short period as obkom first secretary would face demotion. Conversely, most of those with long tenures would receive promotions or transfers to positions of similar scope and responsibility. On the other hand, if the second proposition more accurately describes the situation, most of those with a short tenure should be promoted and the majority of those with a long tenure demoted. Table 30 organizes the data on all those not presently obkom first secretaries.

Considering the totals first, it is obvious that nearly 55 per cent of all those who completed terms as obkom first secretary from 1950 to 1966 failed to be promoted to higher positions so far as is known. On the other hand, nearly one quarter were promoted to more important posts, while about a fifth were transferred to positions at about the same level of responsibility as an obkom first secretary.[51]

When the data are examined in terms of the percentage of the entire group promoted, transferred, or demoted for each period of tenure it is evident that neither hypothesis is entirely validated nor repudiated. Among those with a short tenure slightly more than half were either promoted or transferred, but just less than half were probably demoted. Evidently, a short tenure as obkom first secretary may lead equally to either a political future or obscurity. For those who serve from five to 12 years, however, demotion is nearly twice as likely as either a transfer or promotion, although beyond 13 years service chances again become nearly fifty-

[50] For a conservative Soviet view of the qualities needed in a successful first secretary, see Kochetov.
[51] See Armstrong, pp. 52–53.

fifty. What these data seem to indicate is that both those of exceptional merit and of quite clearly insufficient abilities are moved out
of regional Party leadership posts after a relatively short period. A
large additional group, possessing neither a powerful patron nor
outstanding leadership qualities, is shifted to posts at a somewhat
comparable level after less than five years as obkom first secretary.
Most of those who remain in the obkom more than five years, while
probably capable of adequate performance at the regional level,
possess markedly reduced promotion potential.

The value of this analysis of the promotion patterns of obkom
first secretaries for an understanding of the nature of Soviet regional
politics is that it points up the highly competitive atmosphere
surrounding the political process described in the previous chapters.
The cost of too many errors in political or economic decisions may
mean demotion to positions of little responsibility, while success
may lead to the pinnacle of power—the Presidium. The critical
question remaining unanswered, however, is just what are the
criteria of success for an obkom first secretary? Certainly ability to
attach oneself to a successful patron must be included. Yet, this
alone is not sufficient. Such relations can be of use only so long
as the patron himself remains in positions of power. The very
regularity of the career and promotion patterns described here
suggest further that the significance of personal relations should
not be overestimated. Indeed, although any conclusions on this
score must be somewhat speculative, the educational and career
backgrounds of obkom secretaries indicate that such objective
factors as the ability to meet industrial and agricultural production
plans, the skill to conduct effective propaganda campaigns, and
the capacity to integrate the activities of thousands of persons so
that general guidance may be exercised over the course of events
are probably, in the post-Stalin period at least, the basic determi-
nants of the degree of success an obkom secretary may achieve.
Analysis of promotion patterns by educational background gives
added confidence to this hypothesis. Although the figures in Table
31 must be used with caution, because of the large number of cases
where educational background is unknown, nevertheless it is significant that the ratio of promotions and transfers to demotions is
quite high for those with an industrial-technical and agricultural

Table 30: *Promotion Patterns After Last First Secretaryship by Total Tenure as Obkom First Secretary*

| FIRST POSITION AFTER LAST OBKOM FIRST SECRETARYSHIP | TOTAL TENURE (*in years*) | | | | TOTALS (% of N) (N = 202) |
|---|---|---|---|---|---|
| | 1–4 | 5–8 | 9–12 | 13–19 | |
| *Promotions* | 12.9%[a] | 6.4% | 3.9% | 1.5% | 24.7% |
| INCLUDING: | | | | | |
| member, Presidium CC CPSU[b] | 8[c] | 4 | 3 | 1 | |
| secretary, CC CPSU | 3 | 2 | 1 | 1 | |
| employee, CC CPSU apparatus | 1 | 3 | 4 | 1 | |
| secretary or first secretary Republic CC | 18 | 6 | 2 | 1 | |
| employee Republic CC apparatus | 3 | 1 | 0 | 1 | |
| chairman or deputy chairman USSR Council of Ministers | 0 | 0 | 1 | 0 | |
| USSR minister or deputy minister | 1 | 2 | 0 | 0 | |
| *Transfers* | 10.9% | 4.9% | 2.6% | 0.9% | 19.3% |
| INCLUDING: | | | | | |
| USSR ambassador | 2 | 1 | 1 | 1 | |
| chairman or deputy chairman Republic Council of Ministers | 9 | 3 | 3 | 1 | |
| Republic minister or deputy minister | 7 | 5 | 3 | 0 | |
| position unknown[d] | 4 | 1 | 1 | 0 | |

174

|  | 6.5% | 11.4% | 7.9% | 1.9% | 27.7% |
|---|---|---|---|---|---|
| *Demotions* |  |  |  |  |  |
| INCLUDING: |  |  |  |  |  |
| obkom second secretary | 3 | 1 | 0 | 1 |  |
| gorkom secretary | 1 | 1 | 0 | 1 |  |
| chairman Republic Supreme Soviet | 0 | 0 | 2 | 0 |  |
| chairman oblispolkom | 1 | 5 | 1 | 0 |  |
| chairman oblast or Republic Trade-Union Council | 2 | 5 | 1 | 0 |  |
| position unknown[e] | 6 | 15 | 12 | 2 |  |
| *Unknown*[f] | 15.9% | 5.9% | 3.9% | 1.5% | 27.2% |
| *Retired*[g] | — | 0.9% | — | — | 0.9% |

[a] All figures followed by a per cent mark refer to per cent of total N.

[b] Included in this category are all who served for any time from 1950 to 1966 as obkom first secretaries and who, at any time during this period, were members of the Central Committee Presidium. Since membership on the Presidium is not an occupation, these figures are not included in the calculation of total N, nor in the percentage figures. The value of including these figures is that they indicate that total tenure is not a critical factor in appointment to the most important Party body.

[c] All figures without a percentage mark indicate numbers of individuals. The figures in most categories are too small for percentages to be meaningful.

[d] These figures include those who retained a position in the CPSU Central Committee even after losing their obkom first secretaryship.

[e] These figures include those who dropped from the CPSU Central Committee immediately after losing first secretaryship.

[f] All those for whom no further information is available after removal from an obkom first secretaryship, and who are not included in either (d) or (e) or (g) are included in this category. Most in this category may be presumed demoted, although some may have retired, died, or hold posts not made public.

[g] Although no further information is available about the individuals in this group, each was past 60 years of age when removed from his last position and is assumed to have retired.

*Table 31: Promotion Patterns After Last First Secretaryship
by Education*

| EDUCATION | PROMOTIONS | TRANSFERS | DEMOTIONS | UNKNOWN |
|---|---|---|---|---|
| *Industrial-Technical*[a] | 18[b] | 7 | 7 | 1 |
| *Agricultural* | 10 | 9 | 2 | 1 |
| *Pedagogical* | 4 | 2 | 4 | 1 |
| *Higher Party School* | 3 | 2 | 3 | 4 |
| *Other* | 7 | 8 | 7 | 3 |
| *Unknown* | 9 | 11 | 33 | 46 |

[a] Those who attended the Higher Party School in addition to other higher educational institutions are included in the figures for the latter kind of institution because of the small numbers involved.

[b] N = 200. The two individuals who retired are omitted for convenience.

education and low for all others. This finding does at least suggest some positive relationship between training and experience relevant to managerial work in a major branch of the economy and success as an obkom secretary.

Taking this analysis one step further raises the question of the relationship between these conclusions and the decision-making process at the regional level. That is, what implications emerge from this analysis regarding the likelihood of obkom secretaries to encourage wide discussion, and to listen to alternative proposals from industrial managers or agricultural officials? Again, the lack of concrete evidence, as well as common prudence, suggest caution here. Yet, in the light of the intensive emphasis on the desirability and the necessity of consultation found in the Party journals of this period, and considering the stress on economic successes as a requisite of political advancement it seems warranted to conclude that these factors at least tend to encourage first secretaries to be responsive to alternative suggestions about how best to achieve the goals specified by the Presidium. This tendency would appear to be strengthened by the increasingly large number of secretaries with a higher industrial or technical education who should be capable of communicating intelligently with the specialists who directly manage the economy. In short, the available data on the backgrounds of obkom first secretaries and the requirements for further political success appear, in general, to support the conclusion that those who hold the most crucial position in regional policy-making today are more likely than not to accept consultation with interested officials, and to broaden rather than limit the range of alternative proposals that may receive attention in the process of policy formation.

Organizationally, the channels through which this interchange is most likely to occur on a continuing, day-to-day basis are those provided by the obkom's staff, the secretariat (see Chapter 8). Analysis of the structure and functioning of these communication channels will provide fuller understanding of the ways in which suggestions and ideas arising outside the bureau may find expression in the policies adopted by that body.

EIGHT

# The Secretariat[1]

### FUNCTION

The permanent paid staff of the Party committee together with the five obkom secretaries constitute the secretariat. The secretariat has often been described as the "service apparat" of the Party committee.[2] It serves as a subordinate instrument of the Party committee, carrying on a host of activities under the guidance of the Party secretaries. The secretariat through its otdels provides the Party committee with the channels of communication to the lower Party committees—the raikoms and gorkoms particularly— to the industrial enterprises, the trade-union organizations, the Komsomol organs, the Soviets, and all other organizations in the oblast. The decisions and decrees of the Party committee and its bureau are sent downward and outward to all relevant organizations

[1] Because of a general scarcity of materials in the Stalingrad press on the work of the secretariat, but considering that there appears to be a general pattern of obkom-apparat organization to which the Stalingrad oblast seems to conform, this chapter provides a general desciption of the apparat at the oblast level based largely on the central Party press.

[2] See for example, "Can the Otdels of a Party Committee Give Out Guiding Directives in their Own Name?" *Partiinaia Zhizn'*, No. 6 (1955), p. 61.

through the apparat. It has been stated frequently in Soviet writing that one of the chief functions of the apparat is not only to transmit decisions but to "carry on practical work for the realization of Party decisions."[3] In this sense the Party apparat acts as the executive arm of the Party committee. While this activity is indeed very important in terms of the maintenance of control by the Party over all subordinate institutions, it is not the most relevant function of the apparat in terms of decision-making within the Party committee bureau.

The most significant aspect of the apparat's work in relation to decision-making is the monitoring of all economic, political, and cultural activity in the oblast. This is accomplished through the continuous collection and analysis of statistics and reports from the primary Party committees in industrial enterprises and on the farms as well as in institutions and public organizations. Reports by raikoms and gorkoms on the state of affairs for which they are responsible are investigated through checks and studies made on the spot by Party committee instructors. Finally, letters of complaint from the general population are analyzed. On the basis of this information the apparat prepares reports and project decisions on specific questions at the request of the bureau or one of the secretaries. Or, one of the otdels may bring specific matters before the bureau for its consideration. An interesting example of both of these processes was reported by the Kharkov obkom. During the summer of 1955, the agriculture otdel "studied and brought before the bureau questions of the organization of a vegetable, potato, and livestock base for the city of Kharkov." The otdel also studied on its own initiative questions of the improvement of breeds of cattle and the organization of a feed base. Somewhat later, on assignment from the obkom secretaries, the otdel examined and prepared project decisions on "the construction of silos, on the preparation of the material-technical base for the harvest, the reprocessing of corn cobs in milk-waxen ripeness, and on the electrification of agriculture."[4]

This example seems typical of the way the bulk of bureau

3 "Let's Raise the Organizational Role of the Party Apparat," *Partiinaia Zhizn'*, No. 5 (1955), p. 8.
4 "Current Leadership and the Work of the Party Committee Otdels," *Partiinaia Zhizn'*, No. 20 (1955), p. 31.

decisions are prepared. For the most part they concern relatively minor, day-to-day problems. The work of preparing the materials and project resolutions on which these decisions are based is carried out almost entirely by the full-time Party workers of the obkom apparat. In approaching the solution of current questions, the apparat officials may exercise some degree of discretion. For instance, in supervising the work of a raikom it is up to the workers of the Party organs otdel to decide whether particular actions of the lower Party organ are improper or out of line with obkom policy. However, since the otdels are not empowered to issue guiding directives or to rescind the orders of other Party committees, such questions must be raised before the bureau for a final decision.[5]

On the other hand, when a major policy decision is being formulated, such as the reorganization of industrial administration, a considerably wider group of persons, including factory directors, engineers, technical workers, and others, is brought into the preparation of the project resolution. However, in this case the major outlines of the decision are nearly always drawn up as a "thesis" or a note from the Party Presidium or some similar form before the local officials can begin to work out their own proposals. Under these conditions there is relatively little opportunity for the apparat or other officials to influence the basic direction or content of the policy decision. Rather, the group of people drawn into the formulation of a major policy acts, for the most part, in an advisory, technical capacity, filling in the details and making the general directive applicable to the circumstances of the oblast.[6]

Access to the policy formulation process, then, when it concerns routine, day-to-day problems is limited for the most part to the full-time Party apparat workers. When a major policy change is being formulated, a considerably larger number of groups is brought into this process. However, Party dominance is assured by limiting these groups to an advisory, technical role, by requiring them to work within the policy guidelines established by the Party officials.

[5] "Can the Otdels of a Party Committee Issue Guiding Directives in their Own Name?" *Partiinaia Zhizn'*, No. 6 (1955), p. 37.

[6] For a description of this process in practice, see "How We Prepare for a Plenum in the Party Obkom," *Partiinaia Zhizn'*, No. 21 (1959), pp. 44–47.

ORGANIZATION

The secretariat of the Stalingrad obkom is divided into nine otdels as outlined in Figure 1. The work of the otdels is supervised by the obkom secretaries. From the evidence available of the practice in Stalingrad, it appears that the first secretary devotes most of his attention to whichever area presents the most serious problems at the moment. For instance, Zhegalin appears to have spent the entire spring of 1956 in supervising the current agricultural campaign.[7] In the spring of 1957, it is very probable that the largest amount of his energy was consumed by preparations for the industrial reorganization.

In contrast to the first secretary, each of the subordinate secretaries is assigned a particular area of specialization. The secretary for industry exercises his supervision of industrial production through the Industrial-Transport otdel and the otdel for Construction and the Construction Materials Industry.[8] The secretary for agriculture keeps watch over the work of the kolkhozes and sovkhozes, and, prior to 1958, the MTS through the Agriculture and Sovkhoz otdels.[9] The responsibilities of the secretary in charge of ideology include supervision of the work of the Propaganda and Agitation otdel and the otdel for Science and Schools.[10] The cadres secretary carries out his duties of watching over the work of all the lower Party committees through the Party organs otdel. His competence also includes coordinating with the heads of all otdels the work of selecting, promoting, and removing cadres.[11]

The responsibilities of each otdel are fairly clear-cut. The Party organs otdel, formerly called the otdel for Party, Komsomol, and Trade Union Organizations, supervises the work of these organs on the city and district level. As shown earlier, this otdel also plays a crucial role in organizing the oblast and other Party conferences, especially in selecting the delegates and candidates for election to the committees. The sector of Party statistics within the otdel of

7 See Chapter 6, pp. 101–106.
8 The secretary for industry also probably supervises the work of the Administrative, Trade-Financial Organs otdel; however, this cannot be definitely established.
9 "Party Leadership of the National Economy," *Partiinaia Zhizn'*, No. 3 (1959), p. 18.
10 *Stalingradskaia Pravda*, January 27, 1959.
11 *Ibid.*, May 25, 1957.

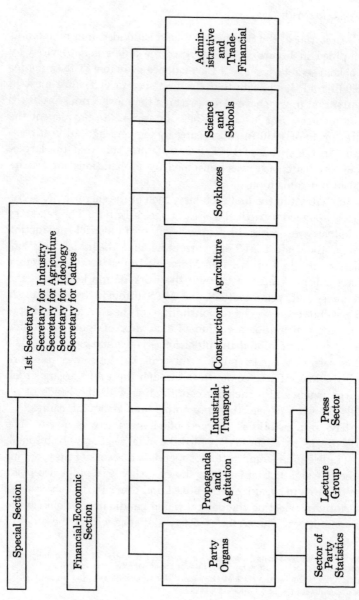

The Stalingrad Oblast Party Secretariat, 1956–1961[a]

[a] *Stalingradskaia Pravda*, January 28, 1960.

Party organs collects data on the age, occupation, social origin, and the like for all communists and submits reports on this once every three months to the Party Central Committee.[12] The Propaganda and Agitation otdel and the otdel of Science and Schools act as the ideological arm of the Party committee, carrying on propaganda campaigns and supervising the ideological and political content of the courses taught in the schools. Within the Propaganda and Agitation otdel there is a press sector charged with reviewing and guiding the oblast and lower press.[13] In addition, within this same otdel, there is a lecture group assigned the task of giving lectures on current propaganda themes throughout the oblast.

The Industrial-Transport and Construction and Construction Materials Industry otdels analyze a continuous flow of statistical data and reports on plan fulfillment by the industrial, transport, and construction organizations of the oblast; transmit Party decisions to the primary Party organizations and managers of these organizations and trusts, and raise before the bureau questions concerning the work of the enterprises for which they are responsible.[14] The otdels of Agriculture and Sovkhozes carry on similar functions in relation to agriculture. These two otdels seem to be particularly engaged with analyzing great masses of details during the agricultural campaigns. For instance, the agricultural otdel of one obkom had to receive and assess each day data on the following indicators from each sovkhoz and MTS in the oblast: How much did each tractor plow? How much of this was done in the night shift? How many tractorists fulfilled their norms? How many did not, and why?[15] The otdel for Administrative and Trade-Financial Organs collects and evaluates data on the work of the state administrative organs, the trade network, and the financial organizations. As is evident from this discussion, nearly every organization and institution, indeed almost every aspect of life in the oblast, comes under the scrutiny of one of the otdels of the oblast Party committee secretariat.

[12] *SPR* (1959 ed.), p. 555.

[13] "For the Activization of Ideological Work," *Partiinaia Zhizn'*, No. 20 (1955), p. 7.

[14] "Let's Raise Organizational Work to the Level of the New Tasks," *Partiinaia Zhizn'*, No. 17 (1955), p. 21.

[15] "A Few Questions About the Work of the Party Apparat," *Partiinaia Zhizn'*, No. 4 (1958), p. 25.

Within each otdel of the obkom there is an otdel chief, one or more assistants, and a group of instructors.[16] The chief of the otdel occupies a crucial position between the secretaries and the bureau who actually make the decisions, and the instructors who collect the information and draw up the reports on the basis of which decisions are taken. The otdel chief directs all the day-to-day work of the instructors, points out to them on what problems it is most important to concentrate and from what perspective questions must be approached. Although the secretaries are also charged with overseeing such aspects of the otdels' work, they are reported as frequently showing little interest in it.[17] Even more important, the otdel chief decides what information is brought to the attention of the secretaries and what project decisions and in what form are raised before the bureau.[18] As one means of insuring that the proper perspective is maintained in the reports, it appears that an assistant chief usually assists the instructors in making up reports and project resolutions.[19] While it is true that the secretaries can be certain of receiving any report they specifically request, and while some otdel instructors have reportedly threatened to go to the secretaries directly, over the head of the otdel chief, with a report they felt was of vital importance,[20] there seems little doubt that the otdel chief is a key person in determining what views will get a hearing in the obkom bureau. This view is given added weight by the fact that some secretaries require the otdel chief to coordinate with them "even the most petty matter."[21] An even more convincing indicator of the importance attached to the position of otdel chief is the fact that the appointment or removal of such officials within the obkom is subject to the approval of the Central Committee of the CPSU.[22]

[16] "Party Leadership of the National Economy," *Partiinaia Zhizn'*, No. 3 (1959), p. 18.

[17] See for example, "Let's Raise the Organizational Role of the Industrial Otdels of Party Committees," *Partiinaia Zhizn'*, No. 5 (1955), p. 12; and "Party Leadership of the National Economy," *Partiinaia Zhizn'*, No. 3 (1959), p. 18.

[18] See especially, "From the Practice of Work of One Obkom CPSU Industrial Otdel," *Partiinaia Zhizn'*, No. 21 (1956), p. 58.

[19] *Ibid.*

[20] *Ibid.*

[21] "Let's Educate Cadres in the Spirit of Initiative and a Business-Like Approach to Matters," *Partiinaia Zhizn'*, No. 18 (1955), p. 6.

[22] "Some Questions on the Training of Cadres," *Partiinaia Zhizn'*, No. 15 (1956), p. 9.

STAFF TRAINING

The rising technical level of agricultural and especially industrial production in the Soviet Union has been accompanied by increased demands that the Party apparat be manned by persons who are capable of understanding and dealing with complex technical problems. This need has been accentuated by the increasingly direct role of the Party in the administration of first agriculture and then industry. As early as 1954, V. Churaev, then an official of the Central committee Party Organs otdel, stated that "Party leadership of the economy can be skilled only when the Party workers have a thorough understanding of questions of the economy. At the present time it is impossible to successfully direct agriculture without the ability to delve into questions of agro-technology and zoo-technology."[23] Shortly after July, 1955, the Central Committee plenum demanded that the Party committees begin to devote more attention to questions of the technology of production; *Partiinaia Zhizn'* stated that in recent years in the industrial otdels there were "fewer and fewer specialists who could delve into questions of technology."[24] By 1958, the same journal could report that "in the past few years the Party apparat has been significantly enriched with specialists with a higher or middle technical education, with people who also have not a little experience in production work at the enterprises."[25] In the same year, the first secretary of the Stalingrad obkom observed that in the raikoms "95 per cent of the first secretaries, 94 per cent of the second secretaries, and 90 per cent of the secretaries have either a higher or an unfinished higher education."[26] In 1962, it was reported that 24 workers of the Party Organs otdel of one obkom had a complete higher education, while nine were specialists in industry or agriculture.[27]

In spite of the definite increase in the technical competence

23 "Instructing as a Method of Concrete Leadership," *Partiinaia Zhizn'*, No. 5 (1954), p. 13.
24 "A Few Questions of the Work of the Industrial Otdels," *Partiinaia Zhizn'*, No. 18 (1955), p. 9.
25 "The Perspective of a Party Worker," *Partiinaia Zhizn'*, No. 21 (1958), p. 49.
26 "Raise Work with Cadres to the Level of the New Tasks," *Partiinaia Zhizn'*, No. 13 (1958), p. 9.
27 "Let's Improve Organizational-Party Work," *Partiinaia Zhizn'*, No. 3 (1962), p. 7.

of the Party workers, it would be rash to conclude that there is developing within the apparat a kind of technical elite whose training would tend to give them a rather pragmatic view of the world more in sympathy, perhaps, with the industrial-engineering intelligentsia and less in line with the more ideologically oriented Party secretaries. In fact, it appears that much of the technical training and higher education received by Party apparat workers and especially by the chiefs and assistant chiefs of otdels is received in special Party schools, such as the oblast Party schools or the Higher Party School within the Central Committee of the CPSU. In 1956, *Partiinaia Zhizn'*, describing the education of Party cadres, cited the following figures:

> During the past ten years the oblast, krai, and republic Party schools have graduated more than 55,000 persons, and more than 40,000 have completed yearly courses; 2,843 persons finished the Higher Party School, and more than 6,000 persons completed this school on a part-time basis.[28]

Immediately following this statement, the journal added that "at the present time among the responsible workers of obkoms, kraikoms, and union-republic Central Committees more than 75 per cent have a higher or incomplete higher education."[29] The direct implication of this statement appears to be that most of the responsible Party workers have received their higher education, or a part of it, in the regional, the republic, or the central Party schools.

At the 20th Party Congress it was announced that since the task of encompassing in the Party schools the basic ranks of the Party and Soviet workers was substantially completed, the Party schools would be reorganized to give significantly greater attention to questions of technology and economics "at least at the level of a technicum."[30] In the newly organized Party school system, the oblast Party schools, one of which is located in Stalingrad, provide a four-year course leading to a higher educational degree. While these courses devote much time to the study of economics and technology, there is still heavy emphasis on what may be called the

---

[28] "The Preparation of Party and Soviet Workers," *Partiinaia Zhizn'*, No. 14 (1956), p. 38.
[29] *Ibid.*
[30] *Ibid.*

*Table 32: Study Plan of the Four-Year Party Schools*

| NAME OF DISCIPLINE | NUMBER OF HOURS |
|---|---|
| 1  *History of the CPSU* | 250 |
| 2  *Dialectical and Historical Materialism* | 200 |
| 3  *Political Economy* | 300 |
| 4  *History of the International Workers and National-Liberation Movement* | 180 |
| 5  *History of the U.S.S.R.* | 150 |
| 6  *Party and Soviet Construction* | 150 |
| 7  *Fundamentals of Soviet Law (Civil, Labor, and Kolkhoz)* | 100 |
| 8  *Economic Geography of the U.S.S.R. and Foreign States* | 100 |
| 9  *The Economics, Organization, and Planning of Industrial Enterprises, Construction, and Transport* | 200 |
| 10  *The Economics, Organization, and Planning of Agricultural Enterprises* | 180 |
| 11  *The Energy Base of Industry* | 80 |
| 12  *Technology of the Major Branches of Industry* | 270 |
| 13  *Productive and Civil Organization* | 100 |
| 14  *General Agriculture and Plant Growing with Basic Agrochemistry* | 240 |
| 15  *Livestock Production* | 140 |
| 16  *Mechanization and Electrification of Agriculture* | 160 |
| 17  *Planning the Local Economy and Cultural Construction of the Raion* | 80 |
| 18  *Trade, Finance, and Credit* | 80 |
| 19  *Bookkeeping and Balance Analysis* | 60 |
| 20  *Mathematics* | 100 |
| 21  *Statistics* | 80 |
| 22  *Production Practice* | 2 mo. |
| Total | 3200 |
| ELECTIVES | |
| Foreign Language | 200 |
| Russian Language | 150 |
| Driver Training | 120 |

SOURCE: *SPR* (1957 ed.), pp. 414–415.

inculcation of the Party point of view. As can be seen from Table 32, 1,430 hours of the total 3,200 in the four-year Party school are devoted to indoctrination courses ranging from the history of the

CPSU to the fundamentals of Soviet law, and to economic geography of the USSR and foreign states.

Rather than providing the Party apparat workers with a technical-engineering background, the economics courses taught at the higher Party schools appear to be designed to provide these officials with a vocabulary and a few basic tools that should enable them to communicate more effectively with the engineers at industrial enterprises and the agronomists on the collective farms. Thus, while the 270 hours spent in the study of the technology of the major branches of industry should make the Party worker qualified to make some judgment about a technical proposal put forward by an industrial engineer, for example, it is very doubtful that the former would have the skill to work out by himself the solutions to technical production problems. Combined with the very heavy emphasis on Party-ideological studies in the Party schools, this lack of real technical expertise would seem to act to set the apparat workers apart from the industrial-technical intelligentsia. There is some evidence to indicate that even those Party workers who have an engineering education are not looked upon as competent members of this latter group. To illustrate his point that Party workers do not have much authority among the industrial officials, an editor of *Partiinaia Zhizn'* related the following incident:

> The director of a certain factory had to decide a few production-technical questions. He was advised to take the matter up with the instructor of the industrial-transport otdel of the obkom, comrade Z. "He won't know anything about this; he has forgotten about such things," objected the director. When they told him that comrade Z is an engineer, this answer followed: "He was a good engineer eight years ago." It may be that this example is not typical, but it shows how the production workers think of those Party workers who do not raise their technical qualifications.[31]

In view of the foregoing, it would seem most unlikely that workers in the party apparat, from the instructors to the otdel chiefs, would have acquired an outlook that differed to any substantial degree from the accepted idea of *Partiinost'*, or devotion to the Party and its principles first, last, always.[32]

[31] "The Perspective of a Party Worker," *Partiinaia Zhizn'*, No. 21 (1958), p. 50.
[32] This point is also supported by Armstrong, esp. pp. 78–79, but see also Chapter 4.

An additional factor that should not be overlooked here is that the instructors and the otdel chiefs are to a large extent dependent upon the Party secretaries for continuance in their positions. Any concerted effort on their part to promote ideas at variance with the viewpoint of the latter would be likely to cost an instructor or otdel chief his job. Of course, it is possible that some Party secretaries may welcome the promotion of policies by the apparat that, while within the general line of the Party, are nevertheless at variance with accepted approaches to particular problems. However, unless these views are adopted by some group other than the professional Party workers, this still does not insure access by outside groups to the decision-making process within the oblast Party committee. In any case, in view of the interpretation of decision-making within the bureau presented in Chapter 5, such occurrences would probably be very rare indeed.

### DECISION-MAKING ROLE

There is, however, another way in which the viewpoints of groups other than the Party officials may find expression in the policy proposals formulated by the Party apparat; namely by the appointment as otdel chiefs of personnel who have spent most of their careers in other professions. Thus, an industrial manager who was appointed as chief of the industrial-transport otdel would probably interpret questions of industrial policy in a quite different manner from one who had always worked in the Party apparat. Unfortunately, little evidence is available on the career patterns of leading apparat officials. It is worth noting, however, that of the 22 persons who held positions as head of an otdel on the Stalingrad obkom in the period under study only two can definitely be identified as having occupied posts outside the Party apparat before becoming an otdel chief. One of these, A. A. Andreev, was identified in 1956, as the head of the construction trust, *Stalingradstroi*.[33] In this capacity he served as a member of the city Soviet executive committee until May, 1958. On the 16th of that month he was appointed chief of the obkom otdel for Construction and the Construction Materials Industry. Although he was a member of the gorkom as early as

[33] *Stalingradskaia Pravda*, March 10, 1956.

1957, Andreev was not elected to the obkom until 1960. While it is very significant that an industrial manager was given such an important position in obkom decision-making as chief of an otdel, it must be pointed out that his views were undoubtedly very similar to the Party professionals. Since the trust, *Stalingradstroi*, is subordinate to the city Soviet, it is subject to considerably closer Party control than are those within the ministerial hierarchy. That the work of this trust frequently came under the scrutiny of the Party officials at obkom plenums and conferences in Stalingrad attests to the Party's direct interest in its work. While Andreev, then, could be expected to promote the viewpoint of the construction industry, in so doing he would undoubtedly remain very sensitive to the guidance of the Party secretaries.

The only other otdel chief to hold a position outside the Stalingrad Party apparat was V. A. Belousov, who was identified in 1954 as the Assistant Chief of the oblast agricultural administration in charge of livestock administration.[34] At the time, he was only 28 years of age. While no information on his earlier career is available, it appears that he had only recently completed either a university education or a course in one of the Party schools, probably with a specialty in agriculture. In January, 1956, he was reported as first secretary of a rural raikom; a position he held until December, 1957.[35] In the latter part of that month he was appointed head of the obkom agriculture otdel. He served in this capacity for about two and one-half years. Then, on May 28, 1960, he was elected obkom secretary in charge of agriculture, to replace Nepokupnoi.[36] Belousov represents what appears to be the desired type of Party apparat worker. With a technical agricultural education and some experience in the practical administration of affairs, he moved into full-time Party work where his technical expertise, it may be assumed, made it possible for him to work out technically feasible policy proposals. Yet his two-year apprenticeship in the raikom presumably served to assure that he had developed the perspective of the professional Party worker before he was promoted to responsible work in the obkom. His promotion to the position of obkom secretary for agriculture at the age of 34 indicates that this

[34] *Ibid.*, May 22, 1954.
[35] *Ibid.*, December 27, 1957.
[36] *Ibid.*, May 28, 1960.

was probably one instance where the desired qualities of technical expertise and a Party outlook toward the solution of policy problems had been favorably combined.

To the extent that Stalingrad is a typical case, then, it is rare that persons who have gained their experience outside the Party apparat are appointed to head an obkom otdel. When this does occur, the tendency appears to be to select persons who, while possessing undoubted expertise in their field, are thoroughly imbued with the Party perspective or at least display a high degree of sensitivity to the wishes of the Party secretaries. From this analysis, therefore, there seems to be little indication that groups other than the professional Party officials are able to achieve a high degree of potential influence on policy through participation in the policy-formation process in the Party apparat. Yet, before any firm conclusions can be drawn in this regard, it is necessary to consider the effects on the decision-making process of the relatively recently organized institutions of nonstaff (voluntary) instructors in the Party committees.

On September 30, 1958, the Central Committee of the CPSU issued a decree empowering the obkoms, kraikoms, and union-republic central committees to establish the posts of nonstaff instructors in the Party committees.[37] By 1962, there were nearly 80,000 nonstaff instructors in the lower Party committees. These include engineers, lawyers, agronomists, teachers, and others who, after completing their normal day's work, volunteer time for work in the Party committee apparat.[38] The wide-scale introduction of communists to voluntary work in the Party committees has as its purpose to "assist the Party committees in all their activities, in carrying out political and organizational work among the masses, in strengthening ties with the primary Party organizations and in improving their activity."[39] In addition, it appears that the institution of nonstaff instructors is seen as one means of making up for the large reductions in the paid staff of the Party committees that occurred between 1956 and 1958.[40]

[37] *SPR* (1959 ed.), p. 555.
[38] Skriabin, p. 44.
[39] "On Non-Staff Instructors in the Party Committees," *Partiinaia Zhizn'*, No. 1 (1959), p. 19.
[40] For the decrees ordering reductions in the staffs of Party committees, see *SPR* (1957 ed.), pp. 405–408, 429, 441; and also *SPR* (1959 ed.), pp. 545–546, 555.

The extent to which the voluntary principle in Party work has been adopted in practice has varied considerably from region to region. In 1960, it was reported that the raikoms and gorkoms of the Ukraine had more than 7,000 nonstaff instructors; Latvia, more than 500; Kirgizia, 400; and Tadzhikistan, 280.[41] Two years later, *Partiinaia Zhizn'* commented that "the greatest development of the voluntary principle in Party work has occurred in the Moscow and Leningrad gorkoms, in the Communist Parties of the Ukraine, Belorussia, Moldavia, and in Volgograd, Ivanovsk, and Novosibirsk oblasts."[42] Although most of the nonstaff instructors are found at the raikom and gorkom level, the Zaparozhe obkom was reported as having 44 nonstaff instructors in 1960.[43]

In particular instances the nonstaff instructors may act as little more than errand boys, transmitting the orders of the obkom to the gorkom, raikom, or primary Party organizations. They may assist the lower organizations to solve minor technical problems or give help in carrying out a propaganda campaign. While the activities of some nonstaff instructors may be of little consequence for the policy-formation process, there nevertheless appears to be little doubt that these voluntary workers may exercise a considerable measure of influence on the formation of policy. This seems to be particularly true in regard to problems of industrial technology. As noted, many of the nonstaff instructors are experienced engineers or other technical workers who labor day-in and day-out with these problems. Describing the qualifications of the nonstaff instructors in the Leningrad Party organization, a Party official stressed that these are people "capable of thoroughly examining matters and bringing positive results in the solution of the tasks of technical progress, ideological, and Party-organizational work in the Party organizations."[44]

In addition to the work of nonstaff instructors, many Party committees have established technical councils and permanent commissions operating on the voluntary principle. These groups, composed of chief engineers, technologists, scientific-research workers and other highly qualified persons, assist the Party com-

41"The Vitality of Leninist Principles," *Kommunist*, No. 6 (1960), p. 78.
42 "Let's Improve Organizational-Party Work," *Partiinaia Zhizn'*, No. 3 (1962), p. 10.
43 Skriabin, p. 45.
44 *VPS*, p. 307.

mittees in an advisory capacity in the working out of technical proposals.[45] In 1962, these commissions and technical councils contained more than 105,000 members.[46]

In assessing the potential influence of these voluntary workers on the formation of policy within the Party apparat certain limiting factors must be kept in view. In the first place, the Party committee bureau selects and confirms the individual nonstaff instructors for its committee.[47] This means that only those persons in full agreement with the general policy line of the Party would be invited into this voluntary work. Secondly, the nonstaff instructors and other voluntary workers are subordinate to the professional Party worker in charge of the otdel. In working out the solution to policy-problems, they must work within the framework or guidelines laid down by the otdel chief or the Party secretaries. And, finally, since the professional Party officials, of course, have the right to determine whether or not, or to what extent proposals submitted by the voluntary workers are acceptable, the monopoly of the Party *apparatchiks* over decision-making within the Party committee remains in effect. Yet, that some Party committees, apparently, are now willing on a regular basis to seek the advice of outside groups in the formation of Party decisions is extremely important. This means that significant new channels of communication are being created. While the advice sought by the Party committees through these channels is largely of a technical nature, and while evidence on the extent to which these channels are actually used is entirely too limited, the very existence of regularized communications channels for outside groups to the policy-formation process within the Party apparat signifies some effort to widen the decision-making group. Although it is still too early to draw conclusions, the extensive use of voluntary workers may be one way in which some significant groups in Soviet society can, in the future, achieve a measurable degree of influence on policy-formation within the oblast Party committee.

45 "The City Party Committee—Organizer of the Masses," *Kommunist*, No. 14 (1960), p. 70.
46 *VPS*, p. 41.
47 "On Non-Staff Instructors of Party Committees," *Partiinaia Zhizn'*, No. 1 (1959), p. 18.

# NINE

# The Influentials

🔲🔲

At the outset of this study, we proposed to inquire into the patterns of participation in the political process within the oblast Party committee of the CPSU. Five primary channels through which major groups in Soviet society might acquire potential influence on obkom policy-making have been analyzed: participation in the Party conference, representation on the Party committee, participation in obkom plenums, membership on the bureau or participation in its sessions, and work in the secretariat on either a full-time or voluntary basis.

What clearly emerges from this study is that a small group of professional Party secretaries, or even the First Secretary alone, can and does control all the channels of access to the decision-making bodies. Although the Party conference is technically the highest organ of the Party at the regional level, the control exercised by the Party officials over the selection of delegates, over the agenda, and over the participants in the discussions effectively nullifies the conference as a means of bringing influence to bear on the Party leaders. Instead of acting as a forum where the Party rank and file, representing all the diverse groups in Soviet society, might call their leaders to account for the way they fulfilled past promises, and where future promises might be extracted in return for assurances of continued support, the conference is a platform for persuading the rank and file of the correctness of new policies and calling to task the leaders of organizations and institutions who fail to fulfill sufficiently the demands made upon them by the Party officials. Of course, it sometimes happens that particular Party officials are criticized and even publicly disgraced and removed from their posts at Party conferences, but this follows only on the decision of the Party committee bureau or the Central Committee of the CPSU and not at the whim of any group of dissident delegates.[1] Although the new committee is elected by secret ballot, the use of a single slate precludes any really effective choice by the conference delegates.

Yet, the conference may provide a certain degree of access to the decision-making process. It does appear that a certain amount of criticism is directed by the speakers at particular officials, or at the way particular policies are implemented, or at the failure of the Party officials to deal effectively with particular problems. At the same time, and this is the crucial point, the participants in the conferences—and in the Party committee plenums also for that matter—speak from a position of extreme weakness. Since all the leading positions within Soviet society come within the *nomenklatura* of the Party committees, or more precisely the Party committee secretaries, there are not, nor can there be, any groups with autonomous political power. All participants in the conference or plenum discussions speak at the sufferance of the Party secretaries, as petitioners who may offer expert advice or circumspect criticism, but who can only take the path of active intervention in decision-making at the risk of losing their positions.

Even a cursory examination of the composition of the oblast Party committee is sufficient to convince one that no effort is being made to give representation to the various groups in the same proportion as their numbers in the Party as a whole. Rather than seek-

[1] It should be noted, however, that normal practice appears to be to make changes in the composition of the leading organ, the bureau, at obkom plenary sessions rather than at the conference.

ing to give a balanced representation to the diverse social and economic groups in Soviet society, the Party officials determine obkom
membership on different criteria. Primary among these appears to
be the desire to assure the dominant position of the professional
Party secretaries. While, for example, the leaders of all organizations and institutions accounted for only five per cent of the entire
Party membership in 1961, the Party officials alone made up 40.9
per cent of the Stalingrad obkom membership in the same year.
The next largest group consisted of those most closely subordinated
to Party control—the officials of the local Soviets.[2] For nearly all
other major groups in the oblast, the only official on the obkom
is the head of the corresponding oblast organization. Thus, the
Komsomol and trade-union organizations may have an official
voice in the obkom in the person of the secretary or chairman of
their oblast organizations. While assuring the Party secretaries'
control over the committee in this way, the existing membership
pattern at the same time provides some opportunities for "access"
to the decision-making process for important groups within the
oblast. But, for the most part, it does not provide these groups with
a very high potential for influence on that process. The access
achieved is a kind of *post facto* entrance into decision-making. As
we have demonstrated above, the locus of decision-making is not in
the committee as a whole, but in the obkom bureau. By virtue of
their membership on the committee, however, the leaders of the
most important organizations in the oblast have the opportunity to
become quickly acquainted with bureau decisions. In this way, they
become transmission belts between the Party committee bureau,
where the decisions are made, and the organizations and institutions that are responsible for executing them. This process is seen
most clearly in the obkom plenums, where major decisions and programs are discussed and particular tasks defined. After the bureau
has adopted a decision, then the committee members enter the
process in the stage where support for it is being mobilized and its
execution organized.[3]

Since the Party committee bureau is the locus of political deci-

[2] See Chapter 4, pp. 41–44.

[3] Brzezinski and Huntington make this same point in discussing the "persuasion" phase
of the decision-making process: "In the Soviet Union . . . persuasion can best be described as the 'mobilization' of support. It is monopolized by the Party, and it normally
occurs not before but after the decision phase." Brzezinski and Huntington, p. 209.

sion-making within the obkom, it is here that access is most crucial. Groups that have the opportunity to present their views before the bureau certainly would have a significantly greater potential for influence on policy outcomes than those who do not have this type of access. While our analysis of decision-making in the bureau has emphasized the dominant position of the Party secretaries and particularly the first secretary in regulating access by outside groups, there also has been observed a highly significant tendency to consult outside groups in open and frank discussion in bureau sessions.[4] This tendency was further noted in regard to the proliferation of nonstaff and other voluntary workers in the Party committees.[5] The importance of this increasing willingness to consult with other groups in the process of policy-formation can perhaps best be understood in the context of the changes in the political process at the regional level in the past 30 years.

On the basis of his study of the Smolensk Archives, Fainsod concluded that during most of the period from 1929 to 1938, the control of oblast affairs was in the hands of the first secretary, the second secretary, and the chairman of the oblispolkom. They dominated the obkom and filled its bureau with their close associates and dependents.[6] Those invited to the sessions of the obkom bureau consisted almost entirely of Party officials—heads and assistant heads of obkom otdels, obkom instructors, gorkom and raikom secretaries. For the discussion of particular problems kolkhoz chairmen, agricultural experts, and industrial managers were invited to the bureau. Although in most instances an invitation to appear before the bureau meant trouble, at times officials participated in a "purely informational or expert capacity."[7]

While outwardly this picture has a close resemblance to that described in regard to Stalingrad in the 1950's, there does seem to be a crucial difference between the two periods. This difference relates primarily to the *tendency* to consult in an atmosphere of open and frank discussion. In describing the arrest and disgrace of the Smolensk first secretary, Fainsod relates that "borrowing a page from his master's book, he had made himself something of

4 See Chapter 6, esp. pp. 129–132.
5 See Chapter 8, pp. 191–193.
6 Fainsod, *Smolensk Under Soviet Rule*, p. 67.
7 *Ibid.*, p. 68.

a little Stalin in his home territory."[8] The significance of this in relation to decision-making in the Smolensk obkom—probably a typical obkom in the Stalin era in this respect—was brought out in the charges against the first secretary: "He ruled with an iron hand . . . his subordinates did not dare to contradict him."[9]

The beginnings of the tendency to widen the circle of those who participate in the political process at the regional level are described in a careful study of the Ukrainian Party apparatus by John Armstrong. On the basis of his analysis of the republican elite for the period from the late 1930's to about 1956, Armstrong concludes that "whatever the reasons for the peculiarities of the Ukrainian apparatus' operation before 1953 as compared to other segments of the Soviet apparatus, they did *tend toward the oligarchic,* as compared to the autocratic system of rule"[10] (italics mine). While Armstrong does not develop his statement further, the thrust of his argument, which appears to be reasonable and to conform to other evidence, is that for several reasons, but largely because Khrushchev's natural inclination lay in that direction, the Ukrainian apparatus developed and displayed a tendency to consult with interested and affected groups in making its decisions, rather than simply imposing them in the Stalinist manner. At the same time, while Khrushchev and the other Ukrainian leaders did not hesitate to work with other groups on a cross-institutional basis, they always insisted on their own, i.e., Party, dominance in such alignments.[11]

After Khrushchev assumed the position of first secretary of the Party in 1953, he conducted a steady campaign to eliminate throughout the Soviet Union the type of autocratic decision-making that characterized the Stalin era. This drive has been documented in this study by many references from the Party journals and press describing the way the Party secretaries are now expected to act: They should listen to other opinions; they should seek advice from many sources in order to avoid one-sided decisions. The difficulty from an analytic point of view arises when an attempt is made to determine the extent to which consultation actually occurs,

8 *Ibid.,* p. 60.
9 *Ibid.*
10 Armstrong, p. 149.
11 *Ibid.,* p. 145.

or the effectiveness of access by particular groups to the decision-making process.

Although for this study it has not been possible to acquire many data on the decision-making process itself, what we have analyzed are some of the political resources that seem to be related to an individual's or a group's *potential* influence on decision-making. Specifically, membership on the various bodies of the Party committee and participation in the public sessions of those bodies are resources the use of which would appear to give their possessors a greater potential for influencing policy outcomes than those who do not enjoy such resources. Of course, these are only one small part of the total arsenal of political resources brought into play in Soviet politics. Furthermore, they constitute only the most general kind of indicator of potential influence. Nevertheless, a summary of the membership and participation patterns examined in this study will at least give some tentative indications of the *variations* in potential influence among the various individuals involved in obkom affairs, and thus indirectly also of the groups with which they are associated in their professional careers. Thus, by comparing official positions and the issue areas—such as questions of industry, agriculture, cadres, etc.,—in which various individuals participate, some tentative conclusions can be drawn as to the relative potential for influence of particular officials and groups in particular issue areas.

Before proceeding to our analysis, it should be pointed out that measures of potential influence do not necessarily indicate actual influence.[12] Regardless of the amount of potential influence an individual may have this cannot be taken as a direct measure of his actual influence. In the first place, individuals with the same amount of political resources may use them differently. For example, one obkom secretary who sits in on all major bureau decisions, but who is not particularly energetic or persuasive in his arguments may have much less actual influence on policy outcomes

---

[12] For a discussion of the differences between actual and potential influence, and the problems of measuring the latter, see Dahl, *Who Governs?* pp. 272–275.

than a raikom secretary who comes from a district of major importance, demonstrates a profound knowledge of his subject, and is exceedingly convincing in his arguments when invited to appear before the obkom bureau. In the second place, we cannot be entirely certain of the amount of potential influence the possession of a particular political resource actually entails. To illustrate, it is simply impossible for us to know whether one would have greater potential influence as director of a major factory, which involves membership in the oblast Party committee but not on the bureau, or as chairman of the oblast trade-union council, which is apparently a less important post than the former, but which normally includes a seat on the Party committee bureau. Keeping in mind that we cannot make many verifiable statements about actual influence, and that even statements about potential influence must remain highly tentative, it nevertheless seems profitable to go as far as the data permit to draw some conclusions about variations in the potential influence of members of the oblast Party committee.

Tables 33 through 37 summarize the *relative potential influence* of various members of the Stalingrad obkom as measured by the criteria specified above, i. e., official position within the obkom and record of participation in obkom plenary sessions. All of those included in the Tables appear to possess a relatively higher potential influence on obkom policy than all other members of the obkom, on the basis of our criteria. Thus, all those included in Groups I through V have formal positions on the obkom, which, on the basis of the analysis presented in this study, appear to give them greater potential access to obkom decision-making than other obkom members, or they have a record of higher participation in obkom plenums than all other obkom members. In other words, Tables 33 through 37 include the 45 persons who, for varying lengths of time during the period 1954 through 1961, possessed the highest potential influence in obkom affairs. This figure includes officials from seven institutional interest groups—21 Party officials, nine Soviet officials, seven industrial managers and Sovnarkhoz officials, five Komsomol or trade-union leaders, two persons in cultural-educational work, and two police chiefs.[13] Taken as a

---

[13] Figures total more than 45 because some officials held more than one position during the period studied.

whole, these officials constitute what might usefully be thought of as the "influentials" in oblast affairs.

This is not to say, however, that all members of this group have equal potential for influence in obkom decision-making. When the criteria discussed above are applied to the "influentials," they divide into five distinct groups on the basis of their relative potential influence. Group I consists of those who were members of the obkom bureau at some time between 1954 and 1961 and who, in addition, participated in obkom plenums in at least one issue area. Group II includes the rest of those who were obkom bureau members but who never participated in the public aspects of the obkom's work. In Group III are those who, although not members of the obkom bureau, are members of the larger committee, participated in one issue area, and occupy positions of oblast-wide importance. Group IV is made up of persons who are not members of the obkom bureau but who are members of both the oblast and the city Party committees. None of the members of this group participated in any of the obkom's public activities. Finally, Group V consists of persons who, while members of the obkom, hold no other major honorary or oblast-level Party positions. All members of this group participated three or more times in oblast Party committee plenums.

To the extent that the criteria of office and participation are useful indicators of potential influence, Group 1 can be said to rank highest, with decreasing potential influence through Group V. Group I includes all those who rank high by both measures. All are members of the bureau and all have high levels of participation, although differing within the group in terms of issue area specialization. Even though the members of Group II have no record of public participation, they are ranked above Groups III through V on the basis of their membership in the obkom bureau. Although they did not participate publicly, that they sat on the highest decision-making body would seem *a priori* to give them a higher potential influence than all those who do not sit on the bureau. The essential indicators that rank the members of Group III above those in Groups IV and V include the fact that they all occupy positions of oblast-wide importance, they hold at least one honorary position such as member of the oblast Soviet, or delegate to a Party

Table 33: *Relative Potential Influence in the Stalingrad Obkom: Group 1*

| NAME AND POSITION | TERM[a] | PARTICIPATION BY ISSUE AREA | | | |
|---|---|---|---|---|---|
| | | INDUSTRY | IDEOLOGY | CADRES | AGRICULTURE |
| *Zhegalin, I. K.* obkom first secretary | (1956–1961) | X | X | X | X |
| *Pankin, I. S.* oblispolkom chairman | (1954–1961) | X | | X | X |
| *Kulichenko, L. S.* gorkom first secretary | (1957–1961) | X | | X | X |
| *Sinitsyn, I. F.* sovnarkhoz chairman | (1957– ) | X | | | X |
| *Nekrasov, K. S.* oblispolkom vice-chairman | (1957–1958) | | | | |
| T. U. council chairman | (1958–1961) | X | | | X |
| *Vdovin, A. A.* T. U. council chairman | (1954–1958) | X | X | | X |
| *Rozhkov, O. I.* komsomol first secretary | (1956–1958) | | X | X | |
| *Sadovski, S. I.* komsomol first secretary | (1958– ) | | X | X | X |
| *Grishin, I. T.* obkom first secretary | (1954–1956) | | X | X | X |
| *Mel'nikov, I. A.* chief, oblast K.G.B. | (1954–1956) | | X | | |
| *Mon'ko, A. M.* editor, Stalingradskaia Pravda | (1954– ) | | X | | |

| | | |
|---|---|---|
| *Nepokupnoi, N. A.* obkom secretary for agriculture | (1954–1960) | X |
| *Zhuravlev, D. P.* obkom secretary for ideology | (1956–1961) | X |
| *Gusev, N. I.* obkom secretary for cadres | (1957–1961) | X |
| *Chmutov, N. I.* obkom secretary for industry | (1954–1961) | X |

SOURCE: Data on which this Table is based are derived from *Stalingradskaia Pravda*, 1954–1961.

[a] This item refers to the years during which the named individual was identified as holding the specified position.

*Table 34: Relative Potential Influence in the Stalingrad Obkom: Group II*

| NAME | POSITION | TERM |
|---|---|---|
| *Andriushchenko, S. A.* | military commander, Stalingrad oblast garrison | (1957–1959) |
| *Antonov, N. D.* | identity unknown | (1954–1956) |
| *Bogatyrev, V. T.* | komsomol first secretary | (1954–1956) |
| | first vice-chairman, oblispolkom | (1958–1961) |
| *Stytsenko, G. N.* | chief, oblast K.G.B. | (1957–1961) |
| *Vovchenko, I. M.* | head, obkom agitation and propaganda section | (1954–1955) |
| *Eliseev, P. P.* | oblispolkom vice-chairman for agriculture | (1956–1957) |
| *Krasavin, V. S.* | obkom secretary for ideology | (1954–1955) |

SOURCE: Data on which this Table is based are derived from *Stalingradskaia Pravda*, 1954–1961.

Table 35: Relative Potential Influence in the Stalingrad Obkom: Group III

| NAME AND POSITION | TERM | PARTICIPATION BY ISSUE AREA | | | |
|---|---|---|---|---|---|
| | | INDUSTRY | IDEOLOGY | CADRES | AGRICULTURE |
| Semenov, V. A. director, Stalingrad Tractor Factory | (1957– ) | | | | X |
| Aleksandrov, A. P. director, Stalingrad Hydroelectric Construction Trust | (1958–1959) | X | | | |
| Larin, I. V. chief, oblast agriculture administration | (1956–1960) | | | | X |
| Merinov, P. V. fourth vice-chairman oblispolkom for culture and ideology | (1954–1960) | | X | | |

Table 36: Relative Potential Influence in the Stalingrad Obkom: Group IV

| NAME | POSITION | TERM |
|---|---|---|
| Zhukov, N. V. | head, obkom industrial transport section | (1954–1960) |
| Dynkin, A. V. | chairman, Stalingrad gorispolkom | (1956–1959) |
| Matevosian, P. A. | director, Red October steel plant | (1954–1960) |
| Atroshchenko, S. N. | director, "machine-building" factory | (1954–1960) |
| Balychev, V. S. | first secretary, Tractor-factory raikom | (1954–1958) |
| Korolev, I. M. | first secretary, Tractor-factory raikom | (1958–1960) |
| Kuznetsov, I. N. | first secretary, Red October raikom | (1954–1956) |
| Bochkarev, N. D. | first secretary, Voroshilov (city) raikom | (1954–1955) |

SOURCE: Data on which these tables are based are derived from Stalingradskaia Pravda, 1954–1961

*Table 37: Relative Potential Influence in the Stalingrad Obkom: Group V*

| NAME AND POSITION | TERM | PARTICIPATION BY ISSUE AREA | | | |
| --- | --- | --- | --- | --- | --- |
| | | INDUS-TRY | IDEOL-OGY | CAD-RES | AGRICUL-TURE |
| *Ivashchenko, I. S.* head, kafedra of the organization of socialist enterprises, Stalingrad Agricultural Institute | (1954–1961) | | | X | X |
| *Zaria, S. E.* chief, goods-transport division, "Glavneft'sbyt' " | (1956–1961) | X | | | X |
| *Krasnov, S. A.* chief, oblast administration of sovkhozi | (1956–1959) | | | X | X |
| assistant chief, Stalingrad sovnarkhoz administration for food and light industry | (1959– ) | | | | X |
| *Troshenkov, D. I.* chairman, Nikolaevskii raiispolkom | (1958–1960) | X | | | X |
| *Sitnikov, V. A.* first secretary, Zhdanov raikom | (1954– ) | | X | X | |
| *Stepanov, A. G.* first secretary, Gorodish-chinskii raikom | (1954– ) | X | | X | X |
| *Borodin, V. P.* first secretary, Kruglovskii raikom | (1957– ) | | | | X |
| *Logunov, I. A.* first secretary, Novo-Nikolaevskii raikom | (1957–1960) | X | | X | X |
| *Makarichev, P. N.* first secretary, Oktiabr'skii raikom | (1954– ) | | X | X | X |
| *Martynov, P. P.* first secretary, Molotov (Krasnoiarskii) raikom | (1956– ) | | | | X |
| *Il'in, N. M.* first secretary, Kalachevskii raikom | (1954–1958) | X | | X | X |

SOURCE: Data on which this Table is based are derived from *Stalingradskaia Pravda*, 1954–1961.

Congress, and, in addition, those in Group III all participated several times in one issue area. Group IV is ranked below Group III because none of the persons included in the former participated in any obkom plenums. Yet, on the basis that each sits on both the obkom and the gorkom and further considering that each is concerned in either a Party, Soviet, or managerial capacity with various phases of heavy and defense industry, the members of this group are ranked in potential influence above those in Group V. Finally, although none of those in Group V holds a position of major importance in the oblast, this group is considered to have greater potential influence on obkom policy than other rank-and-file obkom members on the basis of their high level of participation in obkom affairs. We thus see that on the basis of position and participation there exist at least five distinct gradations of relative potential influence among the obkom "influentials."

The question that naturally arises at this point may be put as follows: If it is true that all members of Group III rank below all members of Group I, does this mean, for example, that Aleksandrov, the director of the Stalingrad Hydroelectric Construction Trust, has less potential influence than Rozhkov, the Komsomol first secretary, the former being included in Group III and the latter in Group I? In order to answer this question satisfactorily, another element must be introduced. As Robert Dahl and others have pointed out, if we wish to be precise in discussing influence we must talk about it in relation to specific issue areas or types of problems. Although this type of analysis was developed to help explain the nature of influence in pluralist societies, it appears that the basic assumption of this approach, namely that "no one group necessarily is most influential in all decision-areas,"[14] may have some relevance to the structure of potential influence in the Soviet Communist Party. Thus, while it makes little sense to talk about Aleksandrov's influence in the abstract, it makes a great deal of sense to discuss this in relation to specific issue areas. On the basis of our measures we may say, then, that Aleksandrov probably has less potential influence in relation to *industrial*

[14] Nelson Polsby, *Community Power and Political Theory* (New Haven: Yale University Press, 1963), pp. 113–114. The pluralist approach to influence is most often associated with such works as Robert A. Dahl, *Who Governs?*; V. O. Key, *Politics, Parties, and Pressure Groups*.

questions than Rozhkov has in relation to problems of *ideology*. This type of statement is more precise, yet even this method of comparison does not appear to be most useful. Most of those persons concerned with ideological work appear to operate in quite different worlds from those dealing with questions of industry, or agriculture for that matter. While there is no conclusive evidence, it appears that the most useful assumption here is that there are different patterns of influence in different issue areas. What holds for one issue area does not necessarily hold for others. So, the most fruitful type of analysis may be to describe the patterns of potential influence in relation to specific issue areas. Where substantial overlap occurs among issue areas, this may be taken as an indication of a general leadership, or line role, either at the oblast or the raion level. Where a high degree of specialization occurs this may be more indicative of a technical or staff function.

Each of the specific groups of "influentials" is worth examining in this light. All of those who appear to play a general leadership or line role on an oblast-wide basis are found in Group I. That the first secretary is the only official to demonstrate by his record of participation a high potential for influence in all issue areas reinforces the concept brought out in this study, as well as in many others, of the first secretary as the major integrating factor of the entire Party committee. Also possessing a high degree of potential influence combined with a general leadership role, although not quite so broad as the first secretary's but including questions of cadres and agriculture in addition to industrial matters, are the chairman of the oblast Soviet executive committee and the first secretary of the city Party committee. Three other officials within Group I exercise a more or less generalized leadership over industry in addition to one other area of interest. These include the Sovnarkhoz chairman and trade-union chairman, both of whom also possess a relatively high potential influence in agricultural questions. The trade-union chairman during the early period of this study, Vdovin, is the third person with a generalized leadership role, including questions of ideology and industry, within his sphere of potential influence.

The only other official in Group I whom our measures indicate as having a relatively high potential influence in industrial matters is the obkom secretary in charge of industry. This is the only issue area in which his participation record indicates a high potential influence however, leading to the conclusion that he probably fills a staff function, with his potential influence being limited to and probably dependent upon his special competence. This same can be said of the subordinate obkom secretaries for agriculture, ideology, and cadres. In addition, the editor of the oblast Party newspaper and the chief of the oblast *KGB* fall into this latter category, with both specializing in problems related to ideology. Other officials in this first group possessing a potential for broad influence include the Komsomol first secretaries and the former obkom first secretary, the former two having potential influence in relation to questions of ideology and cadres in one instance, and cadres and agriculture in the other, while the latter's potential influence related primarily to questions of ideology and agriculture.

This difference between the scope of potential influence of the first secretary in the 1954-1956 period and the scope of the first secretary in the later period has already been noted as reflecting changes in the competence of the Party organs as a whole, particularly their increasing role in industry beginning in 1956.

Looking at Group I as a whole, we see that those individuals and institutional interest groups who have the highest potential influence on obkom policy in relation to questions of industry include the following: (1) three Party secretaries—the obkom first secretary, the gorkom first secretary, and the obkom secretary for industry; (2) two officials of the oblast Soviet—the chairman and the first vice-chairman of the executive committee; (3) the chairman of the Stalingrad Council of the National Economy; and (4) the chairman of the oblast trade-union council. On questions of ideology, those with the highest potential influence on obkom decisions include (1) three obkom secretaries—both obkom first secretaries and the secretary for ideology; (2) the Komsomol first secretary; (3) the chief of the oblast security police; and (4) the editor of *Stalingradskaia Pravda*. On questions of cadres the Party and Komsomol secretaries have a near monopoly of potential influence with Pankin, the oblispolkom chairman and a former Party official, being the only other person with a high degree of potential influence in this issue area. In regard to questions of agriculture, the institutional groups and officials with the highest potential influence include: (1) three Party secretaries—the obkom first secretary, the gorkom first secretary, and the obkom secretary for agriculture; (2) two Soviet officials—the oblispolkom chairman and the first vice-chairman; (3) one Sovnarkhoz official—the chairman; and (4) the Komsomol first secretary.

It is thus evident that in all issue areas examined very few interest groups are included among those with the highest potential influence on obkom policy-making. In fact, outside of the Party and the Komsomol only four groups at the regional level of Soviet society can be said to enjoy a relatively high degree of potential influence on policy-formation—the executive committee of the oblast Soviet; the oblast trade-union council; the chief economic body in the oblast, the Sovnarkhoz; and the security police.

Since Group II by definition includes those bureau members who never participated in public sessions, it is somewhat more difficult to ascertain the scope of their potential influence. Perhaps the most that can usefully be said about this group is to note the types of occupations it includes. Among those in this group are two individuals occupying positions that at another time were included in Group I—the chief of the oblast *KGB* and a Komsomol first secretary. It is entirely possible that during the 1954-1956 period the position of Komsomol first secretary simply was not considered important enough to permit its occupant to join in the public aspects of plenary sessions. Similarly, in connection with the subordination of the *KGB* to Party control, it may not have been considered appropriate to permit public participation in obkom activities by the chief of the security police. Conversely, however, it may simply have been that the individuals occupying these positions were not sufficiently energetic or experienced to seek the opportunity for public participation.

It is interesting that the only military commander ever to be a member of the obkom bureau during the period studied, Andriush-chenko, never took part in an obkom plenum. This tends to confirm the finding of Fainsod for the period of the thirties that the position of the military on the bureau is largely honorary, the military seldom taking an active role in obkom deliberations.[15] Never-

15 Fainsod, *Smolensk Under Soviet Rule*, p. 68.

theless, the military commander's position on the bureau did give him a relatively higher potential influence if he should have chosen to take advantage of it.

The inclusion in Group II of the head of the Agitation and Propaganda section of the obkom for the 1954-1955 period, the highest potential influence attained by any obkom department head, on the basis of our measures, may reflect the increased importance attached to propaganda work at that time in connection with the Central Committee resolution, "On Mistakes in the Conduct of Scientific-Atheistic Propaganda Among the Masses."[16] Yet, in spite of the increased emphasis on propaganda, it is revealing that the obkom secretary in charge of ideology during this period, Krasavin, never participated in obkom plenums. Undoubtedly the major factor accounting for the presence of the oblispolkom vice-chairman for agriculture among Group II of the "influentials" during 1956 and 1957 was the Virgin Lands program, at its height in the Trans-Volga region at this time.

Taken as a whole, Group II consists of two types of officials: (1) those who occupy positions that do not appear normally to be associated with a high degree of potential influence in obkom affairs but which temporarily acquired a relatively high potential influence for several reasons; and (2) those who hold positions that normally were included among those with the highest potential for influence in obkom policy-making but, for other reasons, temporarily became somewhat less important. This points to the possibility that potential influence may also be quite directly related to the issue areas considered important for the moment. When a great propaganda campaign is undertaken, normally at the instigation of the central Party authorities, then the potential influence of the propaganda interest groups is increased in relation to other groups. Conversely, if industrial questions are considered crucial for the moment, then the potential influence of industrial interest groups may experience a relative increase.

The four officials in Group III can perhaps best be characterized as specialists engaged directly in administering a major sector of the economy who enter into oblast politics on the basis

---

16 Central Committee resolution adopted on November 10, 1954. For the text of the resolution, see *KPSS v Rezoliutsiiakh* . . . , IV, 46–50.

of their special competence and specific responsibility. Thus, the director of the Stalingrad Tractor Factory participated in obkom plenums as a major industrial official responsible for the production and delivery of agricultural equipment. Aleksandrov was the official most directly responsible for the largest construction project in the entire oblast, and one of the largest in the country at the time. As chief of the oblast agriculture administration within the oblast Soviet, Larin was most directly responsible for the execution of agricultural policy. The same is probably true for Merinov, the oblispolkom vice-chairman in charge of culture and ideology, although this is less clear. Taken as a whole, this group indicates that those who possess, on the basis of our criteria, the highest potential influence in the obkom aside from bureau members are those administrative personnel engaged directly in carrying out major Party programs. In Stalingrad, this group includes officials charged with responsibility in each issue area examined except for cadres, which appears to be the direct responsibility of the Party cadres secretary.

Group IV tends to be almost exclusively a heavy industry "interest group" inasmuch as all the officials who are members of both the obkom and the gorkom but who did not participate in any obkom plenums are concerned in one capacity or another with problems of heavy industry. This is not to say that they have no relation to light industry or other questions, but the nature of their positions seems to indicate an overwhelming concern with problems of machine-building and steel production. Thus, the director of the Red October steel plant, the largest such plant in Stalingrad oblast,[17] and the director of what was identified only as a "machine-building" plant are obviously concerned with these problems. Since the Tractor Factory and the aforementioned steel plant are the largest and most important enterprises within their respective districts, it may also be surmised that affairs related to them are a major concern of the raikom secretaries in these districts. It further seems reasonable that the head of the obkom industrial-transport sector would spend a major part of his time on questions related to the above districts and plants. The case of the first secretary of the Voroshilov district within the city of

---

[17] *Stalingradskaia Pravda*, January 26, 1959, p. 2.

Stalingrad is less clear. Although it is probably important industrially, there is no available evidence to demonstrate this. Nevertheless, it is quite obvious that those officials whose major professional concern is problems of industry, and primarily heavy industry, occupy a position of relative potential influence subordinate only to those administrators responsible for major sectors of the economy, in addition to members of the bureau. Whereas Group III is divided fairly evenly among the issue areas, Group IV appears to be almost exclusively composed of industrial interests.

Group V, consisting of rank-and-file obkom members not enjoying major honorary positions but nevertheless having a high record of participation in obkom plenums, can probably best be considered as a generalized leadership or line group but on a rather secondary level. That is, none of the officials included in this group holds a position of major, oblast-wide importance, except possibly Krasnov when he was the assistant chief of the food and light industry administration within the Sovnarkhoz. Yet, even this position seems to be of rather secondary significance in comparison with the positions held by the officials in Group IV.

Those who demonstrate by their participation the most generalized potential for influence within this group include four raikom secretaries from rural districts, three of whom participated in all issue areas except ideology. Two raikom secretaries, on the other hand, showed a very specialized sphere of potential influence, participating in obkom plenums dealing with agricultural questions exclusively. The three other officials within this group indicate a moderately generalized scope of potential influence, with two individuals entering discussions of cadres and agricultural questions and one raikom secretary speaking on ideological and cadres problems. At the lowest level of potential influence among the "influentials" then, we find generalist raikom secretaries for the most part. While firm evidence is lacking, it seems probable that the officials within this group owe their potential influence more to personal qualities, such as outstanding leadership and the ability to achieve results, than to the significance of their positions.

Throughout this study we have found considerable variation in the potential influence of various groups and individuals in obkom decision-making. While some interest groups seem to have a relatively high potential for exercising influence, particularly Party secretaries, and the heads of the major Soviet institutions— the Soviets, the trade-unions, the Komsomol,—in addition to major industrial and other administrative groups; others such as literary, artistic, scientific, general educational and engineering groups are noticeably absent from the obkom "influentials." Only one light industry official is included with this group and he is among those with the least potential influence. These measured differences arise from differential patterns of access to the political process. Specifically, they arise from the structure of obkom committee and bureau membership with its heavy weightings in favor of the Party secretaries and the heads of major Soviet institutions, and from the observed patterns of participation in the public aspects of the obkom's work that also favor most of these same groups with more of the "access" such activity provides. Once again, however, it is important to make clear the tentative nature of these indicators; potential influence is no assurance of actual influence.

CONCLUSIONS

In spite of the variety of institutional interest groups included among the obkom "influentials," control over the channels of access to the decision-making process, as this study has amply demonstrated, remains in the hands of one group—the Party secretaries. The ability of any institutional interest group to translate its potential influence into actual influence on obkom decisions depends in very large measure on the receptiveness of the Party secretaries to such activities. Yet, while the importance of these limitations must not be underestimated, the significance of the observed tendency of the Party secretaries to consult with interested groups, to listen to them, to encourage their participation in at least the public aspects of obkom activity must not be overlooked. Compared with the period of the thirties, more institutional interest groups now appear to have the opportunity to exert some influence in obkom decision-making. Although, at the present time, there are measurable differences between the potential influence of the various institutional interest groups observed in this study, and although there exist severe limitations on the ability of all groups to turn their potential influence into actual influence, nevertheless, some of the major interest groups in Soviet society do appear able to make positive contributions to political decision-making through constructive use of their membership on the Party committees and the opportunities available for participation in the Party committees' work.

# Bibliography

🔲🔲

**BOOKS IN ENGLISH**

Armstrong, John A. *The Soviet Bureaucratic Elite*. New York: Praeger, 1959.

Barghorn, Frederick C. *Politics in the USSR*. Boston: Little, Brown, 1966.

Brzezinski, Zbigniew, and Huntington, Samuel P. *Political Power: USA/USSR*. New York: Viking, 1964.

Dahl, Robert A. *Modern Political Analysis*. Englewood Cliffs: Prentice Hall, 1963.

———. *Who Governs?* New Haven: Yale University Press, 1961.

Fainsod, Merle. *How Russia is Ruled*. 2nd ed. Cambridge: Harvard University Press, 1963.

———. *Smolensk Under Soviet Rule*. Cambridge: Harvard University Press, 1958.

Hazard, John N. *The Soviet System of Government*. Chicago: University of Chicago Press, 1960.

Inkeles, Alex, *et al*. *How the Soviet System Works*. Cambridge: Harvard University Press, 1956.

LaPalombara, Joseph. *Interest Groups in Italian Politics.* Princeton: Princeton University Press, 1964.

Labed, Andrew I., Schulz, Heinrich E., and Taylor, Stephen S., eds. *Who's Who in the USSR 1965/1966.* New York: Scarecrow Press, 1966.

Macridis, Roy C., and Brown, Bernard, eds. *Comparative Politics.* Homewood: Dorsey Press, 1961.

Merzalow, Wladimir S. *Biographic Directory of the USSR.* New York: Scarecrow Press, 1958.

Truman, David B. *The Governmental Process.* New York: Knopf, 1951.

Polsby, Nelson. *Community Power and Political Theory.* New Haven: Yale University Press, 1963.

Schulz, Heinrich E., and Taylor, Stephen S., eds. *Who's Who in the USSR 1961/1962.* New York: Scarecrow Press, 1962.


ARTICLES IN ENGLISH

Bachrach, Peter, and Baratz, Morton. "Two Faces of Power," *The American Political Science Review,* 56 (December, 1962), 957–962.

Riker, William H. "Some Ambiguities in the Notion of Power," *The American Political Science Review,* 58 (June, 1964), 341–349.

Nemzer, Louis. "The Kremlin's Professional Staff," *The American Political Science Review,* 44 (January, 1950), 62–71.


BOOKS IN RUSSIAN

Akademiia Obshchestvennykh Nauk. *Voprosy Istorii KPSS.* Moscow: Vysshaia Partiinaia Shkola pri Tsk KPSS, 1959.

Bromberg, M. I., ed. *Iz Istorii Stalingradskoi Partiinoi Organizatsii.* Stalingrad: Stalingradskii Gosudarstvennyi Pedagogicheskii Institut, 1959.

Kochetov, Vsevolod. *Secretar' Obkoma.* Moscow: Molodaia Gvardiia, 1961.

*KPSS v Rezoliutsiiakh i Resheniiakh S'ezdov, Konferentsii i Plenumov Tsk.* Vols. III and IV. 7th ed. Moscow: Gospolitizdat, 1954 and 1960.

Leningradskaia Vysshaia Partiinaia Shkola. *Voprosy Partiinogo Stroitel'stva.* Leningrad: Lenizdat, 1962.

*Plenum Tsentral'nogo Komiteta Kommunisticheskoi Partii Sovetskogo Soiuza 15–19 Dekabria 1958 goda* (Stenographicheskii otchet). Moscow: Gospolitizdat, 1958.

*Programma i Ustav KPSS.* Moscow: Gospolitizdat, 1962.

Slepov, L. A.  *Vysshie i Mestnye Organy Partii.* Moscow: Vysshaia
    Partiinaia Shkola pri Tsk KPSS, 1958.
Skriabin, V.  *Novoe v Rabote Partorganizatsii po Rukovodstvu Pro-
    myshlennost'iu.* Kiev: Gospolitizdat UKSSR, 1960.
*Spravochnik Partiinogo Rabotnika.* Vols. I–IV. Moscow: Gospolitizdat,
    1957, 1959, 1961, and 1963.
*SSSR: Administrativno-Territorial'noe Delenie Soiuznykh Respublik.*
    Moscow: Izvestia, 1963.
Tsentral'noe Statisticheskoe Upravlenie pri Sovete Ministrov SSSR.
    *Itogi Vsesoiuznoi Perepisi Naseleniia 1959 goda* (SSSR). Moscow:
    Gosstatizdat, 1962.
*Voprosy Partiinoi Raboty.* Moscow: Gospolitizdat, 1958.


PERIODICALS IN RUSSIAN

*Izvestia.* 1952–1962.
*Kommunist.* 1952–1962.
*Partiinaia Zhizn'.* 1952–1962.
*Pravda.* 1950–1966.
*Sovetskaia Rossiia.* 1950–1966.
*Stalingradskaia Pravda.* 1952–1962.

## Appendix: Distribution of Total Population by Social Position and Occupation

| SOCIAL POSITION OR OCCUPATION | JANUARY 15, 1959 PER CENT |
|---|---|
| *Workers* | 46.5 |
| *Peasants* | 33.7 |
| *White collar workers* | 19.8 |
| INCLUDING: | |
| Leaders of organizations,[a] institutions, enterprises, construction projects, sovkhozi, RTS, and their structural subdivisions | 1.1[b] |
| Engineering-technical personnel, agricultural specialists, economists and architects | 3.0 |
| Scientific, educational, health, literary, and artistic workers | 9.0 |
| Trade and communal dining workers | 1.8 |
| Control, accounting, and clerical workers | 2.3 |
| Others—communications, communal economy, etc. | 2.4 |

SOURCE: *Itogi Vsevsoiuznoi Perepisi Naseleniia 1959 goda SSSR* (Moscow: Gosstatizdat, 1962).

[a] Includes leaders of Party and Soviet organizations.

[b] Figures refer to percentage of group in entire population.

# Index

Construction and Construction
Materials Industry otdel of
the CPSU obkom
administrative functions of, 181,
183
chief of, 189–190
Consultation as factor in obkom
policy process, 198–199
Criticism, at obkom plenums, 54,
57, 80–83
*See also* Discussions
Cultural workers
participation of, at obkom plenums, 71, 77
relative potential influence of,
200–214
representation on obkom, 42–45
representation at the oblast
Party Conference, 26
selection and distribution of,
200–214

Debates. *See* Discussions
Decision making
access to, within obkom, 133
collective leadership and, 48
effects of competitive pressures
on, 173–177
formal procedures for, in obkom
bureau, 88–89, 100
function of, in obkom plenums,
80–83, 86–87
interest group approach to, 3
obkom bureau role in, 88–89, 100
obkom bureau role in agriculture, 101–107
obkom bureau role in cadres,
119–127
obkom bureau role in industrial
decisions, 92–93, 107–119
at obkom plenary sessions, 53–
54, 57–58, 61, 68, 78
party secretaries' role in, 73
questionaire method of, 128
style of, in obkom bureau, 127–
133
Democratic Centralism as organizing principle of CPSU,
22–23
DeStalinization, 103

Discussions
career factors affecting, in obkom politics, 176–177
at obkom bureau meetings, 128–
133
at obkom conferences, 195
at obkom plenums, 65, 80–83
at obkom plenums, limits on,
57–58
District Party Committee of the
CPSU, secretaries of, 29.
*See also* Raikom
Dneprodzhershinsk Metallurgical
Institute, 147
Doroshenko, P. Y., 145–146
D.O.S.A.A.F., 77
Drozdenko, V., 162

Economic administrators. *See* Industrial officials; Ministry
officials
Education
agricultural, 143, 154, 158–159,
164
of delegates to 23rd CPSU Congress, 142–143
as a determinant of success,
145–147
engineering-technical, 143, 154,
158–159, 163–164, 168
of obkom secretaries, 142–147,
150–151
Party, 143, 154, 158, 164–165, 168
of Party members, 142
pedagogical, 143, 154–155, 158–
160, 165
periods of completion of, 150–
151
Educational officials
participation at obkom plenums,
71, 77, 81
relative potential influence of,
200–214
representation on obkom, 42, 45
Eliseev, P. P., 93–95
Engineering-technical personnel,
representation on obkom, 42, 43,
44, 45, 47
Enlarged plenum, 66, 70, 71, 81–
83
functions of, 81

Oblast CPSU Committee—(*Cont.*)
Secretary, Agriculture—(*Cont.*)
supervisory role in Secretariat
of, 181
Secretary for Cadres, 26, 91, 94,
97
participation by, in obkom
plenums, 65, 67, 78
role in oblast T. U. Council,
90
supervisory role in Secretariat of, 181
Secretary for Ideology, 91, 92,
94, 97
participation by, in obkom
plenums, 65, 67, 75
supervisory role in Secretariat of, 181
Secretary for Industry, 91, 94
participation by, in obkom
plenums, 65, 66, 73
supervisory role of, in Secretariat, 181
size, 25, 37–38
Oblast Party Conference
access to decision making via,
194–195
agenda of, 30–31, 33
election of Party Committee at,
33–36
Eleventh, 25, 26, 51, 93, 95
function of, 27, 29, 33, 36
Ninth, 25, 91
organization of, 27–29
participation at, 31–33
party secretaries' role at, 195
Presidium of the, 27–29, 30–
34
representation of interest groups
at, 26
representation norms at, 26
*See also,* Komsomol
selection of delegates to, 26, 34
Oblast Soviet Executive Committee. *See* Oblispolkom
Oblast Trade-Union Council
Chairman of Presidium of, 89,
93, 95–98
Obkom cadres secretary role of,
90.
*See also,* Trade-Unions

Oblispolkom
chairman of, 57, 89, 93, 95, 97–
98, 102–103
composition of, 68, 90
First Vice-Chairman of, 94–97,
99
joint decisions of, with obkom
bureau, 102, 105, 106
members' role in obkom plenums, 65, 68, 71, 74, 77–78,
84, 85
Vice-Chairman for agriculture,
93–94, 99
Old school ties, relevance to success of, in Soviet politics,
145–151
Organizational Plenums, 91, 92
Central Committee influence on,
63–64
Otdels. *See* Oblast CPSU Committee; *specific otdels*

Pankin, I. S., 85, 89, 95, 97, 98,
102–103
Pankrat'ev, P. A., 84
Participation
frequency of, 10, 83–86
function of, in obkom plenums,
80–82
by guests in obkom plenums, 81
as a measure of potential influence, 8, 10–11, 200–214
at obkom plenums, 65–87
at oblast Party Conferences, 31–
33
in preparations for obkom plenums, 56–57
scope of, 10, 200–214
*Partiinost,* 188
Party cadres plenums
Central Committee initiative in,
62–63
participants at, 78–80
Party officials
controls over, 49, 102
decision making role of, 57
education of, 150–151
industrial role of, 110
participation in obkom plenums
by, 68, 73, 75, 78–81

Soviet officials—(*Cont.*)
  participation in obkom plenums,
    71, 73–74, 77–78, 80
  relative potential influence of,
    200–214
  representation on obkom of, 40–
    47
  representation at oblast party
    conference of, 26
  role in obkom plenums, 83
  selection and distribution of,
    119–127
Soviets, local, 31, 90, 93, 105, 119,
    178
Sovkhoz otdel of the CPSU ob-
    kom, administrative func-
    tions of, 181, 183
Sovnarkhoz, 100, 113, 114
  chairman, 45, 95, 98, 115
  joint decrees with obkom of, 115
  officials, 74, 78–80
  participation in obkom plenums
    by, 65–68
  relationship to obkom of, 114–
    117
  role in cadres selection of, 123–
    125
  role in obkom plenums of, 83–85
Spiridonov, I., 48
Stalin, J. V., 90, 99, 100, 128, 129,
    164
Stalingrad Tractor Factory, direc-
    tor of, 29, 45, 71, 90–91, 92,
    93, 95, 114
*Stalingradskaia Pravda,* 77, 95, 99,
    101, 107
  editor of, 77, 95, 97, 98
Stytsenko, G. S., 93, 95, 97

Tenure. *See* Secretaries of oblast
    CPSU Party Committees
Tolubeev, N., 147
Trade Unions, 31, 38
  cadres, selection and distribution
    of, 119–127
  controls over by obkom, 90, 178

Trade Unions—(*Cont.*)
  as an interest group, 4
  participation at obkom plenums
    of, 77, 84
  relative potential influence of,
    200–214
  representation on obkom, 43–45
  representation at oblast party
    conferences, 26
  role in obkom plenums of, 83, 85

Union of Soviet Writers, represen-
    tation on obkom, 45
*Upolnomochenny,* 101
USSR, Council of Ministers, 110,
    118, 162
  State Planning Commission, 116
  Supreme Soviet, 118, 135
Usubaliev, T., 162

Vatchenko, A., 147–148
Virgin Lands, 164
Vodovin, A. A., 84, 89, 95–96
Vovchenko, I. M., 90, 93

Workers, 34, 109
  participation in obkom plenums,
    71, 81
  rank and file representation at
    oblast Party Conference,
    26–27
  representation on obkom, 40–47
  role in obkom plenums, 83–84

Yengutin, G., 147
Yermin, L. B., 145–146

Zhegalin, I. K., 66, 85, 92, 94, 97,
    102–103, 113, 114, 118, 181
  background, 136–138
  party career, 138–140
Zhuravlev, D. P., 92, 94, 97
"Znaniia" (Society for the Dis-
    semination of Political and
    Scientific Knowledge), 77